513 - v. v

310 - v. v

9/8/19 ~~650~~ v v.

1 5 60 R STN v.

10 80 R STN.

1 8 56 v.

5 60 v

1 1 3 v

Brazil Nuts

Admiral Twn.

FAcy DSP. Facey. Bungles
DSP Bungles, Darley

4TH GENERATION R&D

4TH GENERATION R&D

Managing Knowledge, Technology, and Innovation

William L. Miller

AND

Langdon Morris

John Wiley & Sons, Inc.

New York • Chichester • Weinheim • Brisbane • Singapore • Toronto

This publication is designed to provide accurate and authoritative information in
regard to the subject matter covered. It is sold with the understanding that the
publisher is not engaged in rendering professional services. If professional advice
or other expert assistance is required, the services of a competent professional
person should be sought.

Library of Congress Cataloging-in-Publication Data:

Miller, William L., 1944–
    Fourth gereration R&D : managing knowledge, technology, and
    innovation / William L. Miller and Langdon Morris.
        p.   cm.
    Includes bibliographical references and index.
    ISBN 0-471-24093-1 (alk. paper)
    1. Research, Industrial—Management.   I. Morris, Langdon.
    II. Title.
    T175.5.M55   1998
    658.5'7—dc21   98-12030

Printed in the United States of America.

10 9 8 7 6 5 4 3 2

Contents

9/7/19

Vitamin C
magneseum X

Potassium Salt
Good HBP

Introduction:
Innovation in Crisis

One of the most important and most difficult issues facing today's organizations is the problem of innovation. Although commonly denied in public, it is discussed at length and deeply lamented in private, where top managers acknowledge that their corporations are failing at innovation and particularly at making the substantial leaps that are required for discontinuous innovation.

Although there is universal agreement about the importance of innovation and R&D, and about the vital role that both play in the growth, survival, and success of companies and nations, current practice has fallen into a tenuous state of frustration because the recent track record is so embarrassingly bad. One researcher has gone so far as to suggest that, during the 1980s, American corporations wasted billions of dollars on failed attempts to innovate,[1] which shows that just spending more money doesn't help if assumptions are incorrect or a process is flawed.

Other evidence points to fundamental problems with product conception; detailed analysis has shown that it takes as many as 3,000 raw ideas to produce one lonely commercial success.[2] Measuring downstream, it seems that, of four projects that enter the development stage, only one becomes commercially successful.[3]

Learning from failures may have led to ultimate successes, but the cost is clearly excessive and the returns have not been adequate. In some industries, 80 percent of all innovations originate from customers rather than producers.[4] In the software industry, only 16 percent of all projects are completed on time.[5]

To get a better focus on customers' needs, R&D is often integrated into business units, but this decentralized and incremental approach has also failed to achieve the desired results in most companies. The U.S. Department of Commerce reports that 90 percent of all new products fail within four years, and less than 10 percent of U.S. companies have even bothered to produce a new product in the past ten years.[6]

It is clear that there is a serious problem with the practice of innovation, and it would not be an exaggeration to say that most corporations are pushing a rope at it without success.

The widespread failure of innovation leaves traditional strategists with the following options. First, increase volume in existing global markets through market share warfare. Second, reduce costs through downsizing, process improvements, quality improvements, and outsourcing. Third, use methods and tools such as information technology to enhance performance or customer loyalty. Fourth, make acquisitions for growth. And fifth, exit existing marginal businesses.

But none of these options addresses the fundamental competitive need to increase the value that is provided to customers. In fact, *only* innovation is competent to do this.

Innovation is a difficult and complex problem that is constrained in many dimensions, but it is also an important activity and its mastery is vital for the long-term well-being of nations, companies, communities, and families. Only innovation increases the size of the pie, which means that only innovation leads to improved standards of living.

It is essential, therefore, to understand the problem of innovation and to identify how it can be corrected. It is the purpose of this book to do both. The method of the book is to combine detailed conceptual descriptions with stories and studies that exemplify these concepts. To illustrate many key points, we present the Xerox DocuTech, Apollo 13, NikeTown, the Ford Tri-Motor, Motorola's New Enterprises Group, Hewlett-Packard's Test and Measurement Organization, and Intel.

The Challenge
of Innovation

John Seely Brown has commented: "The great challenge in innovation is linking emerging technologies with emerging markets. If it were just a matter of linking emerging technologies with existing markets (or vice versa), the coupling would be relatively easy. But when both are emerging, it is a delicate, coevolutionary process: as technologies emerge, they affect the markets, and as markets emerge, they influence the technologies."[7]

As new technologies and new markets engage in this dance of complexity, managers must deal with enormous discontinuities, increasing volatility, and the rapid evolution of industries. After more than 30 years of such change, traditional methods for managing R&D and the pursuit of innovation are simply no longer adequate.[8]

For example, in 1970, U.S. companies represented 66 percent of the stock market capitalization of all of the companies in the world. By 1990, even after 20 years of remarkable growth, U.S. companies accounted for only 33 percent of the world's total.[9]

This indicates how the expansion of markets, combined with access to information and choice, has given customers progressively more control. The result is that suppliers must not only listen better and respond more quickly than ever before, but also anticipate change as new technologies and new markets coevolve.

In most nations, however, the management of R&D and innovation remains centered on the incremental development of technology portfolios and products for existing markets, using stage-gate methods. This puts the focus on what is called 3rd generation R&D, and on continuous innovation, while the broader needs and opportunities of discontinuous innovation are poorly understood and rarely addressed.

A complete rethinking of innovation practice is required. We call this new model 4th generation R&D, reflecting research into important new concepts and practices that have emerged since the principles of 3rd generation R&D were first described more than a decade ago.

The techniques of 3rd generation R&D are necessary, but they are not sufficient. The new 4th generation practice enables continuous and discontinuous innovation, both of which are mandatory for dealing with the accelerating change that now pervades the marketplace.

Behind the challenges of new technologies and new markets is the large-scale shift to new rules in a new economy. Technically, this is the shift from the scarcity-constrained industrial economy of the 19th and 20th centuries to the more abundant, technology-enabled knowledge economy that will predominate in the 21st century.

As world markets make this transition, new standards, new ways of thinking, and new ways of working are becoming established everywhere. For example, whereas the industrial economy achieved productivity improvements through knowledge applied to natural resources, machines, and labor, productivity improvements in today's environment depend on the application of knowledge to knowledge.[10]

Ideas, concepts, and capability are today's critical resources. The history of the Dow Jones Industrial Average confirms that knowledge, not hard assets, is now the key to wealth (Figure I.1).

If we accept that a critical role of management is to increase shareholder value, it is clear how this must be accomplished. Managing intangible assets in the form of knowledge is the vital capability. Knowledge is fundamentally different from hard assets, however, because knowledge is created and used only by individuals and communities of

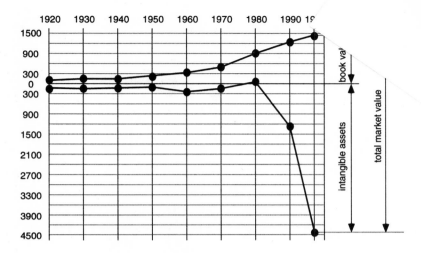

Figure I.I The Dow Jones Industrial Average, 1920–1997.[11] From 1920, when the Dow Jones Industrial Average was first created, until 1980, the value of a company was primarily a function of its hard assets as reflected in its book value. Since 1980, however, intangible assets in the form of knowledge have become much more significant than book value in determining market value.

people, and has no tangible expression beyond what people bring to it. Hence, managing knowledge requires entirely different skills and processes than have been used before.

One consequence is that investments in knowledge and intellectual capital (including learning and R&D) are replacing those in physical capital (including property, plant, and equipment). This trend is evident among Japanese manufacturing companies, where investments in intellectual capital during the 1980s surpassed investments in physical capital (Figure I.2).

Although the Japanese economy is beset by structural problems that reflect paradoxes of Japanese culture, many important principles of the new economy are widely understood and practiced there, including key elements of the innovation process. Not coincidentally, Japanese companies remain formidable competitors in key world markets, and some have earned well-deserved reputations as world leaders in innovation.

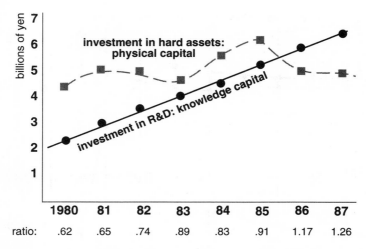

Figure I.2 Japanese Manufacturing Investments, 1980–1987.[12] From 1980 through 1987, investments by all Japanese manufacturing companies in hard assets increased by only 4 percent, while investments in R&D increased by 111 percent. More importantly, the *ratio* of investment in R&D to hard assets more than doubled, from .62 to 1.26. The additional capital invested in R&D came largely from savings achieved by shifting to flexible manufacturing technology, which provided significant reductions in tooling costs.

Clarity and Opportunity

As we make the transition to 4th generation R&D, the complex problem of timing for innovation remains a significant challenge. When ideas for discontinuous products or services are truly new, only weak evidence supports their validity. As time passes, more evidence accumulates in the form of knowledge, but waiting too long for knowledge also kills opportunities (Figure I.3).

The inverse trajectories of these two curves show the temperamental relationship between knowledge and opportunity. Managers

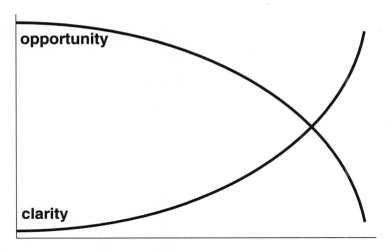

Figure I.3 The Opportunity Curve.[13] Chip Holt of Xerox has noted, "If you wait until all the facts are available, you have not demonstrated leadership."[14] Nor are there likely to be many compelling opportunities left for you to develop.

know that relevant knowledge reduces investment risk. They also know that they must assume investment risk to innovate, but they want to minimize that risk without forgoing opportunities.

Complex decision making and timing trade-offs are therefore inherent to innovation, and these frequently do not involve clear-cut alternatives between competing ideas, but instead a high tolerance for ambiguity and the willingness to live with paradox.

The 4th generation R&D model reduces risk by focusing on the creation and management of relevant knowledge that enables you to grasp the essence of a weak signal and bring it to bear earlier in the innovation process. By achieving clarity earlier, opportunities remain substantial and attractive (Figure I.4).

Successful 4th generation R&D yields significantly improved innovation results, and it does so in advance of the competition because the point of action occurs much higher on the opportunity curve.

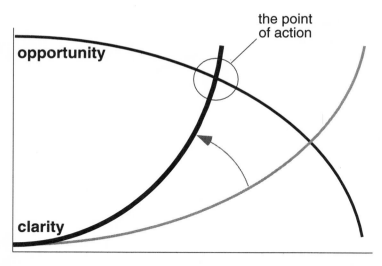

Figure I.4 The Adjusted Opportunity Curve. Successful 4th generation R&D accelerates the trajectory of clarity, moving the point of action higher on the opportunity curve.

A Final Thought

The stakes are high. The transition to new ways of doing business in a knowledge-based economy offers learning opportunities for individuals and new ways to achieve more agile resource deployment throughout society. It also offers the certainty of increasing competition, opportunities for profitable growth, and, through innovation, greater value to customers.

As a critical factor in this environment, innovation is many things. It is inspiration and creation; it is renewal; it is ambiguity and the tension of change in the learning process; and, at its best, it is also a journey of discovery.

You are invited to consider a new system for innovation—one that offers a new approach to the critical issues facing managers in the challenging markets of today and tomorrow.

4TH GENERATION R&D

CHAPTER I

4th Generation R&D

The search for innovation begins at a moment of invention that occurs in response to some combination of practical needs, insights, ideas, technologies, processes, infrastructures, commitments, problems, or possibilities. The search proceeds with an investment in people using tools to find new knowledge. Knowledge, which exists only in people, is then transformed into new capability and is delivered in the form of new technology. The goal, finally, is to provide new value to customers and simultaneously create or enhance a firm's competitive advantage in the marketplace.

While innovation is the result of work by individuals and organizations, its impact extends much farther. Economists, scholars, and executives understand that innovation is at the very heart of any society's sustained well-being, and it is the source of competitive differentiation.

In the words of Japanese professor and innovation researcher Fumio Kodama, "It is the intrinsic productivity growth and innovation rate of businesses that will ultimately determine the economic health of nations and of the world."[1]

Economist and president of the University of California Richard C. Atkinson bluntly states, "Productivity growth is the most important

V

factor governing how fast the economy can expand and how much liv-ing standards can rise over time."[2]

✓ As productivity growth comes only from innovation, Peter Drucker states simply, "The only thing that matters is innovation."[3]

✓ The direct relationship between innovation, productivity in-creases, and social wealth is not a secret. Managers understand the im-portance of innovation for overall economic well-being, just as they know that innovation creates compelling opportunities for business growth.

✓ Although the sum of existing innovations defines current reality for organizations, communities, and nations, it is the capability to in-novate in a progressively discontinuous environment that will deter-mine their futures.

✓ Lester Thurow points out that the Dark Ages were largely caused by a decline in the productivity of agriculture after the Roman organi-zational infrastructure collapsed, which led to a drop in the use of fer-tilizer. Large-scale organized activities came to end for a millennium, and at the end of the Dark Ages (1453), "the Roman roads were still the best on the continent even though they had had no maintenance for one thousand years."[4]

Investment in innovation is required for more efficient use of re-sources, improved productivity, increased global trade, and the in-creased individual and aggregate wealth that the members of society experience as improved standards of living.[5] Innovation is thus the driver of sustainable economic development.

✓ In addition, innovation is a compelling source of competitive ad-vantage for businesses because it represents new value for customers. Value creation is also the core of its definition: An innovation im-proves the value of a product and/or a service in a critical attribute or combination of attributes, all in the context of a knowledge infra-structure (an aggregated body of knowledge or professional discipline) *and* a physical infrastructure. Innovation improves economic value, emotive value, or both.

While the term invention describes the key moment of insight and the concept it evokes, innovation is the process of transforming an invention into something that is commercially useful and valuable. Whereas invention occurs apparently and unpredictably at random, innovation is manageable as a business process—and must be managed.

By this definition, innovation may be simply an expression of fashion, but to earn our full admiration it will certainly also be something more enduring that has to do with improving functionality, reducing cost, or both.[6]

Therefore, when top managers emphasize cost reduction strategies rather than innovation, as they have done for the past decade, it can only mean that they have lost confidence in the ability of their organizations to innovate effectively.[7] With the dismal track record we have seen, this is hardly unjustified.

Most of the disturbing statistics cited in the Introduction were compiled in the early 1990s, and it should be no surprise that in the United States, R&D spending was in decline during the same period.

Since then, however, corporate investment on R&D has been trending slowly upward. Aggregate 1996 spending was about $125 billion, up 3.5 percent from 1995 and 7 percent from 1993.[8]

From this, we conclude that the driving forces of advancing technology, globalization, and increasing competition have made it crystal clear that *sooner or later there is no substitute for effective innovation.*

Behind increases in spending is therefore a hidden search for new methods, new approaches to innovation. Driven by the inexorable, managers are innovating in the process of innovation itself, because they know that to succeed it is first necessary to find effective, practical models.

These must be workable systems that achieve consistency of result and inspire confidence in the minds of stakeholders, including customers, vendors, employees, managers, and shareholders. Further, the goal must not be simply innovation, but a consistently effective, manageable practice of continuous *and* discontinuous innovation.

Continuous and Discontinuous Innovation

The difference between continuous innovations that comply with the standards of existing markets and discontinuous innovations that supplant them is critical.

Continuous innovation is incremental and takes place within existing infrastructures. It builds on existing knowledge in existing markets without challenging underlying strategies or assumptions. We can visualize the domain of continuous innovation as a circle containing the established knowledge of suppliers and customers in a particular market or field (see Figure 1.1).

Strategies for continuous innovation include portfolio planning, five forces analysis,[9] and globalization through regional subsidiaries that stay close to customer needs. The awareness of core competencies also turns the focus inward,[10] while the emerging resource-based view

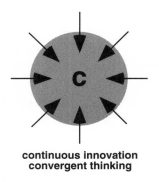

**continuous innovation
convergent thinking**

Figure 1.1 Continuous Innovation. Continuous innovation occurs within the boundaries of this known world. It works when the future competitive requirements of customers can be met within existing industry structures, an existing competitive architecture. As indicated by the inward-pointing arrows, continuous innovation is characterized by convergent thinking—progressive refinements, sharper focus, and therefore increasing specialization.

of the firm proposes integrating internal and external views by better gauging the value of resources.[11]

But continuous innovation is not sufficient unto itself. As Joe Marone, Dean of Rensselaer Polytechnic Institute has commented: "We know that there is overwhelming emphasis on the virtue of continual incremental improvement, yet every time we look at any successful company that has emerged over the last 30 years in a technology in-tensive field, and in fact throughout any period of industrial history, you will always find a pattern of big leaps into major new product lines, which are then followed by the efforts to stay ahead. And yet while we know an awful lot about practices of continual improvement, we seem to know very little about how to manage the discontinuous innova-tions. It may well be that the practices that we have learned for con-tinuous improvement are not only inappropriate for discontinuous innovation, but may actually be detrimental."[12]

Discontinuous innovation brings forth conditions that emanate from fundamentally different new knowledge in one or more dimen-sions of a product or service compared with what has come before, of-fering significantly different performance attributes. The difficulty so commonly experienced in achieving successful discontinuous innova-tion is precisely that it requires new knowledge, which is not available when you are looking only on the inside.

The domain of discontinuous innovation is therefore everything outside of the circle (see Figure 1.2).

Success at both continuous and discontinuous innovation are dri-ven by "forced questioning" about the limits of existing capabilities as well as by asking the right questions and probing at the edges of ex-isting knowledge to understand what new possibilities may exist that have not yet been recognized or considered. It would be trite to say that the kinds of questions you ask determine the kinds of answers you receive, were it not that deep, fundamental questions are simply not being asked in so many organizations. Prevalent cultural barriers widely preclude precisely the kinds of inquiry that are needed. Until and unless such questions are asked, deep and fundamental answers

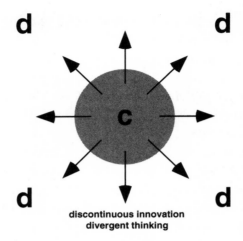

**discontinuous innovation
divergent thinking**

Figure 1.2 Discontinuous Innovation. Discontinuous innovation falls outside existing markets or market segments, and when successful extends and redefines the market, exposing new possibilities. As indicated by the outward-pointing arrows, discontinuous innovation is characterized by lateral or divergent thinking, by looking outside defined boundaries and by discovery of new knowledge related to both market need and technological capability. Discontinuous innovation leads to aggregated domains of knowledge that support new capabilities.

about the evolution of companies, markets, and industries will not be uncovered in time to do anything about it, nor will leadership be achieved.

Discontinuous innovation is more than the shift from horses to automobiles for personal transportation, an inconceivable thought for those focused on four-legged capabilities. It includes the shift from urban to suburban communities that offer new lifestyles created by real estate development that is based, in turn, on new highways that also bring new patterns of traffic and new forms of congestion.

Discontinuous innovation does not just bring change in the simple sense, but change in a deep and systemic way that is fundamental and far-reaching. It affects not only products and services but also the infrastructures integral to their use and extensive chains of distribution that may involve dozens or hundreds of affiliated and competing companies and industries.

Hence, representative changes include the shift from family to factory farms, impossible without the tractor, the truck, the railroad, the ship, and global markets; the shift from typewriters to personal computers, completely unpredictable before the microprocessor; or the shift from live performance to radio and television broadcasting for entertainment, news, and advertising, inconceivable before modern communications.

Discontinuous innovation is dramatic, and it is also inevitable when the requirements of customers can no longer be met within the existing framework of capability. This often happens because *new combinations or aggregations of knowledge, tools, technology, and processes change the underlying character of customer need by changing the boundaries of what is possible.* In fact, new knowledge continually creates new realities.

But discontinuous innovation also brings with it a price in the form of entirely new rules of competition. It invalidates entire companies and even entire industries even as it creates new ones.

There was once, for example, a global infrastructure to distribute kerosene for lighting,[13] and another to distribute ice for cooling.[14] Both were highly developed, extremely sophisticated for their times, and highly profitable for extended periods. But both are now mostly forgotten, displaced by the evolution of technology in the shift from one dominant business model to another.

More recent examples are the rapid evolution of the computer and communications industries that drastically impacted industry leaders IBM and AT&T. Both companies shed hundreds of thousands of employees in the early 1990s as discontinuity reached their worlds, and both still continue to reshape themselves. In addition to its impact in computers and telecommunications, discontinuous innovation is reshaping the airline industry, the auto industry, banking, retail, credit cards, securities, entertainment, and even the staid world of electrical generation and distribution. No business can protect itself fully from the impact of discontinuous change.

In the marketplace, discontinuous innovations are successful only if a new value proposition offers a significant improvement on at least one of the three performance axes: features, benefits, and cost. In the words of Rensselaer Polytechnic Institute Dean Joe Marone, "The performance gain must be five to ten-fold or have a 50 percent reduction in costs, or both."[15]

The switch from the typewriter to the PC required not only the purchase of expensive equipment, but also training in its use. Once a PC user attained experience with particular applications, the investment of additional time that was required to switch to different programs became a significant burden, so users stayed with obsolete software rather than incur the cost of switching to new programs, or even of updating the same program.

Similarly, an audiophile who switches from long-playing records to compact discs must repurchase an entire music library, title by title.

Hence, the new economics of "increasing returns" described by Stanford Professor Brian Arthur suggests that when an innovation does become dominant, so much knowledge is attached to it that it gets "locked in." The cost to switch is too high, showing that the structure of the market, its architecture, is inseparable from the knowledge-enabled capability of end users.

While discontinuous innovations force major shifts in both architecture and capability, continuous innovations are absorbed relatively effortlessly. They are easier to achieve, as they draw on the existing market framework, infrastructure, and tacit knowledge of customers, suppliers, and other stakeholders. As they are more narrowly and incrementally focused, they do not require conceptual leaps, massive amounts of new knowledge, nor the huge risks that accompany dealing with the unknown. Hence, they are also more comfortable innovation targets. As Chip Holt, Corporate Vice President of the Wilson Center for Research and Technology of Xerox has observed, "People have a tendency to focus in on the things they're most comfortable with and work them to death."[16]

In a stable world, there would be no call for discontinuous innovation, and continuous innovation would suffice for every need. But the reality of today is exponential change that takes many forms. One element is the influx of new technologies that drive a positive feedback cycle from which there is no escaping. If you want to remain viable in a competitive market, you must engage in the same cycle of technology development pursued by your competitors (see Figure 1.3).

The threat of unexpected competition, the risks of industry evolution, and compression of the sales cycle make mastery of discontinuous innovation not a desirable adjunct but a vital necessity (see Figure 1.4).

It is no longer enough merely to keep up through incremental innovation in existing markets and market segments (although few companies seem to be doing even that). Today, success is defined by leadership, and leadership is achieved not only by evolving today's products and services, but more powerfully by evolving and even redefining the very industries in which competition takes place. This requires not

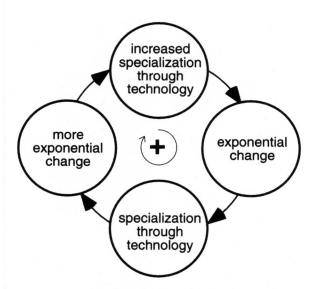

Figure 1.3 Specialization Drives Change.[17] To remain viable in a competitive market, companies inevitably pursue proprietary technical advances. This leads to further specialization, which drives increasing change. There is no graceful way to exit the loop.

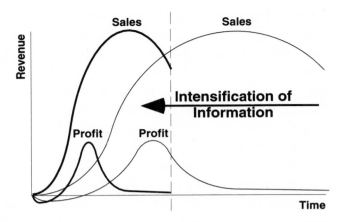

Figure 1.4 Compression of the Sales Cycle.[18]

just managing discontinuities in the marketplace, but *creating new discontinuities.* These are frequently seen as revolutions or ruptures, and achieving them is the true and enduring purpose of innovation; describing *how* to achieve them is the purpose of this book.

Whereas continuous innovation is focused on existing needs, discontinuous innovation is driven by questions about the *future needs* of customers; these needs are rarely articulated. In fact, they may not be able to be articulated at all, and so the only effective way to understand future needs is for customers to participate in the innovation process. Only when researchers work jointly with customers can this hidden knowledge be exposed, and only after tacit needs are exposed and understood is it effective to consider the role that technology should play in fulfilling them.

Therefore, the discontinuous innovation process is a mutually dependent learning process in which customers must experience what is possible to determine what may have future value. The process is driven not by technology itself, but by *how technology is* used.[19] Hence, the role of R&D changes significantly from the 3rd generation to the 4th.

From 3rd to 4th Generation R&D

The thinkers of the Renaissance had the pleasure of rediscovering the scientific method, which had been largely dormant in the European world throughout the Middle Ages. Perhaps Leonardo da Vinci was the first systematic practitioner of research and development in the contemporary sense of the term, in that his fundamental research into the workings of nature led him to envision devices from flying machines to submarines.

During the following three centuries, the continuing advance of science and its application in technologies of increasing sophistication led to the beginning of the industrial era. The practical evolution of industrial era management developed in four major overlapping phases, each initiated by a specific milestone:

1. A systemic approach to manufacturing was defined in 1800 by Eli Whitney as interchangeable parts. This conceptual and management innovation approach constitutes the core architecture of industrialism.

2. Key improvements were made to a critical industrial capability, measurement systems and tools. The micrometer, invented in 1830 by Joseph Whitworth, made it possible to effectively apply the new architecture of precise interchangability.

3. Production capability was progressively developed in the form of machine tools, the factory model, refined materials, and global distribution systems. Beginning with the turret lathe, first used in 1855, critical innovations also include the universal milling machine developed in 1862, electric drives in 1873, Ford's conveyer belt assembly line in 1914, the Japanese Just-in-Time system of the 1970s, and today's agile manufacturing systems.

4. Management capability was developed to handle the finance, accounting, organization, marketing, human resources, R&D,

facilities, and information systems. Methods essential to two centuries of progress have included total quality, process engineering and reengineering, project teams, and now virtual organizations and global alliances. From Henry Ford to Frederick Taylor to Alfred Sloan to Jack Welch, generations of managers perfected the industrial approach.

The advance of industrialism was affirmed when the Civil War ended with the North's defeat of the South in 1865. It was apparent even then that the North's superior industrial capacity was a fundamental factor in deciding the social and cultural conflict between the states, irrevocably establishing the role of industry in the modern world.

Soon thereafter in 1867, German chemical giant BASF established the first industrial R&D laboratory to develop new dye technology, and in 1876 Thomas Edison established a research laboratory in Menlo Park, New Jersey, that became the prototype for corporate research and development in the Industrial Era.

Edison and others such as Henry Ford became wealthy industrialists because their mastery of research methodology, combined with their tremendous (and probably intuitive) grasp of the market development process, enabled them to transform research innovations into commercial breakthroughs.

In the wake of Edison's successes, research and development laboratories were established in corporations throughout the United States, led by GE in 1900, Bell Telephone in 1911, and Kodak in 1913.

Driven largely by technical innovations emanating from these labs, along with university and government labs, the economies of the Western nations completed the transition from agriculture to industrialism early in the 20th century.

Initially, research was managed by scientists who selected and conducted research projects that yielded many significant breakthroughs and led to important and profitable products. In hindsight, the laboratories that were managed by scientists are now referred to as 1st generation R&D labs.

One of the most successful of these labs was operated by Du Pont, where a project by chemist Wallace Carothers led to the invention of nylon in 1939. During the next 50 years, nylon earned the company between $20 and $25 billion in profits.[20]

World War I was a powerful catalyst for R&D, as the development of more advanced industrial technology led to the development of new weapons. The airplane and the tank forever changed the nature of warfare, showing again that war was a matter of technology and production as much or more than an issue of national character or even the sheer number of soldiers in uniform.

Following World War I, Germany invested heavily in the development of new military technologies that gave Hitler's armies a huge advantage at the outset of World War II. Germany's capability in optics was particularly advanced, and it has been suggested that Hitler believed this superior capability would provide an enduring combat advantage for German tanks and aircraft.

However, the management of industrial research made significant advances during the 1930s, and a project initiated by Maurice Holland of the U.S. National Research Council led to the establishment of the Industrial Research Institute (IRI) in 1938. As an international association of R&D directors, the IRI contributed to the development of improvements to R&D management, which helped English and American scientists in the rapid development of capabilities comparable to Germany's. This enabled the Allies to achieve technical parity early on in many fields.

Overall, the concentrated application of R&D in many diverse projects during World War II was unprecedented, and the development of mechanical and electronic technologies in aviation, weaponry, and radar, and chemical technologies such as dyes, fuels, and synthetic rubber were fundamental factors on both sides of the conflict. Once again, superior production capacity contributed significantly to the Allied victory.

The ultimate expression of the wartime R&D projects was the development of the atomic bomb, which involved thousands of scientists and technicians working on the numerous scientific and technical issues at numerous secret laboratory sites throughout the United States.[21]

The important contribution by R&D scientists and engineers to Allied success in World War II was a convincing experience for corporate leaders, and investment in commercial R&D continued to grow after the war. In war and in peace, science and technology were clearly fundamental factors. By 1946, there were approximately 2,000 1st generation corporate research labs in operation, and still more were established in the postwar era.

After nearly a century of steady progress, the practice of systematic research and development was firmly established as a core function of the modern industrial corporation. Nearly every major corporation throughout the world had adapted Edison's model for its own research labs.

By then, corporate managers recognized that they must manage their labs with a greater focus on projects serving the needs of their businesses, and they applied and extended project management practices that were developed during the war. These are now referred to as 2nd generation R&D.

As the scale of corporate R&D continued to grow along with the sophistication of the technology, the cost of R&D increased substantially. Consequently, the inherent risk in R&D investments became a more significant part of a corporation's overall financial exposure.

Long-term success depended to a great extent on the results from the lab, but then as today, R&D work was inherently unpredictable and no one knew when its results would yield products that were ready for the market.

To moderate growing but unavoidable financial exposure, R&D investments were evaluated using tools similar to those used to assess other investments. The concept of the 3rd generation R&D portfolio emerged as a method of balancing high-risk activities that might offer important commercial breakthroughs over the long term, with low-risk activities that represented more modest commercial potential in the short term.

Research projects were analyzed in a family of matrices involving competitive advantage, risk, life-cycle aging, the timing of technology in the development pipeline, fit with core business strategies, and the commitment of resources, all in conjunction with the probability of technical and market success (see Figure 1.5).

R&D management was also concerned with recognizing the changing impact that technologies may have at various stages of their life cycles,[22] as a technology that initially transforms a market may soon be assimilated into basic methodology and lose its distinctiveness. Competitors will copy it outright or find other ways to achieve the same results. Hence, technology road maps helped link the evolution of technology with the products and services in each line of business.[23]

The practice of technology management in the context of financial risk, strategic planning, and technology road maps is called *3rd generation R&D*, which is also the title of the definitive book, published in 1991.[24]

However, the traditional innovation system described by 3rd generation R&D divides the responsibility for knowledge acquisition

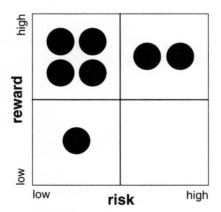

Figure 1.5 3rd Generation R&D. One aspect of 3rd generation R&D shows the relationship between the opportunity and the risk. The "high risk-low reward" quadrant remains mostly empty, while the "high risk-high reward" quadrant receives consistent investment at a moderate level. Preference is generally given to projects falling in the "low risk-high reward" quadrant.

between marketing, which determines customer need through surveys, and R&D, which supplies technology. In this 3rd generation process, only customer needs that can be specifically articulated can be addressed. Such needs, also referred to as "explicit" needs, constitute only the visible tip of the iceberg, the part of need that is above the surface of awareness.

By far the larger mass of need, the submerged part, is "latent" need, and this will probably not be discovered, nor satisfied, in a practice that fragments critical knowledge. Hence, innovations built on fragmented explicit knowledge can only be continuous, where incremental technology is applied in existing markets through traditional stage-gate product development.

In this environment, customers must therefore guess about the products, services, and infrastructures that will be available to them in the future, so their own planning is persistently inaccurate about the investments and capabilities that they would like to develop or will require in the future. Vendors, meanwhile, must guess about market demand for new products and services.

The alternative to this chronic guesswork is the sharing of knowledge gained through experiments in which vendors, customers, and other stakeholders all participate. This takes place in the research process itself, so that when an innovation reaches product development its value has already been proven to all stakeholders, and they no longer have to guess.

This approach exposes latent needs to support discontinuous innovation because individuals from many different kinds of communities and organizations participate jointly in a process of learning about what is possible and what works for each of them.

Here, customer needs and technological capabilities coevolve linked to one another in the 4th generation R&D process of "mutually dependent" learning, in which technologically enabled capabilities and concepts are assessed and refined in the context of real need.

Arie de Geus, formerly the head of scenario planning for Shell, expressed the importance of this most eloquently in his remark, "Learning faster than your competitors may be the only sustainable competitive advantage."[25] However, it is important to qualify this statement, for not all learning is equal: It matters not only *that* you learn, but just as importantly, *what* you learn.

Relevance comes about through careful determination of how the market is evolving, and what capability is required to sustain competitiveness in the face of this evolution. The broad structure of the market and its evolution is called the "competitive architecture" (the subject of Chapter 2), whereas the development of products and services within this market is based entirely on the "organizational capability" (the subject of Chapter 3) that any particular company can deploy in pursuit of its strategic goals.

The learning process for developing these two models must by definition be open-ended (otherwise it is not learning), and because innovation is based on learning, it must also be open-ended. Many of today's organizational methods, however, are biased toward decision making guided by bounded rationale, the practice of using only explicit knowledge. In practice, bounded rationale is inherently limited and limiting, and anything but open.

For example, commonly accepted practices of finance rely on mathematically derived rates of return to determine future value. Guaranteed rates of return cannot honestly be calculated for most innovation investments, however, because their outcome cannot be predicted at the outset, or even in the middle of the journey.

Thus, although "you can't prove innovation in a discounted cash flow model argument,"[26] innovation does require investment, and often in substantial amounts. The methodology of corporate finance must be changed if innovation is to be taken seriously, and the application of options finance to innovation management is an important first step, as discussed in Chapter 5.[27]

Together, these new research practices constitute significant changes in the conduct of R&D, which must now lead the process of determining how new scientific and technical knowledge can be used to identify and satisfy latent customer needs. The 4th generation R&D practice thus defines a broader mission for R&D as leader of technologically enabled discontinuous innovation.

The Approaches
to Innovation

In this chapter, we have described many different approaches to innovation practice, including the 1st, 2nd, 3rd, and 4th generations of R&D practice, and we have also drawn the distinction between continuous and discontinuous innovation.

Another way to describe innovation is to distinguish between breakthrough inventions and fusion innovations. Breakthrough inventions are based on fundamental scientific research that leads to new markets, but which emerge unpredictably and are virtually impossible to manage. They happen when they happen, so relying on whatever is still cooking in the lab is not a reasonable approach to managing for the future.

Fusion innovations, in contrast, are those that come about through the intentional combination or fusion of separate disciplines or bodies of knowledge to create new ones. Biotechnology, nanotechnology, and mechatronics are all examples of fusion innovations that have had (or will have, in the case of nanotechnology) significant global impact. Fusion innovations do not necessarily require new fundamental knowledge as much as they come about through engineering useful combinations of existing knowledge from formerly separate disciplines.[28]

Each of these approaches is characterized by differences that can be presented visually. For example, 1st generation R&D is the unbounded search for scientific breakthroughs (see Figure 1.6).

In contrast, 2nd generation R&D shifts the focus to applicability using project management, while 3rd generation R&D uses surveys to determine existing customer needs, and targeted technology development to create products and services to fulfill those needs. Constrained by the inherent limits of explicit market knowledge, however, 3rd generation R&D is predominantly occupied with continuous innovation (see Figure 1.7).

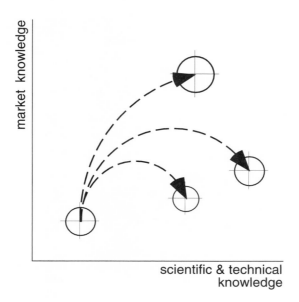

	ideas	trials	beliefs
partners & customers			
r&d	**1st generation r&d**		
marketing			
production			

Figure 1.6   1st Generation R&D. A primary characteristic of 1st generation R&D is that it seeks to leap from current knowledge to new knowledge which *may* be applicable in new technologies, products, and services. The focus is on the leap, not the applicability.

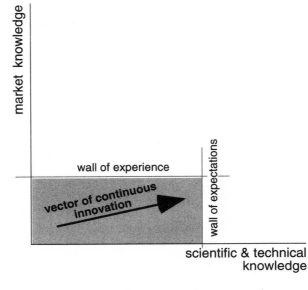

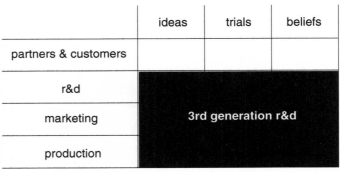

Figure 1.7 3rd Generation R&D and Continuous Innovation. Two dimensions bound 3rd generation R&D and continuous innovation. By focusing on explicit needs determined through experience with existing products and services, the growth of knowledge and experience are limited on the vertical axis, and by staying within the boundaries of existing products and services, the definition of expectations is limited on the horizontal axis.

Although 3rd generation R&D and continuous innovation are bounded within the two walls, discontinuous innovation is unbounded because it is driven by the discovery of unmet, tacit needs (see Figure 1.8).

Fusion innovations are expressions of the fusion of existing knowledge from different disciplines (see Figure 1.9).

The key to fusion innovation is identifying disciplines that are separate but complementary, and this can only be done effectively as the result of extensive examination of the tacit performance elements underlying a new productive domain.

The use of 4th generation R&D combines key elements of fusion and discontinuous innovation into a manageable method (see Figure 1.10).

Because 4th generation R&D is the synthesis of new market knowledge with new technical knowledge, it is not predictable from either

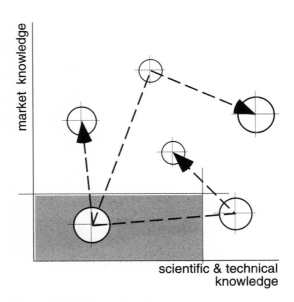

Figure 1.8 Discontinuous Innovation. Discontinuous innovation tends to be undirected and predictable.

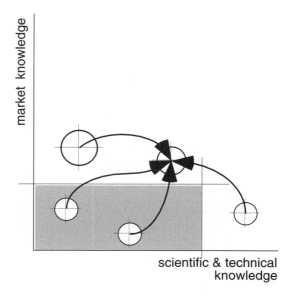

Figure 1.9 Fusion Innovation. Since they are based on existing knowledge in existing disciplines, fusion innovations define new disciplines and avenues of application without necessarily creating significantly new knowledge.

axis alone. And since 4th generation R&D is beyond the scope of traditional R&D practice, creating the conditions for its implementation requires some significant changes throughout the organization.

For example, no single department—including R&D itself—has the full knowledge needed to carry out the responsibility for innovation, which is now obviously an activity involving the entire organization and extending to include suppliers, customers, and other external partners as well.

Thus, one of the key elements underlying this change is the shift of focus from organizational structures within departments to organizational processes that are cross-functional.

"Structure thinking" is instinctively grounded in the familiar hierarchy, and in the patterns of communication that are based on who-reports-to-whom. Structure-bound organizations are highly

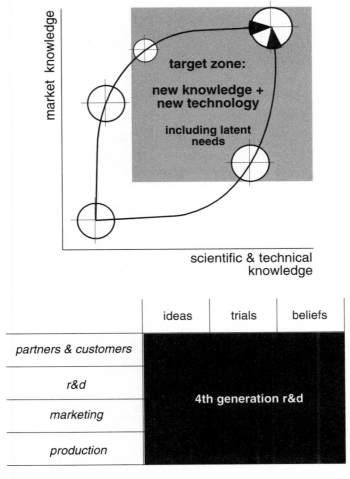

Figure 1.10 4th Generation R&D. Since it is driven by the synthesis of new knowledge, one vector of 4th generation R&D is the creation of new market knowledge on the vertical axis, and this vector has some of the character of fusion. But since that new knowledge provides the context for the development of new science and technology on the horizontal axis, 4th generation R&D also has a second vector. Hence, 4th generation R&D is the convergence of the two vectors as the expression of both new market knowledge and new technology, which occurs outside the domain of existing markets and knowledge, but inside the target zone for new markets and new industries that serve latent needs. The matrix shows that 4th generation R&D integrates customers and other partners in the entire conception and development process, so that when products are ready for market, all stakeholders have beliefs about the new value that is now available.

political, and beset by numerous pathologies in social relations and communications.[29]

"Process thinking," in contrast, is based on the awareness that business results come about not from structures but from business processes and practices that reflect how work actually gets done, and that effective learning is fundamental to effective work.

Historically, innovation has been embedded in organizational structure as the responsibility of the R&D department, focused almost exclusively on the development of technology in supply-driven markets.

As the market becomes fully demand driven and customers are able to assess competitive performance improvements, the old modality is simply not successful, and its failure is well documented.

What is now required is a business *process* focused on *innovation* rather than a business *structure* focused on *R&D, technology development, and product/service development.* A consequence of changes in the economy, in investment, and in management is that 4th generation R&D has emerged as the paradigm shift related to innovation and R&D practice.

Hence, the management of innovation in 4th generation R&D is the synthesis of many threads. Some of them are:

- The management of knowledge from many diverse sources.
- Expeditionary marketing through mutually dependent learning.
- The integration of both explicit and tacit knowledge.
- The development of robust models for competitive architecture and organizational capability.
- New organizational models.
- New approaches to finance, decision making, and accounting.
- The management of technology represented in the form of intellectual property.
- A new innovation process.
- The process and tools through which these elements are integrated.

We expect that the leadership of this convergence will be the role for a new senior officer, the Chief Innovation Officer (CINO) whose responsibilities will encompass the many elements of the innovation process.

The single most important question that the CINO will probably ask is, "What do I know about the evolution of the competitive architecture and organizational capability of the marketplace and in the industry?" From the answers to this question, the search for new value will follow in pursuit of continuous innovation and discontinuous innovation for new products, new markets, and new industries.

CHAPTER 2

Competitive Architecture: The External Framework

In broad terms, there are two possible strategies for dealing with complex problems. You can go in with greater focus, or you can go out for more perspective. Going in means studying the details through deeper and deeper analysis, while going out means pulling back to look for the larger patterns that illuminate a problem in the context that surrounds it.

As participants in an explicit culture that reveres analysis, Westerners usually choose the path of detail. However, the cyberneticians showed as long ago as 1954 that pulling back is actually the superior strategy and will lead to superior results in less time, primarily because complex systems cannot be understood through the analysis of their parts. Developing the overview of the whole system is much more effective.[1]

Since the innovation process necessarily deals with extremely complex situations, this is an important distinction. It means that we must first of all describe the broader system in which innovation is to be accomplished before immersing ourselves in the details.

Until recently the language and conceptual models needed to define these broad characteristics of the market did not exist, which partially explains why innovation practice has become so ineffective. But now the gap is being filled by a new innovation vocabulary whose terms include competitive architecture, organizational capability, dominant designs, and product, service, and distribution platforms; these are the subjects of this chapter and the following one.

The Language of Innovation: Theory and Architecture

As society evolves, its language also evolves, sometimes as a result of new science and technology that introduce new concepts and capabilities that prior terminology cannot convey.

Hence, physics entertains us with "quarks" and "strangeness," while computer science offers "compilers, " "source code," and entirely new self-contained sublanguages such as Fortran, C, and C++.

Economics has brought us "marginal returns," "diminishing returns," and now "increasing returns,"[2] while contemporary management is in hot pursuit of "strategic alliances" that embody "co-opetition," which, when worse comes to worst, become "takeovers" or "takeunders."

In every discipline, in every pastime, in every organization, and in every generation, the progression of specialized knowledge creates the need for new descriptive language that identifies new phenomena. Thus, couch potato Baby Boomers watch as their Gen X children rollerblade, bungee jump, and snowboard in their grunge clothing while listening to hip-hop music. . . .

Describing and classifying new phenomena, new domains of knowledge, new processes, new systems, and new terminology provides new levels of abstraction, which plays the role of theory, which gives coherence to the sum of our knowledge. At their helpful best, these classifications enable us to understand important patterns as they evolve over time. This is critical for innovation, since innovation itself drives evolution: Only when we have established a foundation in correct theory can we be effective at the practical work of innovation.

In the words of W. Edwards Deming, "The theory of knowledge teaches us that a statement, if it conveys knowledge, predicts future outcome, with risk of being wrong, and that it fits without failure observations of the past. Rational prediction requires theory and builds knowledge through systematic revision and extension of theory based on comparison of prediction with observation. . . . Without theory, experience has no meaning. Without theory one has no question to ask. Hence without theory, there is no learning."[3]

For the new innovation business process that yields continuous and discontinuous innovation, we must therefore define both new language to describe the market as it evolves, and its theoretical underpinnings. Without correct theory, it is nearly certain that we will fail to correctly identify the vector of the market's development. Because today's preferences have no inherent predictive value for tomorrow's markets, it is simply not enough to say that customers prefer this or that product.

Therefore, we begin at the highest relevant level of abstraction with three dimensions of theory that are critical for the innovation process (see Figure 2.1). Since innovation takes place in an economic context, we must define the broad patterns in the development of the economy as a whole. We have referred to this in the Introduction as the shift from the industrial economy to the knowledge economy.

The second critical dimension of innovation theory is concerned with learning, which is the core process for the creation of knowledge, and therefore the source from which innovation itself emerges.

The third dimension is management, which defines the organizational structures and means through which innovation and all other activities of an organization are accomplished.

The new innovation process as presented in this book is therefore the integration of these three dimensions beginning with the definition

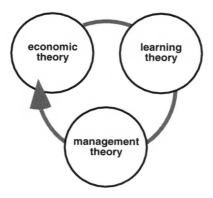

Figure 2.1 Three Critical Dimensions of Theory for Innovation. The new business process for innovation is built on three critical dimensions of theory. Once these three dimensions are correctly defined, practical implementation is possible. Without correct theory in each of these areas, however, effective and successful innovation management is nearly impossible.

of theory and continuing with the description of appropriate practice in each of the three areas.

Selecting the right word to identify the theoretical level in any subject domain requires making a choice. For example, one could refer to a "system" or "metasystem," or the "overview," the "top-level view, the "high-level strategy," or the "pattern language"[4] to represent this level of thought.

We prefer the word "architecture" to express the highest abstraction because it connotes design intention and a sense of order. It comes from the Greek words *archi* for "chief" and *tekton* for "worker," but more importantly in its modern usage "architecture" is a systems term that suggests the overall framework which contains specific and internally consistent syntax composed of specific combinations of terms and concepts. An architecture is a model that enables us to organize and manage complexity by identifying patterns, and more importantly, patterns of patterns. It is capable of describing the evolution of a system over time, and also contains rules for designing new extensions to existing language.

This use of "architecture" to represent this systems view of "evolving pattern of patterns" has been adopted in many fields. Computer designers, for example, refer to "computer architecture" to conceptually organize different configurations and classes of machines and software, from the vacuum-tube mainframes of the 1940s and 1950s to the transistors of the 1960s, the minicomputers of the 1970s and the microprocessor-based personal computers and workstations of the 1980s and 1990s. In fact, nearly every field has some form of architecture at its highest level of abstraction, including law, medicine, physics, engineering, and business.

You may have a different preferred term to describe this overall level of classification, and our purpose here is not to suggest that our choice of terminology is necessarily better. However, we emphatically insist that to be able to work effectively at innovation you must have *some* language that allows you to effectively represent and discuss these levels of thought. Only in such a context can the broad evolution of companies, markets, and industries be understood, and as importantly, predicted.

Defining an architecture requires study and observation, for inevitably some parts of the system are readily evident, whereas others remain hidden from all but the most studious.

Architecture and Capability Development

To manage innovation effectively, a new core process is required in the organization that is focused on defining the overall context in which innovation must take place. This model consists of two elements, one referring to the external evolution of the marketplace, and the other to an organization's response to those evolutionary pressures. These are the important core concepts of "competitive architecture" and "organizational capability."

The competitive architecture defines the broadest overview of a company in the context of the markets in which it competes, its customers and their needs and requirements, and its history, products, services, organization, and goals. Competitive architecture also includes all the other companies, with their own histories, products, services, organization, and goals, and the aggregations of companies and customers that create markets and industries. The competitive architecture shows how external patterns of competition evolve over time.

As this architecture defines the context for a company's future investments, it also clarifies how new internal capabilities must be developed and applied to sustain competitiveness. Hence, the second part of the core process is the systematic development of new organizational capability and the management of the knowledge on which capability

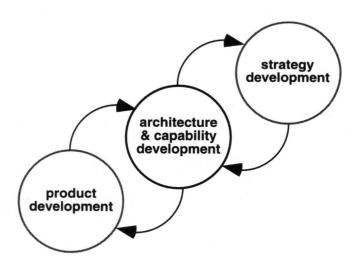

Figure 2.2 Architecture and Capability Development. Strategy development and product development are not sufficient to guide an organization in an increasingly complex business environment. The new core process of architecture and capability development is required to create the correct external and internal context for management and innovation.

is based. Organizational capability is a systems thinking construct that integrates tools, technology, process, and the associated knowledge that people have and create into a manageable unity.

Together, architecture and capability provide the means to properly define the scope for innovation by identifying continuity and discontinuity in the larger process of change in the business environment. Architecture and capability development therefore join strategy development and product development as core management processes for defining strategic intent and the means to get there (see Figure 2.2).

In the pursuit of continuous and discontinuous innovation, competitive architecture includes three additional levels of greater specificity and focus: The economic architecture is the broadest, the market architecture is narrower as it is relevant to industries, firms, and their markets, and the organizational architecture is specific to individual companies (see Figure 2.3).

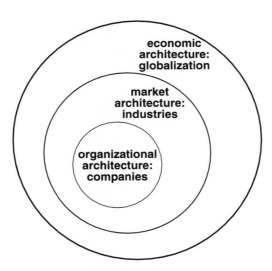

Figure 2.3 Concentric Elements of Competitive Architecture. Competitive architecture consists of the economic architecture at the global level, the market architecture consisting of industries, companies, and customers, and the organizational architecture defining how individual companies function.

Economic Architecture

In the innovation business process, the economic architecture describes broad patterns of investment and development.

The transition from the Agricultural Age to the Industrial Age was accomplished by the parallel development of systems of production and management that began with the concept of interchangeable parts, as devised by Eli Whitney in 1800. This, in fact, was the core of the new economic architecture.

The shift from the Industrial Age to the Knowledge Age that is occurring today is a similar evolution of concepts and tools, but now the capacity to gather, create, and apply knowledge is becoming the critical differentiating factor rather than control of natural resources and manufacturing capacity. In this new economy, the underlying dynamic is the progressive aggregation of more and more knowledge that leads to ever more specialization in science, technology, and trade, and consequently more and more complexity at all levels of society.

In this decade and the coming ones, however, the transition from the industrial model to the knowledge model is a work in progress, not a *fait accompli*. In the transition period, aspects of both economic models coexist, adding further complexity to a difficult and increasingly competitive market situation.

As we study the innovation process and the economic context in which it takes place, we observe many examples of this same dynamic, where contrasting models exist in pairs, or dyads.

Thus, the decreasing returns of industrial economies coexist side by side with the increasing returns of knowledge economies; tacit knowledge exists alongside explicit knowledge; convergent thinking alternates in the creative process with divergent thinking; competitive architecture and organizational capability are necessary complements for effective management and innovation; technologies and markets coevolve; consumer markets are bifurcating into complementary dyads,[5] and we describe innovation as continuous or discontinuous.

These, and many other dyads, are related concepts that describe different but complementary attributes of systems, and they are important for innovation because one of the most critical functions of innovation management is integrating the apparent contradictions that they present. Innovation is not an either-or proposition, but rather the specific and careful accommodation of ambiguity and paradox, and in many cases the coexistence of outright opposites.

In the past, making either-or choices was precisely the role of management, but now the proper focus is on understanding how to live with one foot in each of two worlds. In today's environment, wherever you identify a system with a distinguishing characteristic, you will likely be able to find a complementary characteristic of comparable importance, which makes the process of integrating diverse pairs of concepts a critical element of the economic architecture.

MARKET ARCHITECTURE

At a level of greater specificity within the context of the economic architecture, we can then make the distinction between supply-driven and demand-driven markets[6] as an expression of the "market architecture."

Whether we are talking about mass markets or markets-of-one, the concept of market architecture gives us a tool for evaluating and describing how markets evolve over time, and how different kinds of markets behave in different industries, cultures, and epochs.

The scope of market architecture is the context with which to describe how a company such as Federal Express, an infrastructure such as the Internet, a management approach such as the Health Maintenance Organization (HMO), and products like the personal computer have transformed industries and infrastructures, and thence daily life.

The components of this architecture include the characteristics of the products and services offered by any particular firm, the technologies that underlie them, the behavior of customers, the segments and niches that a firm and its competitors seek to occupy, and how this is all changing over time as technology and social values evolve.

ORGANIZATIONAL ARCHITECTURE

As the market architecture expresses an understanding of the external conditions that affect innovation, we must also describe a comparable model for the perspective inside of organizations. This "organizational architecture" is the set of internal structures and relations among differently specialized individuals and teams, and through which the work of making products, services, and the organization itself is accomplished.

Management consultant David Nadler describes organizational architecture in this way: "By architecture we mean a much more inclusive view of the elements of design of the social and work systems that make up a large complex organization. Architecture therefore includes the formal structure, the design of work practices, the nature of the informal organization or operating style, and the processes for selection, socialization, and development of people."[7]

Within the context of organizational architecture, we can effectively discuss broad issues such as the evolution of a firm, and specific ones such as the choice between command and control organizational models, and other approaches to management and coordination such as "recognition and response."[8]

As the survival of an organization depends on its ability to adapt to changes in the market, and as these changes are driven by broader economic changes, the process of fitting one to the other is one of the great challenges of management. Economic, market, and organizational architectures are therefore necessary complements that together compose a description of the domain in which innovation occurs, and this is why we visualize them concentrically.

Architecture development encompassing all three levels therefore constitutes one of the key management functions of the innovation process itself, as well as the domain in which corporate strategy is relevant for innovation and effective for general management. In some organizations, architecture development is handled concurrently with the development of strategy. More typically, however, those responsible for strategy concentrate on other issues, and architecture development is not practiced at all. Developing these models is one of the first steps in establishing an effective process for innovation.

Defining Customer Value in a Discontinuous Market

As the rate of change accelerates and the marketplace becomes ever more complex, the passage of events is more highly condensed. Futures that were once far in the distance may suddenly be very close at hand.

To manage successfully in these conditions, it is essential to have a good grasp on the emerging future, but the tools that have commonly been used for this are not sufficient.

Trend analysis and forecasting have inherent weaknesses in today's environment. Trends have to be visible to be studied, which means that the invisible is neglected. Those trends that are studied are likely to reveal much more about the present than they do about the future, just as forecasts build primarily on the known past and the visible present to derive assumptions about the future.

Both can be useful tools in continuous innovation, but they are likely to omit the highly improbable and the outright invisible, and these are the very areas likely to be the most important for discontinuous innovation.

Innovation consultant Marv Patterson, formerly of Hewlett-Packard, notes that Hartley's equation shows: "The value of the information carried by an event is inversely related to the probability of the event. . . . The implication is that development energy should be focused on those activities that have an inherent uncertainty. In fact, those elements of a particular development activity that are the least certain will yield the most information."[9]

And concerning the invisible, IBM R&D scientist Praveen Asthana suggests: "In the fast-changing world of high technology, your competitor tomorrow may not yet be a competitor today, and in fact may not even exist today."[10]

Similarly, Fumio Kodama describes a critical paradigm shift facing managers as the threat of new competitors who appear as "invisible enemies" entering into a market without warning from half a world away.[11]

All of this points to a great need for a different way of exploring the future, a tool that will provide an enduring basis for evaluating proposed innovations, whether they are continuous or discontinuous.

For this perspective, we rely on the relatively unchanging viewpoint of customers, as discovered through the consideration of how they experience and define "value." The search for innovation begins with a thorough examination of whatever it is that currently constitutes value, a critical construct of the competitive architecture. Whereas trends and forecasts consider the vectors along which things have been evolving by looking to the past, the identification of value *as it is perceived by customers and other stakeholders* exposes why this has been the case. And "why" is precisely what we must know to make useful predictions about the future.

Value, both perceived and existing, is what motivates people to make choices. They purchase any product or service because of what it offers (or promises) users—is not only the product or service itself, but the embodied *value* as customers perceive it. This embodiment can be literal, as a matter of economic functionality, it can be at the limits of the purely intangible as a matter of emotion or symbol, it can be anywhere in between, and it can be both.

To understand value as perceived by customers, it is necessary to know something of how they intend to use the product or service. It is also important to understand what they need to know (or more precisely, what capability they must have) to use the product or service effectively. Only from this viewpoint do a product's features then become relevant.

Cars, for example, provide the functionality of transportation as well as the symbolic definition of identity for drivers and owners who may wish to cruise the autobahn, cruise Main Street, commute to work, or run errands.

Cars also have significant impact beyond their immediate users, as a larger community of stakeholders is directly affected by the buying, selling, and maintaining of cars as well as the extensive required infrastructure directly affect a larger community of stakeholders.

What, therefore, are all the various sources of value that a product or service might offer to a collection of stakeholders that includes, but is not limited, to owners and drivers?

Identifying sources of value starts at a very high level of abstraction in the development of concepts, and is then integrated with extensive field observations made in many different sectors and contexts. Here, again, is a pair or dyad of activities, and innovation requires not either but both to be effective, a process Fumio Kodama calls "demand articulation."[12]

Concept development begins with definition of the economic, market, and organizational architectures, while useful observation methods may include techniques such as anthropology and video ethnography.

Once identified, grouping and categorizing the sources of value that have been identified make it possible to define a product in terms of what it must enable customers to *do*. Decisions about which elements are mandatory can then be made, and these decisions will also therefore be predictions about how new applications of technology may improve the value proposition and thereby achieve success in the market.

As different categories of value are more or less important in different market segments and to different categories of stakeholders, the information gathered from this process can be presented in a matrix (see Figure 2.4).

Making these criteria explicit is essential for successful product design; the critical functions of marketing and advertising involve addressing these criteria in a way that is recognizable to customers. Note that "recognizable to customers" does not necessarily mean "*consciously* recognizable to customers."

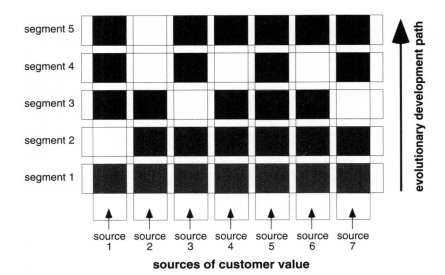

Figure 2.4 The Value Matrix. Successful products and services pertain to core values that are important to customers. The mixture of critical values varies for different market segments, and there is usually an evolutionary development path from more basic segments to more demanding ones. Blank squares indicate that a particular source of value is not important in a particular market segment.

Many or even most of these categories of value may be held in tacit form associated with experiences that have never been examined or analyzed. For this reason, effective advertising messages can be conveyed even though the recipients are largely (or even totally) unaware that any message has been conveyed at all.

In fact, this is a characteristic of all media. As Marshall McLuhan pointed out, the inherent nature of a medium is its predominant message, while the overt messages that are ostensibly conveyed are often of secondary importance.[13]

This suggests that knowing the demographics of customer groups is never sufficient. Value depends on how products are used and what their users want to accomplish, factors that are not likely to be revealed in demographic studies.

A more detailed view of implicit value is suggested by Noriaki Kano, who has described three different classes of features that may be pertinent to a particular product or service. First, there are the features that are presumed, to which the customer pays little if any attention. Then there are features that are expected, which are the focus of competition and which the customer examines when making the decision to purchase. Finally, there are features that delight, often because they are unexpected. It is often these that close a sale.[14]

To innovate successfully and consistently, it is therefore necessary to translate these sources and categories of both perceived and latent value, and of presumed, expected, and delightful value, into an analysis of the marketplace; this value framework is central to the competitive architecture.

This leads, then, to the question of how unique combinations of value elements can be translated into successful products. By exploring the customer's current and future perspective of value in this way, we have found a new way to explore the classic question: "What business are we in?" It is transportation, not railroads; it is personal transportation, not internal combustion engine cars; it is personal illumination, not candles, kerosene, or light bulbs.

Core categories of value such as productivity, comfort, health, and satisfaction tend to remain stable over time. Understanding what they are permits effective targeting for innovation, as new market architectures address enduring values in new ways without changing them.

In the auto industry, a value matrix might look like the one shown in Figure 2.5.

The evolutionary path described by the arrow at the right indicates that individual companies develop by refining their product and service offerings in moving from one segment to the next more exacting one, and this is precisely what the leading Japanese car manufacturers have done.

Following World War II and also later when they began to penetrate the American market, Honda, Nissan, and Toyota all concentrated on making simple cars that were the most basic of transportation. As they developed increasingly sophisticated capabilities, the basic architecture of the industry motivated them to move upstream into new, more demanding and more profitable segments. Finally, in the 1980s, each of

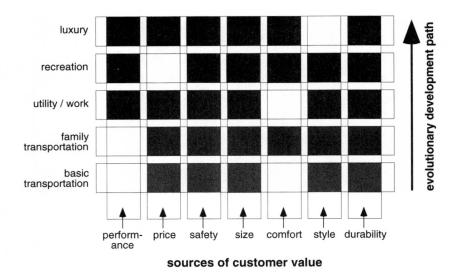

Figure 2.5 The Value Matrix in the Auto Industry. The consistent qualities that provide value to customers are listed across the bottom, while the market segments in which they apply are listed on the right. Some values are not critical in some segments, so these squares are blank.

these Japanese manufacturers established subsidiaries in the luxury segment of the market. Honda established Acura, Nissan established Infiniti, and Toyota created Lexus, all of which defined new standards of excellence in the industry, and all of which put tremendous pressure on existing luxury car manufacturers.

Because the Japanese companies climbed the evolutionary ladder from segment to segment, they had developed and proved their methods in lower price market segments. Their capabilities were inherently lean and efficient, enabling them to sell higher quality cars for lower prices than Mercedes, BMW, and Cadillac. They had created a new market discontinuity that enabled them to capture tremendous market share.

In the consumer electronics marketplace, Sony did exactly the same thing, and after working its way up from the bottom of the market, the company has become one of the world's most highly re-garded brand names.

The relationship between the sources of value and market segments is a critical one, and it is the basis of defining the relevant architecture and managing the capabilities required to create successful products and services.

An existing value proposition will be evident as the generally accepted mix of attributes and features of a product or service; this may also be described as the "dominant design" in a product class or industry.

Dominant Design

A dominant design becomes so widely accepted as the correct combi-nation of features and benefits that it becomes an implicit standard in the marketplace for whatever problems it solves. Because they describe the aggregate of market behavior, dominant designs emerge in all in-dustries and are therefore tremendously useful for understanding how markets evolve, another critical aspect of the market architecture.

The shift from one dominant design to the next is marked by a pre-dictable pattern of events. First, there is a period of instability when competing companies try to capture market share with products and services that reflect their interpretations of three critical qualities: how the product or service should be perceived (including how it should look, sound, and feel[15]), how it should function, and how much it should cost.

Gradually, customers gain familiarity through experience, and de-velop both tacit knowledge and sustained preferences. Products and services that best satisfy these preferences accumulate market share ad-vantages, and eventually any product type in any market segment will stabilize into a state of maturity (even if only temporarily) around a particular approach to solving the customer's problem.

MIT professor Jim Utterback presents this important concept in his book *Mastering the Dynamics of Innovation*.[16] He offers this description: "A dominant design in a product class is, by definition, the one that wins the allegiance of the marketplace, the one that competitors and innovations must adhere to if they hope to command significant market following."[17]

Utterback cites the Underwood Model 5 typewriter of 1899 as an example: "This particular design brought together a number of market-proven innovations into a single machine and very quickly came to command the typewriter industry. It remained the dominant design for decades [until the electric typewriter of the 1950s and 1960s], defining how the typewriter was *supposed to look and operate* in the minds of both typists and other typewriter producers."[18]

There are dominant designs in every conceivable category of products, and in services as well. Wherever it is that you are as you read this book, for example, you should be able to look around and recognize dominant designs embedded in just about every humanly made thing that you notice.

There is the book itself. It is a stack of paper consisting of a title page, a copyright page, a contents page, and then a big pile of text pages, all bound inside a cover. The chair you are sitting in (if you are) probably consists of the elements that have proven appropriate in accommodating the human form, including legs, a seat, and a back, and hopefully it is comfortable.

If you are in an office, perhaps a personal computer is there. It consists of a set of standard components whose overall configuration has hardly changed in two decades, even as the individual parts and pieces have undergone tremendous evolution. On the outside, there is the ubiquitous plastic box, a display screen, and a keyboard. Inside, the pattern is also constant. The CPU (central processing unit) chip sits on the motherboard, which also contains memory chips and connections to a power supply, a hard drive, perhaps a CD-ROM, as well as the keyboard and display. Various standardized ports (always, it seems, on the back) enable the machine to be connected to other devices and net-works, including electric power, telephones (via the modem), printers (via a LAN [local-area network]), and a large and growing assortment of other specialized devices.

Within this accepted dominant design framework for the PC, there are currently two key variants, two different approaches to implement-ing the dominant design. Desktop PCs are one form of packaging for this set of components, while laptops incorporate the same elements in a different configuration. When you go to buy a computer, these are the two possibilities that you have come to expect, and you will there-fore evaluate the various brands on criteria other than these dominant configurations.

Even the teaspoon that you may have used to stir your coffee this morning reflects a dominant design. It was probably a small oval bowl at the end of a narrow, straight or gently curved handle, with a slight bend at the joint between the two. It may have been plastic, wooden, stainless steel, or sterling silver, but that does not change the fact that a teaspoon is a teaspoon is a teaspoon in the eyes of an adult. (When necessary, that same teaspoon may also become a shovel, a drumstick, and a projectile.)

In the hospitality industry, there is an accepted dominant design for hotel rooms, which are placed in rows and contain the same basic furniture with adjacent bathrooms containing the same basic fixtures.

Dominant designs are evident in products as diverse as pens and pencils (a tip, barrel, top), scissors, shovels, and knives (handles at-tached to blades), doorknobs (handles, barrel, and strike), and calen-dars (rows and columns of dates on pages of months).

Dominant designs are also prevalent in services, in distribution systems, and in the design of organizations. To send a letter in any country, you put a document in an envelope, write the address, and affix postage in the form of stamps or an airbill, and the postal service of your choice takes over from there.

Dominant designs emerge in mass markets and niche markets as an unspoken consensus expressed by the aggregate of individual choices in the marketplace. It is intuitively obvious to both competing suppliers and interested customers when a dominant design has been established, because at some point it is suddenly clear that there is near-universal expectation about what a product is, what it looks like, what it does, and what it costs.

There is also implicit agreement about what it does not look like. In describing the failure of the Toyota Previa minivan, a Toyota engineer commented: "It didn't fit American consumers' accepted formula of what a minivan should be."[19]

Once a dominant design has taken hold in the behavior and expectations of both suppliers and customers, those pursuing innovation are confronted with a choice, as any new product that is intended to serve the same function as an existing one will necessarily have to conform to the existing standards of dominant design, or break with those standards and challenge that design with a new one.

Each company must therefore choose to innovate within this existing framework via continuous innovation, or attempt to transcend in some significant way a combination of limitations that is inherent in the existing model, and thereby define a new dominant design that is discontinuous.

There are risks both ways. Does the current dominant design still satisfy the fundamental needs of customers? If so, then any attempt to supplant it with a new dominant design may be doomed. On the other hand, is today's design simply the best that can be done with old technologies whose constraints can now be overcome? What advantages would be gained by a new dominant design? And if this organization does not take the risk, will a competitor seize the initiative and thereby take the lead?

Sometimes new dominant designs change not only the character of products and services, but the very industries in which companies compete. Recognizing when new dominant designs are emerging is a critical management function, and s-curves and bell curves are often used to help visualize the progressive market acceptance of products that eventually become dominant designs (see Figure 2.6).

Having defined a model of market architecture consisting of value frameworks and dominant designs, there is now a clear context in

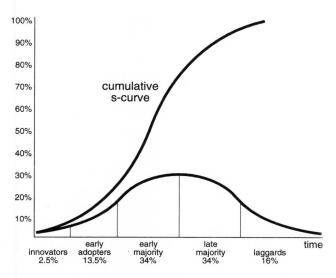

Figure 2.6 Diffusion of Innovations.[20] Research by Everett Rogers has shown that the process of adoption can be divided into five periods, and in each period a different type of consumer behavior is prevalent. The point at which the s-curve tapers off at the end defines a window of opportunity, and it is here that a new product or service may be able to capture the imagination of the market and become the next dominant design.

which to pursue both continuous and discontinuous innovation. Going forward, therefore, these theoretical constructs must be continually validated through experiences that confirm the model, or revised based on experiences that contradict the model.

Product, Service, and Process Innovation

Utterback also observes that once a dominant design has emerged in the marketplace, the focus of competition shifts from the characteristics of the product itself to the production and distribution processes by which it is made and delivered to the market. The objective of this intense cycle of process innovation is to lower the critical cost factors that determine pricing strategies while improving the performance attributes that shape customer experience. This rationalization and optimization of the product itself and its production and distribution processes become the basis on which firms seek competitive advantage (see Figure 2.7).

In the early days of the auto industry, dozens of companies marketed cars with steam engines, electric motors, and internal combustion engines. Only after more than a decade of competition did the internal combustion engine emerge as the dominant design, after which the focus of competition shifted to the manufacturing and distribution processes rather than the base product configuration.

After a full century of consolidation around the internal combustion engine, about 10 companies dominate the world market for cars, and a massive global infrastructure has developed around the fueling and maintenance of gas-powered cars and trucks, activities that together account for some 15 percent of global production. In any given

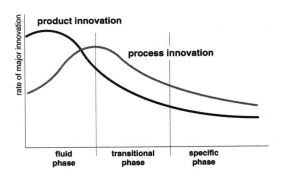

Figure 2.7 Dominant Design Progression.[21] The fluid phase is defined by the development of the dominant design in the form of the product concept. Once the concept has been accepted, the focus shifts to innovation in the processes by which it is manufactured and distributed, as these become the critical cost factors that determine competitiveness.

segment of the auto market, the products of one company are nearly indistinguishable from those of its competitors.

As the basic technology of internal combustion has been applied to dozens of other markets, it is also the key to dominant designs of products as diverse as lawn mowers, motorcycles, and even electric generators.

But with the advent of global warming and the worsening of urban air pollution, many in the auto industry believe that electric or hybrid cars are inevitable and are working on discontinuous innovations to make them a reality.

At Honda, 33 percent of the budget for engine research has been allocated to electric and hydrogen-powered vehicles. In 1992, Honda's head of engine development Hideyo Miyano suggested that gasoline engines would only be prevalent for two more decades,[22] and within five years Honda had already introduced an electric vehicle, as had numerous other manufacturers as well.[23]

In contrast, many continuous innovations are entirely process-oriented, and their importance is not immediately visible to customers, except as they permit greater efficiencies that may result in cost changes. At Wal-Mart, numerous innovations in the management of the supply chain enabled the company to significantly reduce its distribution costs. The company then passed some of these savings on to its customers in the form of price reductions, and by doing so developed tremendous customer loyalty. Much of this loyalty was obtained at the expense of Wal-Mart's competitors such as Montgomery Ward and Sears.

For companies like Sears that are already established in the marketplace, discontinuous innovation that is well received by customers represents one of the greatest threats. In the history of commerce, particularly during the rapid changes of the past century, the shift from one dominant design often accelerates the demise of companies that cling too long to the old standards.

Failure to adapt to new conditions in the marketplace, as reflected by a change in the dominant design, may be crippling because it often takes years of investment in learning to build the necessary competitive capability. Although some advocate the "fast follower" strategy, the reality is that when dealing with changes in dominant design, this approach is rarely successful because learning always takes time.

Followers also face a critical handicap in that market leaders have the opportunity to aggregate their knowledge of market needs and business processes into product, service, and distribution "platforms" that provide significant operating efficiencies.

Product, Service, and Distribution Platforms

We have noted that desktops and laptops are two commonly accepted approaches to the design of personal computers. These two variants of the base dominant design perform the functions that are expected, but the specifics of how they accomplish this and the particular configurations are different from one to the other, even as the software that runs on each is interchangeable. These are therefore derivatives of a basic dominant design as expressed in different "product platforms" that address different segments of customer need.

For manufacturers, the principle of the product platform offers a useful and efficient way to manage diversity in a product line. A product platform as defined by the originators of the concept, consultants Marc H. Meyer and Alvin Lehnerd, is "a set of subsystems and interfaces that form a common structure from which a stream of derivative products can be efficiently developed and produced."[24] Platforms are generalized aggregations of technology that can be applied in a diverse range of specific applications.

The reason this is so important is that through design leverage and the reuse of standardized elements, derivative products can be produced for as little as 10 percent of the cost using nonplatform approaches. The competitive implications are obviously enormous.

At Black & Decker, the concept of product platforms was used to rationalize the manufacturing process for an unwieldy line of power tools that was expensive to produce. Before introducing the platform concept, 122 Black & Decker power tools required 30 different motors, 60 different motor housings, and 104 different armatures. After rationalizing around a common platform, a universal motor system had been devised that provided motors varying from 60 to 650 watts of power. While the old motor assembly line required 108 people, the new one needed only 16, and the labor cost per unit therefore declined by a factor of seven, from 14 cents to 2 cents each.[25]

Its new product platform gave Black & Decker a tremendous cost advantage over its rivals, which the company leveraged as a competitive weapon and literally drove most of its competitors out. Over a five-year period, Stanley, Skil, Pet, McGraw Edison, Sunbeam, General Electric, Wen, Thor, Porter Cable, and Rockwell all departed the consumer power tool market, leaving Black & Decker and Sears as the only companies left standing.[26]

Using platforms as a manufacturing strategy resolves one of the most difficult innovation dilemmas, the necessity of addressing a complex and diverse marketplace while maintaining simplicity in the manufacturing process. This, another example of dyadic complexity, shows how innovation must respond to inherently conflicting requirements.

An example of the utilization of platforms in a much different kind of market is the auto industry, where intense competition has continued for decades on many fronts, including all the key value dimensions—performance, price, safety, size, comfort, style, and durability. As noted, the leading Japanese manufacturers established new high standards in all these areas, and in the late 1970s their American and European counterparts found themselves scrambling to catch up.

Many of the techniques developed by Japanese companies significantly reduced manufacturing costs, and these were eventually copied throughout the industry. There are also significant costs in the other aspects of the business, including the design and engineering processes, and companies including Ford and Chrysler applied the platform concept to reduce these costs as well.

Before the application of platform thinking, new cars originated in product planning and proceeded sequentially through design, engineering, procurement, manufacturing, and finally to marketing. Concept and design changes made at each step required rework at the previous steps, and the tedious back and forth process was expensive and time consuming.

To better manage new car development, Chrysler organized its design and engineering efforts around five platform teams: small car; large car; minivan; Jeep and truck; and special projects (such as the Viper sports car). New cars in each platform segment were developed by multidisciplinary teams that included participants from all the company's departments. By working concurrently rather than sequentially, development cycle time was reduced by 27 percent, from $4\frac{1}{2}$ years to $3\frac{1}{4}$.[27] Not only was labor cost reduced, but by improving time to market the company could capitalize on its ideas sooner while reducing the sunk cost of development.

To optimize its investment in platform teams, Chrysler then invested $1 billion in a new facility to house the 7,000 people who participate on platform teams and their related support functions.

Hence, the evolving market architecture of the auto business drove the shift to product platforms as a competitive strategy, which then changed the very nature of the organization's capabilities, its organizational structure, and the processes by which work is done. Here we see how the concurrent and interacting development of competitive architecture and organizational capability drives adaptation to change and creates the conditions for improved performance and competitive advantage.

The platform concept is useful not only in defining a path to rationalizing existing businesses, but also as a strategy for creating new products. When the Sony Walkman was introduced, it defined a new product category and also became its dominant design. Between 1980 and 1990, more than 160 kinds of Sony Walkmans were introduced, which averages to one every 27 days over the span of years. Along the way, significant improvements were made to all the components, even though during the entire period the basic configuration of the device was almost unchanged. The 1990 Walkman looked nearly the same as it had 11 years before, and it still set the standard against which competing products were evaluated.

The cost savings available from the platform approach can be significant in many markets. Figure 2.8 has been adapted from Meyer and Lehnerd, and it shows the cost savings in the development of derivative products.

Another use of the platform concept is in modeling the evolution of an industry. For example, with the enormous market for computing devices as the enticement, new designs for computers are being developed that manufacturers hope will become next generation product platforms. These new product platforms are derivative rather than revolutionary, as network computers that use client-server architectures

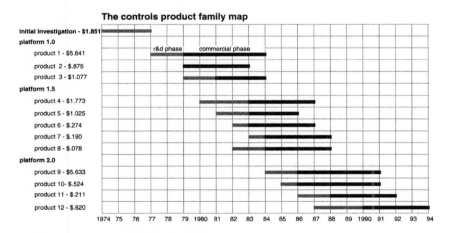

Figure 2.8 Product Platforms for Derivative Products.[28] Product platforms are families of products that share key attributes and base technologies within the framework of a single dominant design. Derivative products can be produced for as little as 10 percent of the original development cost, thereby creating significant cost advantages for companies organized around the platform model.

are now proposed as alternatives to stand-alone desktop PCs, while palmtops are offered as alternatives to the laptop.

The concept of a platform refers not only to the appearance and functionality of a product, but also its design and manufacture, the design and manufacturing processes and facilities, the services that are provided with it, and even its distribution.

In distribution, existing wholesale, retail, and direct channels define current platforms, while companies such as Wal-Mart have pioneered new platform concepts that have redefined practices for large retail chains. For example, rather than warehousing many of its products regionally before shipping them to stores, Wal-Mart has connected its cash registers directly with the computer systems of its suppliers so that products can be shipped as needed directly from factories to stores without intermediate warehousing steps, saving time and money and defining a new EDI (electronic data interchange)-enabled distribution platform.[29]

The Internet could also become a significant new channel for the distribution of information and knowledge directly from content producers to end users, replacing existing systems including bookstores, newspapers, and magazines, as will be explored in more detail in Chapter 4.

New service platforms also evolve through innovation. The delivery approach taken by Federal Express is itself an example of a new service platform, which has aggregated the knowledge needed to run an airline, a trucking company, a sorting and distribution system, and an information system to support a cycle of pickup and delivery that occurs across the continent in less than 24 hours. Once the basic service platform was established, the company was able to expand into new classes of service that include early morning, afternoon, and 2nd day deliveries for envelopes and parcels of all sizes and weights. The company then created another platform by offering to warehouse and manage inventories for its customers, in addition to its delivery services. A third platform has also been proposed, an Internet shopping mall infrastructure enabling small retailers to reach national and international markets, for which FedEx is happy to deliver the parcels (see Figure 2.9).

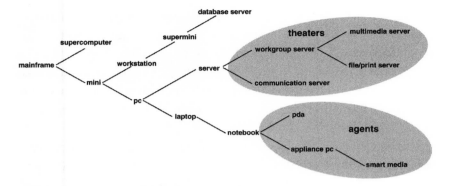

Figure 2.9 Platforms in the Computer Industry.

Together, the value framework, dominant designs, and platforms are three critical, functional elements of the competitive architecture. Each describes an important aspect of the market and the competitive approaches that companies take in pursuit of market share. To manage innovation in this context, it is important to recognize how these concepts are interrelated and how the decision-making process advances through the innovation cycle.

The Innovation Cycle: Architecture, Capability, Platforms, and Products

As Utterback shows, the survival of any company depends on the performance of its products and services in the marketplace relative to the dominant design, and on the effectiveness of the underlying processes by which they are created and delivered. Just as important to competitive success is the awareness that to achieve success with new products and services it may well be necessary to develop significant innovations in product, service, and distribution platforms as well.

However, the design of platforms, products, and processes must take place in a coherent context that is established by management and is expressed through models of competitive architecture and organizational capability.

In fact, the innovations in competitive architecture and organizational capability become the enduring basis by which firms adapt to changing conditions in the marketplace. Innovations in capability and architecture create vital organizational knowledge through which new needs can be recognized, and on which additional and continuing new product, product platform, service, and distribution innovations will be based, and this is the enduring pattern of the innovation cycle (see Figure 2.10).

As we study the histories of the successful and unsuccessful companies of the past few decades, this pattern shows up consistently and almost without exception.

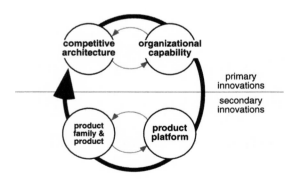

Figure 2.10 The Innovation Cycle. Competitive advantage can be obtained from a continuing stream of innovation in new products, services, and platforms, but it is also clear that developing and delivering the right products and services comes about as the result of the right competitive architecture and organizational capability models.

Xerox, for example, recognized the great importance of product innovation to its future, and the company established its Palo Alto Research Center (PARC) to be a source of new ideas. Since its founding in 1970, PARC has achieved a magnificent track record as the source of a long line of significant new product concepts and prototypes in high technology. In the 1970s, PARC created the Alto, a robust predecessor of the personal computer with numerous features including the mouse, windows, the graphic user interface, and text editing. Soon, the local area network and the laser printer were also invented at PARC, all far in advance of any competition.

Nearly all the innovations developed at PARC gained acceptance in the marketplace, but unfortunately for Xerox they have not done so in Xerox products. Instead, they have appeared in products of and earned billions of dollars in profits for other companies, including IBM, Apple, Microsoft, Novell, and Hewlett-Packard (HP).

This happened precisely because Xerox did not have a process to develop competitive architecture and organizational capability and therefore did not accompany its innovations in product platforms and dominant designs with new capabilities in business processes, organization, and management. The missing process would have enabled Xerox to transform itself and successfully exploit the new products in the marketplace. An entire book has been written about Xerox's inability to profit from the Alto, its own intellectual property.[30]

Xerox attempted to sell its new computer products using the same organizational architecture and organizational capability that sold mainframe computer services, Xerox Computer Services (XCS). The result was a miserable failure, as XCS understood neither the product nor the emerging market for what was, in truth, a new dominant design that subsequently became the personal computer industry.

Although the product itself was quite advanced, XCS was unable to market it effectively, and finally sold its excess inventories at enormous discounts to employees and exited the business.

A second issue, and also an important one, was the lack of market development. Perhaps Xerox entered the market prematurely or gave up on it too early. But soon after Xerox abandoned the market, Apple

Computer incorporated many of the same features into the Lisa and then the Macintosh computers, and more than a decade later the Mac is still selling hundreds of thousands of units each year.

Had Apple gone to an open operating system architecture in the 1980s before Microsoft incorporated many of the same features into its Windows software, history might have picked "Macrola" rather than "Wintel" as the dominant worldwide design for the PC. Thus, Xerox innovations are now integral to the operating system software of nearly every one of the hundreds of millions of PC throughout the world. For want of the correct competitive architecture, Xerox's share of the revenues from all this has been negligible, and Apple's is declining.

Although Xerox PARC was technically and conceptually far in advance of any potential competitor, the company was burdened with a learning disability, for just as learning is the core process that leads to new products and services, so it must also lead to new processes and new forms of organization where they are needed.

A satirical view of PARC's failed innovativeness is offered by *Upside* magazine: "On the first day, Xerox PARC created the PC. On the second, it created the OS [operating system]. The third, desktop publishing. The fourth, the key to laser printing. On the fifth day, it realized it had no marketing. On the sixth, it gazed deep into its navel. On the seventh, it gave everything away."[31]

What will happen in the strategic battle for the next dominant design? Competitive architecture and organizational capability will again play a decisive role. Innovations in processes and management are vital aspects of organizational capability and must stand beside technical proficiency, knowledge management, and marketing prowess as critical core competences.

At Xerox, the lessons of the Alto have been carefully studied. Among the conclusions offered by John Seely Brown, now head of PARC, is the realization that "as much, if not more, creativity goes into the implementation part of the innovation as into the invention itself."[32]

The innovation cycle does not just apply in high-technology industries. At Honda, for example, the initiative to establish manufacturing operations in the United States was undoubtedly a significant managerial innovation that was based on a correct model of the competitive architecture: "Early in the 1980s, while U.S. industry was searching for excellence, along came Honda. In late 1982, just three years after the company started manufacturing motorcycles in the United States, Honda became the first Japanese company to manufacture automobiles on American soil. . . . it was Honda's managerial innovations that transformed a group of central Ohio people into a highly motivated and inspired work force."[33]

Today we chuckle at Henry Ford's shortsighted and condescending statement: "They can have it in any color they want as long as it's black," because we know that the days of supply-driven markets are long gone. But then we behave exactly the same way when introducing new products and services without considering the organizational architectures and capabilities required to deliver them to the market.

Consequently, those who are unwilling to undertake the necessary organizational and architectural innovations and cultural changes have, in effect, already decided not to be innovative. In these companies, old organizational forms have been allowed and even expected to take on an aura of permanence. It is honestly (and naively) expected that while products and services change over time, the organization and its tacit set of accepted beliefs about its markets and its management will remain fixed and unchanged. Products and services come and go, while departments, procedures, distribution channels, the scope of technological capability, and staff positions have their own inertia.

Once this inward-looking way of working and thinking has become embedded in tacit knowledge and the internal structures of budgeting, decision making, and operations management, it is nearly impossible to change an organization itself, except at great cost and great trauma. Hence, at General Electric it was said, "Many of GE's best managers devoted far more energy to internal matters than to their customers' needs. As GEers sometimes expressed it, theirs was a company that operated, 'with its face to the CEO and its ass to the customer.' "[34]

The underlying beliefs about how to create value and how to earn money in the market must change. The innovation cycle reverses the direction of causality that is normally supported in organizations. It switches the emphasis from permanence of organizational form to a managed process of mutual learning with customers and business partners to enable transitions between fluid organizational forms. Organization is understood to derive from and adapt to the specific requirements of an evolving mix of products and services.

The benefits of organizational fluidity and the risks associated with a rigid organizational structure are also exemplified by two chapters in the history of the IBM personal computer.

To develop and market its breakthrough PC, IBM created a new division that had the autonomy to quickly create and manage a product whose tremendous success was quite unexpected.

The group was given so much autonomy because the initial sales forecasts were very modest, but if IBM had tried to push the product through its existing organizational structure, the new venture almost certainly would have failed.

Ironically, having achieved great success through architecture and capability innovation combined with platform, product, and service innovation, IBM then ignored the important consequences of its success. The company failed to recognize that the very existence of the PC and the wide scope of its market acceptance changed how people thought about and organized their computing functions: the competitive architecture was changing.

Hence, the PC began to have implications for IBM's mainframe business, but instead of embracing this change, IBM struggled to preserve the structure of the mainframe market for nearly a decade beyond its natural lifespan. By its own actions, IBM had created a fundamental shift in the competitive architecture of the marketplace but then failed to recognize the consequences.

Fighting a futile rearguard action, its stock price tumbled from a high of 168 in 1987 down to a bargain basement 56 only five years later.

By 1993, the company's leaders realized and admitted their predicament, but by then it was too late to save hundreds of thousands of jobs, and there followed one of the most costly and gut-wrenching processes of recovery ever seen in corporate America. Only after writing off a staggering $8 billion did IBM began to rebound.

Meanwhile, as IBM had failed to recognize what it had caused, the market was wide open for new competitors such as Sun Microsystems, Silicon Graphics, and HP to earn hundreds of millions in profits in market niches that IBM chose not to address. "Customers used to say to me, 'I have a mainframe, so go away,' " said Glenn Osaka, general manager of the commercial systems division of Hewlett-Packard. "Now they say, 'I want to get rid of this mainframe. Can you help me?' "[35]

To sustain or improve your market position you must enter the iterative process of the innovation cycle by creating the proper context through architecture and capability development. This leads to platform development, and thence to innovations in product, service, and distribution. Having then accomplished any form of innovation that affects the marketplace, your own actions have changed the very dynamics of that marketplace, and you must then enter a second cycle of innovation and reconsider how the architecture itself must be reframed.

The innovation cycle also describes what happens when innovations are introduced from outside. As mentioned in Chapter 1, global industries once thrived around the distribution of kerosene and ice. Both progressed significantly over many decades, with profound innovations leading to significant reductions in operating costs. However, the advent of electricity killed the kerosene business, and electricity-driven refrigeration killed the ice business. Like Black & Decker's competitors, both victims were unable to respond to the new competitive architectures, and they disappeared.

From this, we can generalize that any mature industry dies when its leaders do not go back and fix their models of competitive architecture and organizational capability to reflect the impact of innovation. Thus, we augment Utterback's model of dominant design evolution to reflect the importance of architecture and capability development (see Figure 2.11).

Hence, it is at the level of architecture and capability development that competitive forces are first manifested, and it is here that strategy development is relevant as an expression of managerial intent.

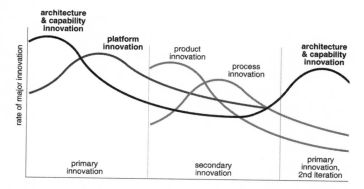

Figure 2.11 Architecture and Capability Development as the Source of New Dominant Designs. The development of competitive architecture and organizational capability leads to innovations in product platforms, from which product and process innovation follow. The impact of new products in the marketplace then creates new consequences for competitive architecture.

Market Architecture as a Business Process

Innovation is driven by asking the right questions in facilitated dialogs that are designed to expose critical gaps in existing knowledge. In the words of John Pepper, CEO of Procter & Gamble, "Just by having the dialog we can see our business like we've never seen it before."[36]

In this context, consider a decision-making scenario in which two proposals are being considered. One describes an apparently continuous innovation, and the other seems to be discontinuous. How shall we come to a decision about whether to pursue one, both, or neither?

Some individual or group (we suggest the Chief Innovation Officer, CINO) must be responsible for identifying the impact that they are likely to have both externally and internally. Here are some of the questions that must be asked:

What value will it offer customers?

How does this differ from what is currently available?

What is the trend of customer demand?

Does the innovation conform to an existing dominant design, or does it represent a new one?

From the customer's perspective, is it a continuous or discontinuous innovation?

Will the likely development path of the innovation intersect with customer demand in the future?

Is it derived from an existing product platform, or is it a new one?

Does it require a new service, or distribution platform, or does it rely on existing ones?

Finally, the most critical questions pertain to organizational capability. Since most organizations are accustomed to practicing only continuous innovation, they do not have established processes for defining and developing new architectures and new capabilities, and consequently they tend to filter out new efforts that go beyond existing and familiar technologies, services, and distribution platforms. If new capability is required to perform design, engineering, manufacturing, distribution, sales, or support activities, how will this be developed? And how will it be measured?

There are also questions about how the product should be introduced to the market, and then supported. There are questions pertaining to the scope of investment that will be required to do the necessary work, and the timing of when that investment will be required.

As more proposals are brought forward, this decision-making exercise will not be an isolated activity, but one that is undertaken regularly. This raises organizational questions about issues such as knowledge management and asset management, the responsibility for the processes of evaluating, preparing, and disseminating innovations, and the systematic development of new organizational capability, which are the topics of subsequent chapters.

But first we will present a case study of the Xerox DocuTech to see how the competitive architecture is reflected in the process of innovating in the office equipment industry. At Xerox, a new dominant design was envisioned far in advance of its ever being accomplished, and with the introduction of the DocuTech in 1990 the company was positioned to develop important new markets and industries.

THE XEROX DOCUTECH: THE DEVELOPMENT OF A NEW DOMINANT DESIGN AND A NEW PRODUCT PLATFORM

Xerox is well known for developing leading edge technologies, but the company's track record is decidedly mixed with respect to marketing its technological advances.

Xerox did invent the copying industry, and by 1960 it had transformed this invention into innovation as a new dominant design that took the company from $50 million in annual sales to over $1 billion. During the 1970s, Xerox invented the Alto personal computer, but failed to bring it to market successfully and left billions in profits for Apple, Microsoft, and others.

In the 1980s, Xerox saw the possibility of merging its capabilities in copiers and computers, and launched a project to integrate these two technology streams. Chip Holt, now Corporate Vice President of the Xerox Joseph C. Wilson Center for Research & Technology, was responsible for managing the 400-person team that developed and launched the company's DocuTech product platform, which debuted in 1990.

DocuTech is the first "print shop in a box," a high-volume copy machine that accepts digital input, and the result has been the creation of new industry called printing-on-demand. With more than 12,000 DocuTechs installed worldwide, Xerox has about 90 percent of the market in this new industry it has created.

At a price of $240,000 to $400,000, three different versions of DocuTech, all variants of a common platform, provide Xerox with more than $2 billion per year in revenue, while typical users are running about 1.5 million copies per month and achieving handsome 46 percent gross margins.

Here, Chip Holt tells the story of DocuTech.[37]

I'm an electrical engineer by background. I wrote a thesis on the design considerations of the control unit for a general purpose computer, 110 titillating pages of knowledge that today wouldn't even qualify for an introductory paragraph. That's just an indication of the pace of technology change.

I characterize a lot of my efforts as the pursuit of productivity. I'm amazed at how many perspectives can be brought to bear in the pursuit of that one word. In its simplest form productivity is the measure of the output divided by the input. The output management, which is associated with growing revenue, is an exciting one. But many times corporations get overly excited about the ease by which investment can be reduced and therefore the productivity equation increased. As an engineer and scientist, I come down squarely and strongly on the side of making investments in innovation which increase the output part of the equation.

If you look back over its 35 years, Xerox has been propelled by miraculous product events that only a few technologists saw coming. The first was Xerography itself. Chester Carlson invented it in 1938 and it didn't reach the marketplace until 1959 in the form of the 914. It changed the way the office worked and it democratized information.

The second miraculous event was the invention of electronic printing that created the electronic printing industry. Too bad we didn't have the foresight and emphasis that Hewlett-Packard did on the low end, but we created another billion-dollar industry with that invention.

And then the most recent miraculous event, DocuTech, which created the print-on-demand business that is very vibrant today.

In the early 1980s, our products were managed in an evolutionary way. We would plan the development of those products over time, with slight increases of speed, increases of image quality, but essentially rooted in the same kind of paradigm.

In early 1983 I was asked to review a block diagram of a product and report on whether the technologies would emerge that would make such a product feasible. This product was proposing to digitize the reprographics function, to replace the photographic process with a digital process.

We believed that the competition had photographic products and printing products, but we didn't believe that anyone had perfected the marriage of computational image processing and reprographics the way we were going to do it. We really thought we were about to embark on a new journey. The question, although we didn't fully appreciate it in those days, was, could we build a revolutionary product?

We convened the best electronics and systems people to simply ask, "Could we build a computer big enough to move the data that would be required for a fairly high speed printer, and still manage the relationship with a scanner that was trying to capture the information electronically, store it, and then push it out the back end to make prints?"

The answer that we had in July of 1983 was yes, we thought such technologies were available, but it would be a fairly large job in commercializing this cutting edge technology.

That became the beginning of DocuTech. I found myself at the very point 15 years later that I think I had joined the company to do, but couldn't articulate at the time. This was the strategy I thought Xerox was on in 1968 when they acquired the computer company, SDS.

But the product was very controversial from its inception. We were not on anybody's planning charts, relative to the annual plan process. This was really an exploration. Our boss, Bob Adams, had to actually tuck it away out of the reach of both the existing Xerox product organizations to allow nesting. It was a big secret that I had been assigned to this thing and that it was officially funded.

In 1984 we started to articulate the functional capabilities of the product. The image processing in the old products was done photographically. We now were rendering the image electronically, just like the data and the control instructions of a computer. We could marry the image information with the control information and create stuff that wasn't possible without thinking that way.

The first feature was concurrency. We knew that productivity was important, so how would you improve it in the days before DocuTech? In centralized print shops, the manager is paid for how much production they get out. Using offset presses and the best duplicators, the job has to be moved on and off the press, and somebody's got to do the set up between jobs. There was nothing you could do about the inter-job time, which was incredibly important.

Because we were acquiring information electronically and storing it, we had the ability to build an infinite queue, thereby allowing the printer to never stop. So right off the bat the DocuTech was going to run 10 to 15 percent more productively. A print shop would kill for 6 percent, so 10 to 15 was a real bell ringer.

The second feature was electronic sourcing of the print file. The document recirculating mechanism in those days would cause damage to the original, and that was a big dissatisfier to customers. On DocuTech we only had to image the original document once on a scanner, and all subsequent prints were made from electronic files. The increase in reliability of not having to recirculate the original, and the improved customer satisfaction of not damaging their original documents were the keys.

The third feature was that we put the graphics arts process online. This process was originally done in the camera room or the make-ready shop, where you touched up your originals, brought in photographs and pasted them up with the text, rotated or reformatted, all with scissors and tape and drafting tools.

Everything you could do in a drafting room or a camera shop, we could now do online. And the quality that we could achieve in these documents had never been achieved before, because we started to appreciate and understand the value of the information that was electronically captured and what we could do with it.

A complete appreciation of interfaces and crossovers had never before been available, but now they were available and revealed to us as we started to move image information around with different technologies. And still the printer always ran.

So now we were bypassing entire departments in the work process, and one of things we argued about was how could you put a feature like this on a product that is run by people that are used to getting dirt under their fingernails, keeping the toner hoppers filled, keeping the paper trays filled?

What we found when we went to the marketplace was that we had uplifted the job with very little increase in skills requirements, because all of this functionality was hidden behind fairly easy to use icons. So the operators of the press took a higher liking to their job, they had more pride in what they did and they all wanted to run a DocuTech.

The fourth feature doesn't look too interesting, but it is also a real bell ringer. Because DocuTech sourced its images from electronics, if you had an error during a duplex copying job, you only had to purge about seven sheets of the paper track in the machine, as opposed to two hundred and fifty sheets in a paper tray. So the improvement in waste and productivity was great. For large documents, like 11 × 17, the staging tray wouldn't even fit the product due to the 250 sheet storage requirement.

The fifth feature was the ability to automatically improve images to create signatures and create books from those signatures.

While we were working on this, Xerox CEO David Kearns came to visit me without an entourage and we sat down and talked about what this potential product would do. He understood from the very beginning that if such a product materialized it could damage both our printing business and our reprographics business. He said he wanted us to be the first company that did it because if someone else leveraged that product against our established businesses we wouldn't know what to do.

One of the technical challenges we were talking about in 1983 was the requirement for 130 Megabits a second of throughput so that the printer never stopped. We were selling this productivity, so the ability to capture information properly through the scanner, to keep the print queue filled, managing that information, and getting it into the proper format was consuming incredible amounts of bandwidth.

We knew we needed a computer bigger than any of us had ever seen. We scoped the requirements of the computer to be a speed of hundreds of mips ["millions of instructions per second," the basic speed measurement for computers]. This was in the days when the best you could buy were one mips processors, so we thought hundreds of mips were going to be a real stretch. We were going to have to make up the difference between the processor's capabilities, and the speed required to keep the print engine working.

It turned out that the processing requirements of that computer required a *thousand* mips. Ultimately we put together a multiprocessing system that connected 8 of these 1 mips processors together, and got the rest of the thousand through hardwired silicon and Asics [customized computer chips, or "application specific integrated circuits"] of our own design.

So the key components were lasers, scanners, integrated circuits, the basic mechanics of moving the paper, the software, and the user interface, which used a gray-scale display and a touch screen that we also had to develop.

For a year and a half we pursued the planning implications of these features, and in the spring of 1985 we had the features of the product defined, and the first working prototype was running.

In 1983 we had thought we were going to need a hundred thousand lines of code, but on the actual product we have a million and a half lines of code. The management of just the software endeavor became a technology in itself. When you get a million and a half lines you're dealing with human dynamics and interfaces that are almost indescribable.

To get this product to an acceptable cost of ownership value, we had to get to the point where we had about 7 failures per million copies, which was equal to or better than the equivalent reprographic product, so all these technologies had to be brought together and commercialized. We had to get the hardware and software the computational functions to a point where they didn't have any bugs, running the electro-mechanical almost flat out.

Until 1986 I had serious concerns about technology, and between 1986 and 1988 I had serious doubt that the engineering effort could put a product that big together. By 1998, however, I knew the product would meet its goals.

From 1988 to 1990 we were engaged in tests with users, first internal then external. In 1988 I went to our own internal print shop and I described the product to them and asked them if they would like to be the first customers. I exaggerated all the bad things about the product by a factor of three, and asked if they would still be okay with having a product like that, because I did not want to give them false expectations.

As we got more and more confidence in the ability to put these features together in a product, we began to see what the product itself could do, relative to the work process of different market segments. The product took us higher up the food chain of our customers' work processes.

By the end of the project, we had two program teams. One was associated with the technical development of the product, the other with launching the product. The two teams met every Saturday for a full year and a half before the product was launched. The perspective gained by blending the technical and market teams together was excellent and made the product launch very successful.

Our marketing people started to address specifically how this product could be applied to various market segments, such as pharmaceutical markets, aerospace markets, university markets, and started to develop a real belief about how powerful this product could become. The features of DocuTech and the market opportunities they addressed gave birth to a new industry, print on demand.

The implications of print on demand are taking the industry by storm. That business is presently creating in excess of $2 billion dollars a year on DocuTech alone. All of our estimates of both revenue and placements where vastly exceeded by the product, and the print on demand industry is big, big, big, billions.

The business we're in continues to have an insatiable appetite for speed, image quality, and productivity. What that means ultimately is that we're going to be in the advanced-customization-of-production-documents business, where every individual will get lithographic quality brochures that are specifically tailored to their interests. This means tapping the enormous databases that are emerging out of the information infrastructure, the continued marriage of the technologies of computation, communication, and presentation.

What's the next generation of systems integration that leads to a product beyond DocuTech? How do you make an offset press look like a variable data machine? It can do all those things. In units of one.

All the critical elements of competitive architecture are reflected in this story. The project originates because the evolution of technology implies the possibility of a new competitive architecture, a new external framework that threatens the established product lines of the company. Rather than circling the wagons to defend the existing revenues, however, Xerox boldly investigates to understand what the new architecture may be. Competitive architecture and capability development are the beginning points for the innovation process.

The new architecture implies the fusion of two domains of technology that had heretofore been separate, computation and photography-based reprographics.

The outcome of this investigation affirms the threat and also a significant opportunity, but it is one that neither of the two major businesses of the company are competent to address themselves. Therefore, the DocuTech project is set up to report to neither existing business, and it is thus protected from internal competition while the new architecture is being developed.

The critical element of customer value around which the entire project is structured is the opportunity to provide customers with improved productivity, and this metric is used to determine the seminal features of the product in a context that is relevant to (and attractive to) end users. With the emphasis on productivity, DocuTech addresses the main stream of innovation's importance in the broad economic context, in addition to its value for individual customers.

Only after the critical customer values are identified is technology developed to fulfill the requirements that customer value dictates.

And the process of developing this technology is a demanding exercise in capability development that harnesses the creative powers of hundreds of people. In addition to the DocuTech product platform itself, Xerox also gains the capability to manage huge software development activity, and learns how to get 1000 mips of performance out of 8 one-mips chips. Neither is a small accomplishment in itself, and neither is likely to be soon matched by its competitors.

One of Xerox's largest customers is Kinko's, which has the largest fleet of DocuTechs outside of the U.S. government, with more than 230 machines running in its 830 U.S. locations.[38] When asked about the DocuTech, Mike Sihilling, Kinko's Director of Production Systems noted that the DocuTech is the only machine in its class, that it is the cornerstone of Kinko's digital marketing strategy, and that it has significantly helped the company compete effectively with offset printers.[39] He also notes that three Xerox competitors are approaching rapidly—IBM, Lanier, and Océ—and all offer products that are superior to DocuTech in some ways, although none has yet matched DocuTech as a complete system.

In the end, then, DocuTech becomes a new product platform *and* a new dominant design. Xerox has used technology fusion to create significant competitive advantage and to create a new industry, printing-on-demand. The company has taken significant market share from competing industries such as offset printing, and as Chip implied, further erosion of the offset industry lies ahead on DocuTech's development path. But having established a new industry, Xerox has also created an attractive market, in which it already faces competitors who have significant capabilities in their own right.

With the integration of the formidable technologies underlying DocuTech, it is not an exaggeration to say that this project reflects innovation at its finest. After the missed opportunities of the Alto, it shows a significant turnaround in the company's management of the critical process of discontinuous innovation that drives the development of competitive architecture. Now Xerox faces the challenge of the continuing evolution of its markets, for innovation never sleeps.

CHAPTER 3

Organizational Capability: The Internal Framework

Two critical and complex dimensions of any business are the external structure, as defined in terms of customers, suppliers, and competitors, and the internal structure, defined by people and their knowledge, tools, technology, and work processes.

The competitive architecture is primarily concerned with external structure, and is ultimately a function of how stakeholders perceive and define value, both consciously and unconsciously. It consists of the dominant designs that customers accept as standards, and the platforms on which products and services are based. These key elements of the broader environment largely define the external context in which innovation is pursued.

The internal context for innovation, in contrast, is a function of knowledge, and how it is engendered and used within an organization to create the products and services that will be offered in the marketplace as well as the organization itself. In these terms, technology is one specific kind of knowledge among many.

The methods by which knowledge is sought out, documented, shared, managed, and applied are all aspects of organizational capability. The purpose of this chapter is to explore many of the facets of organizational capability,[1] including the nature of information and knowledge, the relationship between learning and knowledge, the learning curve, tacit and explicit knowledge, and the aggregation of knowledge, tools, technology, and processes into organizational capability.

Information, Knowledge, and Capability

To begin, we examine the difference between "information" and "knowledge," for although these terms are often used interchangeably, their meanings are quite different.

There is a commonly held myth that providing individuals and groups with information will lead them to appropriate personal and organizational actions and performance, but this is far from true. "The right information to the right person at the right time" is not nearly enough, as was shown in research conducted by the military intelligence community.

During World War II, the Allied armies had broken German codes and often knew in advance what the Axis armies were going to do. In some cases, this information was given to field commanders prior to battle.[2]

At the end of the war, a comprehensive survey of how field commanders used this information resulted in a shocking discovery, as in more than half of the cases the field commanders had done absolutely nothing with information they knew to be accurate.

Further analysis discovered that there were three reasons for these lapses. The first was overconfidence: the information was not needed. The second was underconfidence in dealing with a system of extreme complexity: the chain of command and the planning cycle were so in-tricate that last-minute information was disruptive. The third reason was related to the inherent ambiguity of information, as it was often not apparent until much later what the information meant, so it could not be used.

The same thing happens in the daily course of business. Hence, we recognize that far more useful than information, and consequently far more difficult to obtain, is the right *knowledge*.

"Information" is defined as the description of "what," which can exist in a documented form that stands by itself. "Knowledge," how-ever, which is held only by people, contains instruction in "how" things are accomplished. This is more complex, more valuable, and also more elusive.

While information about a product or service is the awareness of its existence, knowledge is usually required to use it effectively. There is a huge gap, for example, between the individual who is aware that air-planes fly and another who knows precisely how this is accomplished, and who can actually fly the plane. The knowledge of the second is a superior capability precisely because it is much more than information.

For organizations of many individuals to sustain their competi-tiveness in changing environments, the fact of rapid change creates a continuing need for new knowledge. This knowledge always resides in individuals, and the aggregate of all the knowledge in the mem-bers of an organization is the critical attribute we call "organizational capability."

This is more precisely defined as "people applying explicit and tacit knowledge to the use of tools and technology in processes of work as learning, and learning as work" (see Figure 3.1).

Having a particular capability, or lacking it, determines whether the people in an organization can perform a particular activity within an effective context.

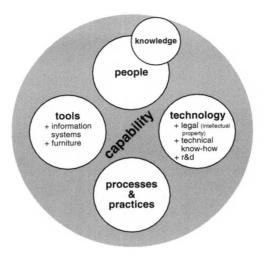

Figure 3.1 Capability: Applying Explicit and Tacit Knowledge.

While most organizations have processes for strategy development and processes for product development, few organizations have a process for defining competitive architectures and organizational capabilities, or for developing them.

In the context of today's highly competitive world markets, differences in capability separate leaders from followers, as capability is the basis on which work is accomplished. Adding processes to develop both enables organizations to do things they currently cannot and do not know how to do, which makes them critical functions of management.

Capability and architecture development can be targeted to improve speed, quality, or costs within existing product platforms, and it can be targeted to generate discontinuous innovation and new dominant designs.

In the context of a world that is changing exponentially and will therefore be different tomorrow, the ability to develop the right new organizational capabilities will be the fundamental source of competitive advantage. This is done through learning.

Learning and Knowledge

In our definition of organizational capability, we used the phrase "in processes of work as learning and learning as work." However you look at it, there is an intimate link between "learning" and "knowledge," and both are tremendously important as they are also tremendously complex. These fundamental concepts are central to the mysteries of what it means to be human, how we as individuals grow, develop, and express ourselves, and how we together create the communities, cultures, and societies that envelop us throughout our lives.

To have knowledge, as defined in this chapter, is not just to know that something can be done, but more usefully to know *how* to do it. Gaining new knowledge comes through the process of learning, through which each individual integrates the elements of information, theory, and experience (see Figure 3.2).

I approach you to ask if I can borrow your old F-117 Stealth fighter for a quick trip across the country. Since I have carefully read the very detailed instruction manual from cover to cover, I am certainly qualified to do so. Or am I?

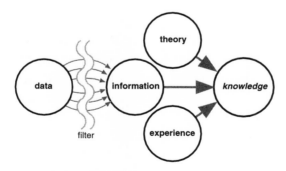

Figure 3.2 Learning. Knowledge comes about through the integration of information derived from data, plus theory that puts the information in the proper context, plus experience of how things work in the real world. This process of integration is also called learning.

Hardly.

It is true that the instruction manual contains a very complete description of the aircraft and its controls, but if I attempt to fly the plane based solely on what I have read, the plane and I will most likely be destroyed during the takeoff, if we even make it all the way from the hangar to the end of the runway.

After you stop laughing at my silly request, you quite rightly insist that to be qualified as a pilot I must first master the theory of flight as expressed through concepts such as lift, drag, aerodynamics, and control. This mastery will only then be augmented by the information in the manual, which describes the application of the broader theory in the specific case of the F-117.

Further, I cannot begin my flying career by going from theory class directly to the Stealth flight line; instead I shall progress from theory to a small and slow trainer. There I will learn to handle the controls while sitting beside an instructor who will correct my numerous mistakes at a sedate 150 knots, at which speed it is possible to recover, rather than at the blurry Mach 2 where these same errors would be fatal.

After this practice, perhaps augmented by practicing in a flight simulator or even using simulation software on a computer, I will learn to fly progressively more powerful and more complex aircraft, accumulating the necessary experience to eventually be able to fly the F-117 safely.

"Come see me again in a few years," you suggest with a chuckle, after I have thoroughly integrated this enormous body of information, theory, and experience. Then will I have learned to fly the Stealth, because only then will I have the *knowledge* that is required. Only then will I have the know-*how*.

In this exchange, the three elements of learning are all evident: information from published materials and teacher instruction, theory from ground school, plus many progressively more complex stages of experience all integrated together in the making of a pilot who is qualified to fly a propeller-driven plane. When the time comes to learn to fly a jet, the cycle is repeated with this more powerful technology.

This is the same process that, in our schools, is called "driver's education," and on the sports field is called "practice." All are critical to effective performance in complex activities.

Lacking any of these three critical dimensions of information, theory, and experience, learning does not take place, and knowledge simply is not created.[3] Therefore, when we describe organizational capability as the aggregate of the knowledge of the members of an organization, we recognize that this knowledge has been obtained through countless learning processes that have occurred inside and outside the specific context defined by the organization.

Just as a greater capacity to learn distinguishes some individuals, so, too, does the aggregate of individual learning reflect important differences between organizations.

For example, if the members of one company's R&D staff are experts in existing technology x, which is expected to continue as the foundation for the new dominant design in its industry, but in fact the new design turns out to be based on technology y in which none of the staff has competence, then this firm could be in big trouble. Hence, there is more to knowledge management than just accumulating knowledge. Relevance is critical, and the companies that survive from one dominant design generation to the next are those that develop capability as it is required, and before.

In Dr. Deming's terms, having the correct theory to guide the process of figuring out what is relevant and what is not is the core of an effective innovation program. Without correct theory, work is a random process in which you sometimes win and frequently lose.

The Learning Curve

The learning curve model shows that with careful attention in a complete cycle of activity in a complex process, it is possible to develop new knowledge through which quality improvements and/or cost reductions of between 10 percent and 30 percent per cycle can be achieved.[4]

For manufacturers, this cycle may be "research-design-manufacturing-distribution-and-sales," while for service companies it may be more simply "research-design-deliver." For both, the faster each cycle is completed and its learning applied, the faster the products and services can be improved (see Figure 3.3).

The results of the learning curve are reflected in the relative performance of competing companies in interesting ways. For example, at the beginning of the 1980s, General Motors was rapidly losing market share to Japanese manufacturers, and GM's leaders realized that significant changes would have to be made for the company to remain competitive.

A key statistic frequently cited at the time indicated that compared with Toyota, GM required about twice as many person-hours to assemble comparable cars. Since Toyota's assembly lines were significantly robotized, GM committed itself to robotizing also.

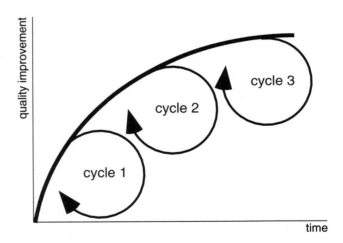

Figure 3.3 The Learning Curve. Each complete cycle creates new opportunities to learn. Applying that learning defines an improvement curve that typically results in 10 percent to 30 percent improvement per cycle.

During the 1980s, therefore, GM invested the massive sum of $77 billion to automate its factories. This figure includes the acquisition costs of two high-technology companies, Hughes Aerospace and Ross Perot's firm, EDS. With Hughes, GM acquired a world leader in advanced electronics hardware, while the acquisition of EDS brought state-of-the-art capabilities in software development and information systems management.

By the end of the 1980s, however, GM's market share had continued to decline, and GM's automated factories were not performing well. At one point, $500 million worth of robots had to be scrapped because they were not performing up to expectations.[5] But what do you do with large manufacturing robots when you cannot use them? GM's unusable robots were simply pushed to the side of the factory floor to get them out of the way, and there they sat as monuments to a failed idea.

One critical reason for the failure was that GM's model of implementation was not managed as a learning process. The program was clearly implemented from information and theory, but lacked the critical step of experience. Experience would have shown, and later did, that GM's concept of robotization was far too rigid to be effective, whereas the Japanese implementation of flexible manufacturing systems was tremendously effective and saved huge amounts of money that were then applied in R&D.

In addition, GM's competitive problems were not properly diagnosed in the first place. Although the labor factor was a critical difference between the two companies, another factor was equally if not more important: the time required not for manufacture, but for the design of new cars.

During the 1980s, Japanese manufacturers typically required 48 months to design, engineer, and prepare a factory to manufacture a new car. GM, however, took nearly 84 months to complete the same process. Over a span of 14 years, therefore, GM completed only two generations of new cars, while Honda, Toyota, and Nissan were completing nearly 4 generations each (see Figure 3.4).

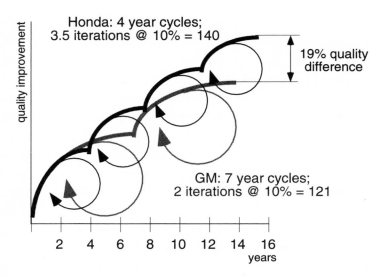

Figure 3.4 Theoretical Learning Curves for GM and Honda. Assuming a 10 percent improvement per cycle (and that is admittedly a generous assumption), every 14 years Honda would complete 3.5 cycles while GM would complete only 2. Starting with equal quality levels arbitrarily assigned a value of 100, Honda would therefore achieve a quality value of 140 while GM would only achieve 121.

In the famous phrase that economists rely on so much, "all other things being equal," this difference would enable the Japanese to achieve a quality advantage of 19 percent or more, a huge difference that readily translated into better performance on the road and greater appreciation by consumers. Many people believed that Japanese cars were better, and they were generally correct.

A great deal of the valuable learning in the product development cycle comes at the point of new product introduction. As Marvin Patterson points out: "Every time a company introduces a new product into the marketplace, it receives a rush of feedback that is unavailable to competitors. Customers describe what they like about the new product and what they do not like. They apply the product in ways never dreamed possible, and these new applications suggest new opportunities for future products. The more often a company introduces new products, the better it learns the dynamics of its marketplace."[6]

While the Japanese companies understood the learning curve and applied it as a focused management strategy (remember that Sony introduced a new Walkman an average of every 27 days for 11 consecutive years), the American manufacturers were generally ignorant of the principle and its potential impact on their businesses.

This is obvious when you consider why GM required 36 additional months to complete the same work. A first thought might be that the Japanese designers and engineers were simply more skilled than those at GM, but in fact GM designers and engineers required about 48 months, just as they did at Honda.

The difference was that GM used an additional three years for the decision-making process of senior management. During the GM design and development cycle, senior managers reviewed each project regularly, and the aggregate time wasted in these reviews was typically about *three years* (see Figure 3.5).

Whereas they believed that Toyota's key advantage was in its application of technology to auto assembly, far more important was the

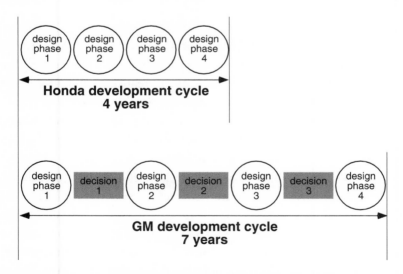

Figure 3.5 Honda and GM Development Cycles. GM's development cycle was three years longer than Honda because of three years of management decision making in the development process, not because of differences in engineering capability.

application of the learning curve to the cycle of design and development for new cars. While GM practiced strategy development and product development, the company neglected entirely the importance of the learning curve, a critical aspect of the linked processes of architecture and capability development.

Thus, GM's senior management had misunderstood the real Toyota strategy, and were killing the company's competitiveness by suppressing the learning process. This gave GM's Japanese competitors a tremendous learning advantage that the Japanese adroitly transformed into a significant advantage in the marketplace.

The application of the learning curve has been and remains a key to Japanese success in the world markets in which they compete. Japanese companies thoroughly understand and effectively apply the principle of learning faster than your competition.

Eventually, GM's management realized that a significant problem lay with the learning curve, whereupon the company reduced its design cycle time to 48 months, as indeed all auto manufacturers were doing at that time.

But no one stopped there. In the late 1980s, Ford's Taurus, the car that saved the company, was designed and brought to market in only 36 months. And noted in Chapter 2, Chrysler invested more than $1 billion in a new building to house its platform teams, a capability development strategy that resulted in similar time reductions.

With the development of new cars now requiring between 30 and 36 months throughout the auto industry, the learning curve and its application has become an accepted management principle.

The model applies as well in other industries. Cambridge Technology Partners, a contract software firm, has grown rapidly during the 1990s, in large part due to its capacity to complete work quickly. In the words of CEO Jim Sims: "Speed changes all the fundamentals of business: how we train our people, how we relate to our clients, how we manage projects. . . . Five years ago, this company had about 100 employees. Today we're adding nearly that many people every month. We've established a hiring cycle of 60 days between when we recognize a need and when a new hire reports for duty. That timetable—that focus on speed—forces us to be creative and disciplined about how we recruit, interview, and evaluate people. . . . The time dimension has shaped how we grow the business."[7]

But it is not enough to know about the learning curve and begin applying its lessons. Another major issue is how to catch up with competitors who are already using the learning curve as a management tool. As long as Toyota managers understand the importance of the learning curve, they will continue to compress their cycle times and their lead may be insurmountable.

The best competitive strategy in this situation then has two elements. Of course, Ford, GM, and Chrysler must continue to chase after Toyota, Honda, and Nissan to sustain their existing business operations as best they can.

But the second part has a different character. Toyota, Honda, and Nissan have created their learning advantages in the existing dominant design, but that advantage may not necessarily be transferable to the next generation. When a new dominant design arrives, the playing field will suddenly be leveled, and there will be a prime opportunity for innovators to seize the lead based on their grasp of the new paradigm.

In such an environment, success will be primarily a function of the "unlearning curve," a measure of how rapidly the members of an organization can abandon their obsolete knowledge. Only when unlearning is complete can the learning curve apply in the quest to grasp and apply the new rules, as discussed in greater detail in Chapter 6.

Perhaps this is what led GM to create its Saturn subsidiary. By starting over from scratch, Saturn did not have the organizational burden of correcting counterproductive habits from the past. Instead, the new company could simply do things right the first time by developing a corporate culture in which the qualities that were critical for success in the marketplace were also the ones that were valued in the company.

By reinventing the processes of selling and servicing cars, Saturn has defined a new dominant design that does not pertain to the product, but concerns the relationship between the company and its customers. As other companies strive to copy Saturn's approaches, the new dominant design it created is having considerable impact.

The next test for Saturn will come when a new dominant design emerges and it becomes necessary for the company to respond by changing its ways of working. If the company can adapt to such a challenge, then perhaps it will endure as a worthy global competitor.

Meanwhile, judging from their unsatisfactory performance, it is apparent that the other GM subsidiaries still suffer from acute lag at both unlearning and learning, and they must find a way to overcome this disadvantage or risk going out of business altogether.

The Path to Wisdom

As we noted, the knowledge embedded in successful innovations comes about through the integration of three essential dimensions: information, theory, and experience. As important as it is, however, even this knowledge alone may not be sufficient. Beyond knowledge, and even more valuable, are understanding and wisdom, as illustrated by the "path to wisdom" (see Figure 3.6).

It is apparent that value increases as we move from left to right, as there is more value in Understanding *why* things work as they do than in Knowledge of *how,* and still more in the Wisdom that is able to distinguish between what *can* be done and what *should* be done.

Perhaps this insight also underlies T.S. Eliot's 1934 pageant play *The Rock:*[8]

> Where is the wisdom we have lost in knowledge?
> Where is the knowledge we have lost in information?

As with the creation of knowledge from information, theory, and experience, each transition requires work. Data, for example, must be

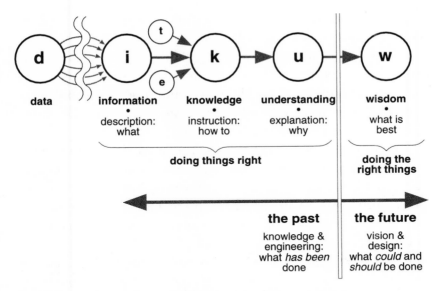

Figure 3.6 The Path to Wisdom.[9] The path to wisdom is described by Russell Ackoff, who observes that the distinction between doing things right and doing the right things is the difference between understanding and wisdom. This distinction, which he attributes to Peter Drucker, is crucial for our society in these times of rapid change. Adding to Ackoff's model, we observe that this distinction divides the past from the future: Knowledge comes about only from what already exists and what has been done; wisdom concerns the future and what *could* and *should* be done.

filtered to become useful as information. Hence, the information printed in the F-117 instruction manual has been filtered by a writer from what was probably a much larger mass of technical data. To a great extent, the pilot's survival will depend on how skillfully the filtering has been done. If critical data have been omitted, even a highly competent pilot might crash the jet, and while the feedback might not be so immediate in the management of your company, the consequences of poorly filtered data may ultimately be just as decisive. What information does and does not get communicated through the filter of the organizational hierarchy is critical, as is the interpretation given to it.

Likewise, effective filtering of today's massive computerized databases is critical if they are to yield useful information.

Progressing from the left we see that the elements of data, information, knowledge, and understanding together compose the capacity to engineer effectively, as credible engineering prescribes with the certainty what can be done based solely on the knowledge and understanding of what *has been done* in the past.

Hence, we rely on the knowledge and understanding of a structural engineer to specify precisely how large to make the beam holding up the roof of a house, or how to configure the truss that holds up a bridge. An electrical engineer knows what kind of wire or fiber to use in a high speed data network, or how to connect the new streetlights that are being installed in our neighborhood.

As engineering looks to prior accomplishments to substantiate future plans, it usually involves the recreation or adaptation of something that already exists.

Lord Kelvin, President of the Royal Society and inventor of the Kelvin temperature scale, made what could be the ultimate back-firing statement in the history of engineering in 1895 when he said, "Heavier-than-air flying machines are impossible."

What he really meant was that heavier-than-air flying machines had not yet been invented. The Wright Brothers remedied that situation only eight years later, and clearly it was not only their prowess as engineers that drove them to create the Wright Flyer. Just as important was their capacity to envision something that had not yet been done, and then to develop new capabilities in aircraft design, manufacture, and testing to transform their vision into the first flying machine.

It was precisely because these capabilities did not exist in 1895 that Lord Kelvin could be fooled into thinking that they could never exist. Yet the Wrights' disciplined approach to engineering led them to create a wind tunnel in the back of their bicycle shop in 1901 to test more than 200 different wing shapes, each about 4" long. They were the first aircraft designers ever to conduct systematic tests in this way, and after only three weeks of testing they determined the curvature and shape that would provide the needed performance attributes. Their tests results provided accurate, and their gliders and airplanes fly as anticipated.[10]

After successfully testing their wing design on a glider, they also used the calculation tables and the theories they had gleaned from their wind tunnel and flight test experiments to design the twin propellers for the Wright Flyer. "As we were not in a position to undertake a long series of practical experiments to discover a suitable propeller . . . it seemed necessary to obtain such a thorough understanding of the theory of its reactions as would enable us to design them from calculation alone."[11]

Sometimes, as shown here, innovators must not only apply theory, but first *devise* it to be successful. In the process of doing so, innovators act out the future, envisioning what can be done and then applying their vision backward to shape a course of action in the present that will achieve the desired outcomes in the future. In this way, the path to wisdom is bidirectional, as the wisdom of what could be done in the future shapes both the present and the future. The path to wisdom is in fact two paths, stretching from the present to the future, and back.

This creates a compelling need to refine and realize visions in the form of creative tension. And so, driven by the creative tension that grows between the way things are now, the current condition, and compelling visions of the future, innovators are motivated to create the theories and the knowledge that are the basis of innovation (see Figure 3.7).

Wisdom also reflects creative tension, for it is oriented toward the future, toward what *could* and *should* be done even though it may never have been done before. It is wisdom that enables individuals to make correct choices for the future.

In contrast with Lord Kelvin's 1895 opinion, the words of Henry Ford from 1926 express a visionary's perspective on the future, and also illustrate how much the world had changed in 31 years: "Now the fact is that a generation ago there were a thousand men to every opportunity while today there are a thousand opportunities for every man."[12]

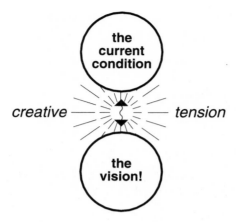

Figure 3.7 Creative Tension. Creative tension drives innovators to enact the future and translate what they see in their mind's eye into something they can touch, use, and share with others.

Thus, we hope that our leaders are wise, that they have the vision to accurately foresee the future, and the charisma to prepare us for it. The president of a nation or the CEO of a company is expected to be wise, to correctly envision the future and to make the proper decisions in the present that will guide the nation or the organization toward that preferred future. Likewise, the effective innovation process is guided by compelling visions of the future, and by the compulsion to create new products and services that will be successful in the marketplace in the coming months and years.

As the state of one's knowledge advances, however, the accomplishment of wisdom also leads one to discover new levels of ignorance. Hence, the path to wisdom can more precisely be visualized as a spiral, with one iteration leading to another (see Figure 3.8).

Another model of the progression of knowledge has been defined by Roger Bohn, who shows how the idea underlying the path to wisdom can be applied to particular processes.[13] As the state of knowledge advances, different forms of management and learning are required at each stage (see Figure 3.9).

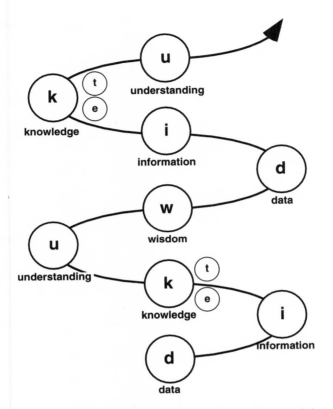

Figure 3.8 The Spiraling Path to Wisdom. It has been suggested that the more you learn, the more you also discover that your ignorance is vast. Developing wisdom therefore leads to new questions which reinitiate the learning process. Through many learning iterations, wisdom becomes deeper and broader.

Bohn shows how these stages can be applied in many different industries, including high-tech manufacturing, consumer marketing, and professional services, providing a means of evaluating the state of knowledge in any particular area of focus. This capability is essential to knowledge management, as it gives direction to the process of capability development.

	name	comment	typical form of knowledge
1	complete ignorance		nowhere
2	awareness	pure art	tacit
3	measure	pretechnological	written
4	control of the mean	scientific method feasible	written and embodied in hardware
5	process capability	local recipe	hardware and operating manual
6	process characterization	trade-offs to reduce costs	empirical equations (numerical)
7	know why	science	scientific formulas and algorithms
8	complete knowledge	nirvana	

Figure 3.9 The Stages of Knowledge. From complete ignorance to complete knowledge, knowledge has many gradations that become progressively useful for the management of complexity and the determination of the correct path for the future.

Tacit and Explicit Knowledge

In Bohn's stages of knowledge chart, the typical form of knowledge at the level of awareness is tacit. However, when we speak of "knowledge," most people assume that this refers to knowledge that is written in books and discussed in classrooms and conference rooms, a form referred to as "explicit" knowledge. The distinction between these two forms is critical for innovation, and indeed all aspects of management.

We look to the ancient Greek philosophers, to Plato, Socrates, Pythagoras, and Aristotle, and to their antecedents and peers among the Arabic and the Chinese cultures as the sources from which our traditions of knowledge have come. With reverence for logic and rhetoric and ethics, our high regard for the rational Western mind embraces explicit knowledge to the exclusion of nearly everything else.

Extending thousands of years of this intellectual tradition are today's intelligence tests that assess the capacity to recognize rational truths that are hidden in word games and mathematical problems. Measurements such as the Scholastic Aptitude Test (SAT) are widely used by colleges and universities to gauge the academic potential of applicant students. While SAT scores are useful for predicting how successful students are likely to be in college, the test is quite incapable of predicting how well they will do after college in their professional careers.[14] This is because the SAT measures only a student's explicit knowledge, whereas professional success depends on much more. Although it is little recognized or understood in the West, the complementary dimension of tacit knowledge is critical to success in the "real world."[15]

Scholar and professor Michael Polanyi demonstrates the prevalence and importance of tacit knowledge in our daily experience simply by challenging us to express how it is that we can invariably recognize the faces of those we know.[16] It is not their particular shape or color, but something else, some other essence perhaps, something very specific that nevertheless remains undefinable enabling you to pick out the faces of your family or your colleagues among a sea of faces in a crowd. The ability to recognize these faces, those of celebrities whose pictures we have seen, and even people we have only seen once (and perhaps long ago at that) is astonishingly unerring.

The consistency of this ability is reflected in our system of laws, for recognizing someone's face is considered to be "positive identification" and is among the most compelling forms of evidence that can be entered in a court of law.

On the other hand, those who are unable to recognize faces are considered severely handicapped, as is the case for many persons with Alzheimer's disease.

Tacit knowledge is part of everything that we do and say, and as it is inherent in our very thinking, it is deeply embedded in the way that we work. When you ask someone to describe what they do, whether it is a task at the office, the manufacturing plant, or in the kitchen at home, their best attempt at a description will most likely be incomplete. What will be missing is the important tacit knowledge.

It is tacit knowledge that enables us to recognize the correct "feel," the right way to hold and use a hammer, a kitchen knife, or the controls of the F-117 as it shakes in a turbulent airflow. It is tacit knowledge that is critical to producing a desired outcome when the task is complex. Hence, we recognize that tacit knowledge is involved in a task when we are reduced to trying to explain the "feel" of something, particularly the way that it feels when it feels "right." In many cases, this feel eludes all our attempts to describe it, and so success in tacit domains comes, ultimately, to a matter of doing it.

Only after you have done it will you know what it feels like, and perhaps only after you have done it repeatedly will you know how to get it to feel just right, especially when you cannot specifically define what "just right" is.

Among the three components of knowledge, information tends to be explicit, but as we rarely take the time to reflect back and bring all the elements of our activities into full awareness, most experience is tacit. Hence, a Ford engineer notes, "When people look at a car in the showroom, the first thing they do is open and close the doors. They may not even realize it, but if they don't like the sound, they'll just walk away from the car."[17] Knowing this, Ford and its competitors now engineer the sounds a car makes, including doors, latches, and of course engines.

The distinction between tacit and explicit knowledge is well expressed by David Pye in his discussion of the difference between design, which is explicit, and workmanship, which is tacit: "Design is what, for practical purposes, can be conveyed in words and by drawing; workmanship is what, for practical purposes, can not. . . . The *intended design* of any particular thing is what the designer has seen in his mind's eye: the ideally perfect and therefore unattainable embodiment of his intention. The design which can be communicated—the design on paper in other words—obviously falls short of expressing the designer's full intention, just as in music the score is a necessarily imperfect in-dication of what the composer has imaginatively heard."[18]

The intended design and the workmanship used in its pursuit are within the tacit domain, whereas the words and drawings are explicit, and as Pye suggests, often insufficient.

Another expression of the same idea is offered by David Packard, who notes simply, "Written instructions are seldom adequate."[19]

As tacit knowledge plays a critical role in the definition of what constitutes workmanship, it also plays a critical role in a customer's definition of what constitutes value. However, since tacit knowledge exists in an inexpressible form, it does no good to ask customers to ex-plicitly state what they want because they probably cannot tell you much about their tacit sensibilities.

So while the quest for innovation is directed toward providing new value for customers, those very customers are usually unable to express the factors that constitute the value that they require. The implica-tions of this are fundamental for marketing, product development, re-search and development, and indeed for all the activities that constitute management and innovation.

This means, for example, that market research conducted in the traditional way using focus groups and interviews with customers is likely to keep the innovation in the domain of existing experience and block the search for discontinuities. "Standard market research techniques—focus groups, questionnaires, telephone research—are extremely weak ways of predicting how people might behave with a product they barely understand."[20] Because these methodolo-gies do not enable potential customers to actually experience new technologies, they have no tacit experience of what the true value could be.

While such research uncovers what customers already know based on experiences that they have already had, this is likely to be irrele-vant to the use of a breakthrough product or service. Hence, in 1876 an internal memo at Western Union proclaimed, "This 'telephone' has too many shortcomings to be seriously considered as a means of com-munication. The device is inherently of no value to us."[21] Lacking the context that comes only with experience that they had not had, the utility of the telephone was not recognizable.

Similarly, before Fred Smith founded Federal Express, his university management professor rejected the idea with the comment, "The concept is interesting and well-formed, but in order to earn better than a 'C,' the idea must be feasible."[22]

And when the Saturn automobile was being designed, market researchers queried focus groups about nearly every aspect of the car's design. At the time, customers said that they preferred the accepted standard, motorized seat belts that engaged automatically when the car was started. Soon after this research was completed, however, air bags accompanied by manually operated safety belts became widely available and immediately became the dominant design.

The Saturn designers then realized that their market research had led them to an incorrect decision. They had not created a research context in which a future technology, the airbag, could be understood, so their research overlooked the tacit and as yet unrecognized demand for airbags.

In addition, there were operational problems with motorized belts that the Saturn designers had not recognized, which caused neck and head injuries to some users. It took two years before the company could correct the error and install airbags.[23]

Regrettably, the story does not end there. Only after airbags were installed in more than 60 million cars did the evidence emerge to suggest that airbags may cost lives as well as saving them. The standard airbag design is intended to protect a 165-pound man, but it has proven lethal to smaller individuals, including at least 85 children and small adults.[24]

In hindsight, it is clear that the product was forced into mass production before being fully tested. "The air bag became an all or nothing experiment with the American driver as the guinea pig."[25] This shows that there is no substitute for a rigorous innovation process, and that assumptions can only be confirmed through extensive real world testing, as discussed in greater detail in Chapter 8.

In contrast with the Western absorption in explicit knowledge, many Asian cultures reflect a refined appreciation of tacit knowledge. In particular, many Japanese companies have applied a profound grasp of tacit knowledge to their use of the learning curve in the development of leading products in consumer markets throughout the world.

By recognizing and exploiting the implications of new technologies to address new, unrecognized, or unmet needs, Japanese companies have produced many product breakthroughs using technology that originated in the West. For example, the basic technology of the transistor was invented in California in the 1940s, but the transistor radio was commercialized by Sony before American and European manufacturers did so because Sony Chairman Akio Morita identified a new market for portable radios whose unmet needs the existing radio manufacturers had not recognized.[26] Sony's product immediately became the dominant design, as did its Walkman 30 years later.

During the 1960s, the technology of video recording and playback using modular cassettes was developed in the United States, but a successful product never materialized despite many attempts to do so. The designers never understood the tacit requirements of users, and the controls they provided were too complicated. However, a Japanese company, JVC, persisted in the development process and after 20 years produced the system that was quickly accepted as the dominant design in the market because it was user-friendly (enough) to attract a following. The same design still dominates today.[27]

Success at creating new dominant designs depends to a significant degree on discovering new tacit knowledge, and then transforming it into an explicit form so that an innovation team can discuss it, refine it, and apply it in their work. Through iterations of hands-on experimentation and analysis in the research phase of early and rapid prototyping, fuzzy uncertainty is progressively eliminated and the innovation process is properly targeted.

To visualize how designers share and transform tacit and explicit knowledge, Japanese professors Ikujiro Nonaka and Hirotaka Takeuchi developed a matrix that describes these transitions (see Figure 3.10).

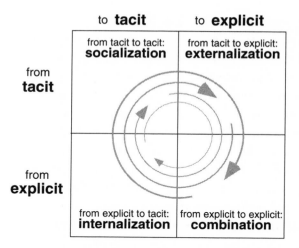

Figure 3.10 Tacit and Explicit Knowledge. The upper right quadrant shows that when tacit knowledge is made explicit it is externalized, made manifest in spoken words, writings, or tangible objects. Researchers seek to do just this, rendering the hidden tacit forms explicit and therefore applicable in the innovation process. Explicit knowledge is made tacit when it is internalized through experience. A pilot reads the F-117 instruction manual and then flies the aircraft to develop a feel for flight that cannot be expressed. Through such experience, the descriptions in the manual are translated into an appreciation of the actual flight characteristics of the plane. The matrix also shows that tacit knowledge can be shared from one person to another without being made explicit, the process of socialization that is used in advertising to convey social meanings that are powerful even as they are intended to remain at the unconscious level. In the fourth quadrant, combination occurs when explicit knowledge is shared and integrated through learning.

Just as the advance of knowledge is represented in the path to wisdom as an iterative spiral, Nonaka and Takeuchi point out that as knowledge moves through an organization or a society, it often moves from one quadrant to the next as indicated by the spiral that connects the four quadrants. Until knowledge is represented in all four quadrants, it is not thoroughly embedded in the reality of the society, and the learning process is therefore incomplete.

We do the same thing when we become conscious of new facets or dimensions of our own experience. In extreme cases, we may develop awareness of the vast amount of knowledge being processed in our minds at any given time.

For example, Craig Breedlove builds rocket-powered cars in quest of the land speed record, but often the outcome is not what he wanted. In 1965, his Spirit of America crashed at 620 miles per hour, but Breedlove emerged unscathed from the wreck and immediately spoke about what had transpired during his failed test run. He remarked, "It's amazing how much information you actually pull in and how much you can pull back. It's the kind of thing where you can have your attention interrupted for just an instant and miss some type of data input, a marker or location. At the speed that the vehicle's going, that could be a fatal mistake."[28] It took Breedlove 93 minutes (5,580 seconds) to account for what happened in the 8.7 seconds of the test run, indicating just how much is going on in our minds at any given time that we are dimly aware of, or not aware of at all.

One way to overcome these limitations (without racing cars at hundreds of miles per hour) is to establish teams of people to work together in communities that share critical knowledge.

Communities of Practice

In the complex social milieu of all organizations, both explicit and tacit knowledge are continually present, and they evolve concurrently in the course of accomplishing work.

Dr. Brigitte Jordan, an anthropologist at Xerox PARC and its affiliate the Institute for Research on Learning, studies the modern workplace and seeks to expose and understand the tacit behaviors and actions that can make the difference between new product success and failure; "Anthropologists learned to learn not by explicit instruction but by participating in the routine activities of people's daily lives and by immersing themselves in the events of the community, thereby coming to appreciate what the world looked like from the point of view of 'the natives.' Today, there are few unstudied exotic peoples left, but ethnographic methods have been found to be exceedingly useful whenever one needs to understand complex functioning systems within a holistic perspective. . . . While in exotic settings one might learn how to build a canoe, weave a hammock, make rain, or deliver a baby, in industrial work places one gets insights into the intricacies of returning customers' phone calls, adjusting a piece of machinery, smelling a vat of chemicals, or negotiating with co-workers about a useful software strategy."[29]

Hence, while learning is an intellectual activity that can only be done by people, this does not mean that it has to be done by people working alone. In fact, research into the learning process shows that a great deal of the most important learning occurs in a social context that is self-defined among groups of people who share interests or responsibilities. They create joint endeavors and the unique language that describes it, and in so doing form themselves into communities around their shared intents, knowledge, and practices.

These communities provide the social and intellectual context in which learning occurs because it is here in a social context that information, theory, and experience are actively integrated in the continual process of doing, of getting work done through practice. Thus, it is in these "communities of practice" that a great deal of today's learning is useful and important.

As literature from the Institute for Research on Learning explains, "People are learning all the time, but what they are learning is not necessarily in their best interests or in the best interests of society. People learn what enables them to participate in communities of practice—not just any communities of practice, but those that appear to them to be real, to be available, and to hold possibility of meaningful participation. It is this need for meaningful participation that motivates both the gang member and the honor student, the scientist and the soloist, the public servant and the entrepreneur."[30]

This helps to explain the persistent complaint that high school, college, and even MBA graduates do not have the skills that their employers need. There is almost always an adjustment period after leaving school precisely because skills in school have been honed in the academic community of practice whose goals, constraints, and measures of success differ greatly from those on the job.

At work, we therefore augment or substitute much of the information and theories that we learned in school with experiences that enable us to create the knowledge that is relevant and useful in the communities in which we are now becoming participants.

This principle has many implications for the development of organizational capability and the design of work teams. Communities of practice have definite boundaries, and therefore differences in culture and terminology can be significant barriers. Thus, it is simply not enough to have members of different communities sit around a conference table together and expect useful understanding or meaningful work to result. When we recognize that knowledge is literally embedded in communities of practice, we also realize that effective communication between teams working to build new capability requires each to experience the other's environments to understand the meanings embedded in their languages.

Conversely, breaking up established interdisciplinary work teams can dramatically reduce an organization's effectiveness. For example, at one time GM's manufacturing department was extremely capable, largely because it was structured as a multidisciplinary team. A complete, embedded information systems (IS) capability participated on the team, and their role was to support automation in GM's manufacturing and assembly plants.

When GM acquired EDS at the start of its major automation initiative of the 1980s, the information systems specialists in the manufacturing department were transferred into the functional IS department under EDS. This change reduced GM's capability to automate effectively exactly when it was most needed. Since EDS was structured as a separate data processing department that got paid based on the number of CPU cycles that were being used on its computers, there was no organizational incentive to learn how to paint cars faster, or to use vision systems, or to apply any computer technology that was required in an automated factory to control machines or measure their performance.

Inappropriate social design also contributed to the failure, since the computer technicians were removed from the shop floor to the front office, isolating them from the very communities of practice that they were expected to support, and cutting them off from the only place where they could have learning experiences that would enable their work to be successful.

This also illustrates the multidisciplinary nature of innovation, in which the integration of critical knowledge from different communities of practice, as with the DocuTech, often provides the most fertile ground.

When the Wright Brothers invented a discipline that had previously been assumed by people including Lord Kelvin to be impossible, they created a new aircraft industry in the process. The key to their method was aggregating knowledge from many disciplines into a single, coherent new discipline that defined a new transportation architecture.

The core elements of the aircraft, even in its earliest development, consisted of its aerodynamics of the wings and the means to control of the aircraft in flight, the structural design of the airframe, power supplied by an internal combustion engine and delivered through the propellers, and the ergonomics of piloting the craft including the placement of the control levers in relation to the pilot's body. These disciplines had never been brought together in an effective way before, but after the Wright Brothers, they could never again be understood as completely separate (see Figure 3.11).

For those who are new to a community there is a process of initiation, a period during which to learn the values of a community and its interaction protocols, and to understand what is important and how to achieve those behaviors or results. If we fail at this or choose not to engage, we remain outsiders.[31]

Each action that we take is therefore an opportunity to test existing information and theories against new experiences that confirm and

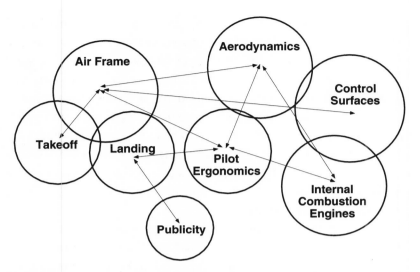

Figure 3.11 Overlapping Communities of Practice in the Wright Flyer. Innovation comes about by aggregating knowledge that originates among different communities of practice. This is "mutually dependent learning" that leads to new products, new market segments, and new industries. Hence, we ask the question, "Which came first, the Wright brothers or the Aeronautical Engineering program at Purdue University?" And we realize that innovation creates new disciplines, not the other way around. The creation of an academic department only follows the expansion of knowledge, as driven by practical needs and the creative tension that they inspire.

validate them, or conversely throw them into question, forcing us to seek a more coherent explanation of our experience.

Through continual action and error-correction in pursuit of their goals, individuals participating in communities of practice actively define, and then redefine, what is appropriate and inappropriate. This basis of experience also defines what is "possible" and what is "impossible," for this kind of experience is the most compelling source of our knowledge about how the world works and what is "real."

The intent to create an innovation affects this knowledge precisely by bringing reality into question, by *redefining* what is possible, and transforming the formerly impossible into something that is at first perhaps only a plausible idea, and later perhaps a reality. Hence, innovation is the transformation of the impossible into the commonplace by transcending the existing boundaries of knowledge.

Since an innovation can be brought into existence only when one, two, or all three of the variable components of knowledge are somehow changed, we must therefore have new information, new theories, and/or new experiences to innovate. Thus, "A U.S. Honda design team, stalemated on a trunk design project, spent an afternoon in a Disneyland parking lot observing what people put into and took out of their car trunks and what kind of motion was involved . . . and ultimately came up with a new design."[32]

In the language we are defining here, we would say that the members of the community of practice called the Honda design team obtained new experience by observing the behavior of members of another community, families visiting Disneyland. By experiencing the overlap between the two communities of practice, Honda designers created new knowledge that became the basis of a new design.

The same dynamics are prevalent among scientific researchers, who seek to confirm and extend existing scientific theory. But when their observations conflict with the existing theoretical framework in their discipline, they must develop new theory to account for their observations. Hence Dr. Deming's observation that theory always comes with the possibility of being wrong.[33]

Thomas Kuhn calls this transition the creation of a new paradigm, and he cogently describes the tumultuous and awkward period when conflicting paradigms happen to coexist, when an old paradigm has been brought into question but before a new one has been widely accepted among the members of the community.[34]

Like all other scientific disciplines and communities of practice, cosmology has had its share of paradigm shifts, all driven by the conflict between existing theory and new, conflicting knowledge: "The 1965 discovery of background radiation by Arno A. Penzias and Robert W. Wilson of Bell Laboratories proved to be the crucial evidence in establishing the big bang theory as the preeminent theory of cosmology. . . . As investigators developed the theory, they uncovered complicated problems. For example, the standard big bang theory, coupled with the modern theory of elementary particles, predicts the existence of many superheavy particles carrying magnetic charge . . . magnetic monopoles. . . . monopoles should have emerged very early in the evolution of the universe and should now be as abundant as protons. In that case, the mean density of matter in the universe would be about 15 orders of magnitude greater than its present value. This and other puzzles forced physicists to look more attentively at the basic assumptions underlying the standard cosmological theory. And we found many to be highly suspicious."[35]

Stress is also present during periods when society or the economy are undergoing change, and certainly today we are experiencing both the fundamental changes of perspective and the resulting stresses in the transition from the Industrial Age to the Knowledge Age.[36]

Among businesses, the fact of change is often exposed in hindsight through the discovery that customers have adopted new behaviors, needs, or expectations. New products and services change the way that customers, as members of communities of practice, react to the suddenly old products and services, thereby permanently changing the dynamics of the marketplace.

In this milieu, managerial and organizational theories are tested day by day, and this continual shifting of the experiential framework can be very unsettling for those whose organizational structures were constructed on the expectation of stability in the marketplace. Constant change and new experiences mean that the foundation of theories and information upon which organizations are built are far less stable than we ever imagined them to be.

Since impending change is often revealed first in smaller and more narrowly drawn special-interest communities, studying the surprises that emerge in these groups becomes an early warning strategy. In the words of Peter Drucker, "Systematic innovation consists in the purposeful and organized search for changes, and in the systematic analysis of the opportunities such changes might offer for economic or social innovation. . . . No other area offers richer opportunities for successful change than the unexpected success."[37]

For example, laser technology had its initial impact only among theorists and researchers in the scientific community, and then later in the few technical research domains where lasers could be usefully applied. Only after many years was this technology refined and adapted to produce the mass market laser printer that has had so much importance for the personal computer industry. Still later was the technology further refined to create consumer compact disc devices, which then displaced the market for vinyl records in a period of only 18 months.

Even as the search for innovation is necessarily an activity that occurs in communities of practice, it is precisely because communities of practice are built on prior experience that they are often blinded to the possibility that there may be another way, and perhaps a better way.

It is for this reason that a significant percentage of all innovations are made by people who are working outside the discipline for which they were trained. After all, a considerable proportion of professional training is really an extended lesson in the limits of existing knowledge. This separates the world into the possible, what we do now, and the impossible, which is what we don't do.

The reason that we don't, of course, is that we don't have the knowledge.

We don't, that is, until we do. So as communities of practice are the context in which learning occurs, they can either be a trap that impedes even the pursuit of new learning that might contradict established norms, or a context in which enthusiasm for learning leads to new knowledge.

Hence, the creation of new knowledge can be accelerated by bringing the members of two communities together. Done skillfully, this may lead to the creation of a new community, an integration of complementary knowledge sets that will lead to opportunities for innovation (see Figure 3.12).

The development of new communities of practice is more than just creating teams. It is a method of countering overspecialization by maintaining a dyadic tension between the specialization of particular

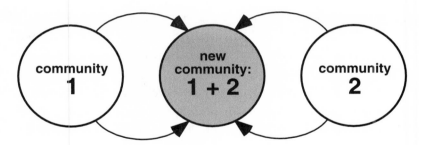

Figure 3.12 New Communities of Practice. New communities of practice come about through the integration of knowledge from existing communities in the interstitial spaces between them.

disciplines and the breadth that can be fostered when those from different disciplines integrate their distinct knowledge bases together.

Thus, it is important to recognize that today's innovations are rarely conceived within the framework of a single community of practice. In an environment of complex technologies and complex markets, products and services often are composed of elements developed in many different communities of practice. NASA and University of California scientist Mike Wiskerchen observes: "Simple innovations which represent one technology usually do not flourish. Integrated sets of technologies which can be assembled together into a product and then delivered to the marketplace are the only things that modern innovators can really be successful with. What that means is that individual people starting things have a very tough time. Groups of innovators coming together for an integrated product seem to be necessary today."[38]

This process is also called "knowledge aggregation," and it is evident in every product that you are likely to find in any store, anywhere in the industrialized world. Even the most basic of them are likely to use components made of many different materials, including new metals, plastics, and fibers, each of which is technologically advanced compared with the versions of these materials that were used even 5 or 10 years ago.

Every year more and more knowledge is being created and applied in new products and services, and in new disciplines that are emerging at the points of intersection among two or three or many disciplines that were once considered separate.

As noted in Chapter 1, Japanese researcher Fumio Kodama describes the broad tendency of separate disciplines to converge in new combinations as the process of "technology fusion." Thus, mechatronics (digitally controlled manufacturing equipment) is the fusion of mechanical and electrical engineering, biotechnology is the fusion of genetics and physiology, and nanotechnology is the fusion of physics and mechanics (see Figure 3.13).

Kodama suggests that this process offers the greatest opportunities for economic growth in the decades ahead: "For years it has been said that innovation is achieved by breaking through the boundaries of existing technology. Recent innovations in mechatronics and optoelectronics, however, make it more appropriate to view innovation as the fusion of different types of technology rather than as a series of technical breakthroughs. Fusion means more than a combination of different technologies; it invokes an arithmetic in which one plus one makes three."[39]

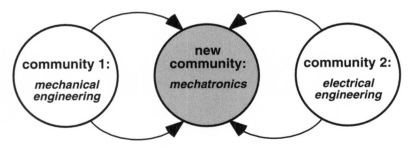

Figure 3.13 Technology Fusion: Mechatronics. By integrating mechanical engineering with electrical engineering, a new discipline was created, mechatronics. Mechatronics applied to digital machine tools has proven to be a significant advance in production environments as a means of increasing quality while reducing costs.

Fusion innovations emerge when the complementarity between the two (or more) knowledge sets is exploited. By creating useful interdependence, the members of different communities create new shared language, and in so doing they also create a new community of practice whose unique knowledge may have distinct value in the marketplace.

In the language of marketing, customers who fit a particular demographic pattern are members of a community of practice, and the core characteristics of this community can be identified and ranked in importance to create the possibility of predicting future behavior, always a favorite topic.

Recognizing and fulfilling needs that have not yet been made explicit, future needs, requires mutually dependent learning involving all the participants in the innovation process, including the customer. Working together they can create experiences that expose the critical elements of tacit knowledge that may lead to new products and services.

In Dr. Jordan's words, ". . . research that focuses on work *practice* requires a radical conceptual switch from seeing knowledge as a property of the individual, as a kind of quantity that can be measured, assessed, and 'transferred,' to seeing knowledge and meaning as socially constructed within ongoing communities of practice. Taking this view seriously means to investigate the ways in which people in the workplace 'co-construct' knowledge and skill by drawing on the social and material resources available to them."[40]

Communities of practice play a critical role in developing knowledge and also provide a method for managing large bodies of knowledge. Since everyone cannot know everything, individual and team specialization within communities of practice is a way for organizations to accumulate useful knowledge.

Managing such specialization has also been described by Gary Hamel and C.K. Prahalad as managing "core competences." "A competence is a bundle of skills and technologies rather than a single discrete skill or technology. As an example, Motorola's competence in fast cycle-time production (minimizing the time between an order and the fulfillment of that order) rests on a broad range of underlying skills, including design disciplines that maximize commonality across a product line [which we might also identify as a product platform], flexible manufacturing, sophisticated order-entry systems, inventory management, and supplier management. The core competence Federal Express possesses in package routing, sorting, tracking, and delivery rests on the integration of bar-code technology, wireless communications, network management, and real-time linear programming, to name a few. It is this integration that is the hallmark of a core competence. A core competence represents the sum of learning across individual skills sets and individual organizational units."[41]

Recognizing the relationship between the learning process, its integration as core competences, and the way both are embedded in communities of practice suggests a fundamental change in what it means to be employed. Whereas the Industrial Age worker had an explicit "job" that was to be done (according to Taylorism) to the exclusion of learning and only according to explicit knowledge, the Knowledge Age worker "participates in overlapping communities of practice" that richly embed learning and the use of both explicit and tacit knowledge.

These differences are also reflected in differing models of learning investments. Industrial education was directed at explicit knowledge held by individuals through formal workshops and classes. Knowledge Age investment is directed toward developing and exposing tacit knowledge in groups, which requires investment in all four quadrants (see Figure 3.14).

This shows why corporate training is of limited value, and why real learning is so rare in the classroom, while the lower right-hand quadrant is the domain of learning by doing, which is still insufficient because it is accomplished only by individuals.

To support effective learning and successful innovation processes that are organizational in scope, it is necessary to identify, create, and apply knowledge that lies in the upper right quadrant, the domain of tacit knowledge held by groups.

To achieve this transition from lower left to upper right there must be dialogue directly between members of the different communities of practice to explore the overlaps and limits of existing

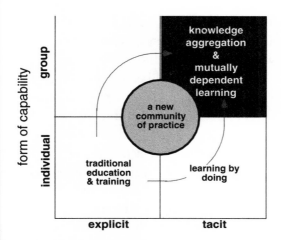

Figure 3.14 Models of Learning. Capability is represented on the vertical axis, starting with capability in the individual at the bottom and in groups at the top. On the horizontal axis, explicit knowledge is at the left leads to tacit knowledge at the right. The lower left quadrant is where knowledge is held by individuals in explicit form, which is dealt with in a typical classroom. This form of knowledge tends to be passive, both in terms of the learning process and certainly in the value that may be applied in developing innovations.

knowledge, as well as direct, hands-on experience of the artifacts of their collaboration.

In the innovation process, this means that field trials with actual customers are necessary. Through these trials, a new community of practice may come into being that consists of all the people who are participating in the project, both as customers and as developers. The circle in the middle of the matrix therefore represents this new community the practice, which defines a new domain in which innovation may be found.

The way the matrix is drawn implies that there is a 50–50 balance between an individual's tacit and explicit knowledge. At first glance this seems to be perfectly reasonable, but perhaps it is not an accurate perspective. "Recent studies show that the conscious mind can process between sixteen and forty bits of information per second. But the sub-conscious mind can handle eleven million bits per second. In other words, we're aware of barely a millionth of the information that our brains process. While you were deliberately focusing on the movement of your arm, your brain was rapidly and efficiently dealing with the enormous amount of information needed to manage your body."[42]

Relating the terms "conscious" and "unconscious" mind to "explicit" and "tacit" knowledge is problematic, as these terms may have quite different meanings in the various communities of practice wherein they might be used. Nevertheless, there is certainly some correlation, and the implications are significant.

If more than 99 percent of the brain's activity is not recognized consciously, then you only have 1 percent of the system to work with

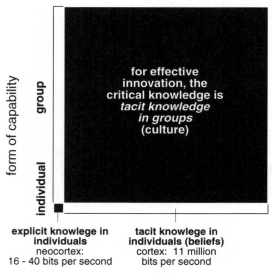

Figure 3.15 Tacit Knowledge in Groups. No wonder it is so difficult to lead change in organizations. It is almost impossible to change people's beliefs when the explicit "input channel" is so small compared with the tacit input channel. This shows why "walking the talk" is so critical, as its messages are largely tacit and exemplary rather than explicit and therefore necessarily reductionist.

(see Figure 3.15). What, then, are the proper functions of "management" and "leadership"?

Further clarification of the distinction between explicit and tacit knowledge has been developed by Harvard Professor Howard Gardner,[43] who has identified not just one form of intelligence, but seven (see Figure 3.16).

The implications of this research are significant for all researchers, as it suggests critical issues that must be identified and addressed in any form of product and service development. It specifies, for example, that the sound of a car is so important not just because it is a tacit dimension that we are concerned with, but also as an intelligence that can be identified and addressed.

For products and services that are more complex, the need to balance tacit and explicit knowledge can be even more critical. An extreme example of such complexity is the Apollo program of the 1960s, an ultimate expression of large-scale engineering that literally changed the relationship between humans and the universe we inhabit.

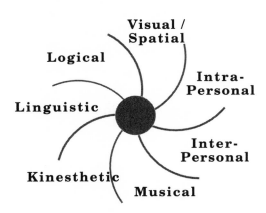

Figure 3.16 Seven Intelligences. In addition to the logical and linguistic forms of intelligence that are typically thought of as explicit, five other kinds of intelligence can be specifically identified.

The Story behind the Story of Apollo 13

Building on the knowledge developed in the Mercury and Gemini space programs of the early 1960s, the Apollo program resulted in the transforming Moon landing by Apollo 11 on July 20, 1969. The successful Apollo 12 mission followed in December 1969. Among the many successes and inspirations of all the Apollo missions, the failure of Apollo 13 stands out, nevertheless, as a triumph of spirit, of insight, and of engineering.

Apollo 13 was launched on April 11, 1970. The next day, however, an explosion occurred that damaged the spacecraft so severely that its mission to land on the Moon was aborted. The immediate challenge was to figure out how to use the crippled spacecraft to return the crew safely to Earth, which required considerable improvisation by the crew and the support workers on Earth.

Ken Cox was Technical Manager of the Primary Flight Control Systems for the Apollo program in the mid and late 1960s, and later Shuttle Technical Manager for Integrated Guidance, Navigation and Control. (They tend to be specific about their job titles at NASA.) He is now Assistant to the Director, Engineering Directorate for NASA at the Lyndon B. Johnson Space Center, Houston.

The story behind the story of Apollo 13 that he narrates here from his personal perspective reflects many of the concepts introduced in Chapters 1 through 3, and shows one instance of how they pertain in a world of professional innovators when the stakes are despair and inspiration, life and death.

When the explosion occurred on board Apollo 13 in April of 1970, I got a call at my home across from The Manned Spacecraft Center (now called the Johnson Space Center) at about 1:00 in the morning and I was told to get to Mission Control right away. I listened to the whole drama unfold, and I was part of the process of figuring out what to do to bring the spacecraft and the astronauts safely back to Earth. I was part of that activity on the ground, listening as the life support system began to drain out of the Command Module, as we realized that we must use the Lunar Module as a lifeboat.

When I saw the movie *Apollo 13,* the emotions, my experience, how people felt...*Apollo 13* was a very emotional film for me to watch. It depicted, in my judgment, with very great credibility the spirit of everyone trying to save that mission and bring the astronauts back.

To do this required us to use the Apollo spacecraft in a way that it was not designed to be used, and I'm going to tell part of the story of how this was done.

Most of the fundamental decisions about how to design the Apollo spacecraft were made in the early 1960s. The Apollo system consisted of three spacecraft, the Command Module, the attached Service Module, and the Lunar Module.

The command and service modules were built by North American (later Rockwell), while the lunar module was built by Grumman.

One of the main design issues was that if you launched a rocket toward the Moon you would swing around the Moon and come back toward the Earth, but you wouldn't make it to the Earth and get a good entry. So Apollo was designed to inject into lunar orbit by firing the big engine of the Service Module, a major Delta V propulsion burn, and then to later achieve a good Earth reentry trajectory with another engine firing.

The original designs for the engine control systems called for analog controls, because the Mercury and Gemini systems prior to Apollo were analog. They were built like airplanes had always been built. Digital computers as we know them today, digital systems, had never been built for an aircraft or a spacecraft.

A major decision was made in approximately 1964 after the original designs were essentially completed, because someone realized, "Wait a minute, computers are coming and they give us a lot more capability." So NASA made the very fundamental decision to go to digital primary control systems for all three modules, with backup analog systems which would be built as planned by the spacecraft contractors.

The primary system, though, was the beginning of the new digital avionics, digital flight control systems for Apollo. There was no precedent since previous spacecraft—none had never flown with digital systems. Because of my prior background in digital systems, I was given the responsibility to develop the primary control systems for all of the Apollo vehicles.

Since the primary contractors did not have experience in digital control, MIT Instrumentation Lab (later the name was changed to Charles Stark Draper Lab) was given responsibility for the primary control systems software, computer, and digital computer implementation that was used for all three modules, and my role was to manage the project.

Right from the beginning, I had one heck of an integration job, and I did it from scratch. There was no precedent. There were no reports saying "Here's the way we have built these systems in the past," and so it was a brand-new, open ball game.

I had gotten advice from Grumman and from North American, but they both wanted to use the digital capability, the new capability with exactly the same filters, exactly the same gains, exactly the same feedback loops as an analog system. They both advised me that the only way to do it was to stick to the tried and true, the analog design techniques, and just digitize it.

I did not want to do that. I realized that there were inherent properties of digital systems that were not available in analog systems. There were some good properties and some bad properties, but if you used the digital systems right, you got some capabilities that are not at all equivalent, positive capabilities. So there was a big, roaring debate which I was right in the middle of, on this whole question of the philosophy of how do you develop digital systems.

The great advantage of going digital was flexibility. You could make your control systems independent of the hardware sensors and effectors. You could change your control parameters after receiving actual flight test data. For example, we found out later that we didn't model all of the atmospheric properties correctly at the initial edge of the atmosphere. No airplanes had ever gotten up to that altitude, so we didn't have any real flight data. For all of the spacecraft, the mass properties were constantly changing, but once you built an analog control system you had no flexibility to make adjustments. You would find out when you got up in flight that the basic modeling was different than what you designed to.

With analog control systems, you would have had to physically remove the hardware and build new hardware. But because we had a digital system, we immediately changed the programming after the first Apollo flight and adjusted for extra firings and extra activity on the flight control system. In a digital system, it's a snap. You just go in there and adjust a few figures. So it was definitely the right thing to do because it gave Apollo mission flexibility with extremely low impact on the overall program.

I should mention that the computers that we were dealing with were very primitive by today's standards. The total memory of the onboard computers was about 32 K, and flight control only took about 35 percent–40 percent of that. The rest of the code was concerned with navigation, guidance, targeting, and communication between earth and the spacecraft. It was programmed in HAL, which was developed at MIT.

So now we are in late 1967, about 21 months before the first Moon landing with Apollo 11, and 30 months before Apollo 13. We were working on the digital control system, and the people at MIT and I discussed the idea that we really ought to have a contingency mode for coming back from the Moon if something happened and you could not fire the big command service module engine. What happens if there is a problem, and you cannot use the big engine? That was the drama of Apollo 13. Do we have contingency flight control, or contingency capabilities if something happened and we could not use the big engine? If you had the lunar module and command service module docked, the main engine on the lunar module could provide the incremental burn that was required so that we could get on the right trajectory to come back to Earth.

We said, "Look, we think we have the time to add this capability to the digital control system, and we don't think it's that big a deal." It wasn't like we were running hell-bent for leather and we were up against schedule constraints, and so I pushed real hard to say, "Well, let's put it in, damn it. This is an enhanced capability if something happens."

Now mind you, we could not define with any credibility or any predictability what the probability was that something would go wrong with the big engine, but it was obvious to us that if anything happened to the command service module and the big engine was not available to make this required burn in order to loop around the Moon and come back, the spacecraft just should have the capability to use the engine in the lunar module.

I had even talked to some of my counterparts in the propulsion engineering design group, and they said, "Oh, no, we would never have an explosion like that. No, no, no. That's not a credible scenario."

Based purely on good design practice and prior experience, there was no specific reason to protect against this happening. But we went ahead and we designed the thing anyway. We had the capability, and to us it was just the right thing to do.

Then we had to decide whether or not to include this contingency flight control capability on the lunar module into the backup analog flight control systems. We brought it up with Grumman, and they said, "In order for us to have the backup analog system, it's going to cause hardware to be changed and we cannot afford the impact on our schedule."

So we said, "Okay, we won't require it to be a function of the backup analog system, but the digital part can be done without changing hardware, or even changing code in the computer."

We took this idea to the Apollo program office, but they wanted us to prove that something might happen: "What is the problem, and what is the probability?" We didn't have the foggiest idea what the probability was that something might explode on the way over. So the initial response was, "Well, but you haven't proved yet that it is really needed."

But I went ahead and requested the Lab to go ahead and code it for simulation and testing. When we had done the software coding and knew that it wasn't that big a deal, that it would work, I brought this issue up before the Apollo Software Control Board, which was run by Chris Craft (before he became head of the center).

I made an impassioned plea to put it in, and I really believed that it was important enough, and it was logical enough, and even though we didn't have the explicit criteria for what we were protecting against, I made the argument this it was the right thing to do.

Chris listened to all this at the formal software control board meeting, and much to my surprise and chagrin, he said, "Ken, I think that you've done good work here, but you haven't proven that you need it, and therefore your request to put this in the basic capability of the Apollo program is disapproved."

I couldn't believe it. I said to myself, "I don't give a damn whether I can prove it or not! It's the right thing to do!" I was just crushed. But as I was walking out the door to leave, Chris motioned me over to the other side of the room, and he got me in a corner where there was just me and him. He looked me right in the eye, and there was a twinkle in his eye, and he said, "Put that mother in as soon as you can."

Immediately I realized that because of project politics, Chris did not want to open the gates for a lot of other changes that people had proposed that were not nearly as important as this.

So I called the MIT Instrumentation Lab and I said, "Put it in, put it in!" At this point it was a joint thing, it wasn't just me directing them. This was an interesting relationship between a civil service person and a contractor out to do something. We were totally, absolutely committed in a partnership sense to doing the right thing.

We agreed that we would put the design in and test it in the main program. Now this was totally against the rules, totally against the bureaucratic trend, but we did it. And when I came back three or four months later to the Software Control Board, I said, "We have done this action, we have put it in the main line configuration control and if you turn this proposal down at this point, it will impact the program because *you will have to take it out.*" And Chris had a twinkle in his eye, and he just said, "Well, if that's the case, I think we just ought to keep it in and accept the design." So that's how it was done.

When the explosion occurred on Apollo 13 in April of 1970, it did render the main propulsion system of the command service module inoperable. Had we tried to use that engine it probably would have exploded. It was definitely not something we could have risked. So once they transferred to the lunar module, it became abundantly clear that we had done the right thing.

Of course I was very happy because I knew that I'd made a major contribution to the program itself. That's part of the intrinsic spirit and working together as a collective community that just flowed in the Apollo program. I think we were able to accomplish things like this because we had a very fluid organization in Apollo. We all had clearly defined goals, and we knew that this was an important, international and national endeavor.

We're second-guessing history here, but I believe that it is probably the case, just in a probabilistic sense, that if we had not gone ahead and developed the digital control systems, Apollo 13 probably would not have made it back to Earth.

Apollo 11 astronaut Michael Collins was much more direct in his assessment. In his 1974 book, *Carrying the Fire*, he wrote, " . . . when a tank exploded and Lovell, Swigert, and Haise lost most of their oxygen on Apollo 13, they clearly owed their lives to the Houston computer and trajectory gnomes."[44]

The astronauts and the gnomes were engaged together in a tremendously complex learning activity that profoundly reflects the language of innovation that we are developing here. In our terms, the overall design of the Apollo system, with the spacecraft, its crew, and the ground support people and systems (including Ken Cox and his fellow gnomes) is the third iteration of vehicle design which became the third generation dominant design, following the prior generations of Mercury and Gemini spacecraft.

The 3rd generation design includes the basic configuration of the three major components, the Command Module, the Service Module, and the Lunar Module, and the way these modules connect together and "fly" in response to the physics of the Earth-Moon gravitational system and the relative vacuum of space. It includes the life support requirements for the crew, and the plan for and management of the mission. In sum, this design is everything that came together to compose the design of the Apollo program architecture, and Apollo 13 in specific as it was launched on April 11, 1970.

The Apollo dominant design is an expression of the accumulated knowledge of each individual and team that participated in the program, from the chief designers and engineers to the technicians, mechanics, security guards, and janitors. It reflects their capabilities in mathematics, physics, rocketry, physiology, safety, and nearly every other practice and discipline that one could possibly identify.

As an overall compilation, such a dominant design is realized upon the knowledge of individuals as manifested in their actions, for such actions bring systems into existence, and then sustain them. Spacecraft, companies, markets, and economies all exist because of the knowledge that people express through their actions.

Therefore, the necessary complement to a dominant design is the sum total of all of this knowledge, plus the technology, tools, and processes that are created and utilized by all the people in all the communities of practice that constitute an organization. We refer to it in aggregate as organizational capability.

At the beginning of the Apollo project, there was a vivid intent expressed by President Kennedy, and a specific overall design concept that we would therefore refer to as the architecture. However, only a small fraction of the knowledge that was needed to actually build and launch the spacecraft and conduct a successful Apollo mission existed at the outset. Through persistent research and experimentation, a tremendous amount of new knowledge was created that extended the capability of NASA and its contractors toward the fulfillment of the intended architecture.

This learning process was certainly not smooth and straightforward, and in fact a great deal of knowledge was developed at a very high cost in money and human lives. Three astronauts died in a fire in an Apollo capsule during a ground test exercise in 1966, which led to significant changes in the design of the system.[45] Such accidents, as well as the much more numerous successful experiments, led to new knowledge that had been outside the boundaries of existing knowledge provoking Apollo's designers to reconsider the architecture.

In his role as technical manager of primary flight control systems, Ken Cox began with a computer system architecture that was based on analog flight control techniques. The possibility of putting a digital computer into the spacecraft was a complete break with the past, something that had not been done before. This new architecture came with certain costs, but application scenarios suggested that it also offered what seemed at the time to be significant potential benefits, although their true value would only become evident later.

Many of the costs had to do with learning, with developing the capability to make use of the new technology. But as NASA did not have the capability to program the computer, Ken contracted with the MIT Instrumentation Lab to perform that work, and the first thing they did at MIT was to extend the existing computer architecture into software by creating a new programming language, HAL.

Here we see clearly how two overlapping communities of practice worked together to extend the boundaries of knowledge in the development of architecture and organizational capability that are inextricably linked. One simply cannot advance without the other, and their parallel and mutual advancement is an essential outcome of the innovation process. Learning creates new knowledge that is manifested in new technologies, which then require new learning to use effectively, and which then results in additional new knowledge that calls for the redefinition of the architecture, as described in Chapter 2 with the innovation cycle (see Figure 3.17).

Properly managed, the cycle can be an unending source of new value for an organization and its stakeholders, or as in this case a global society and its citizens.

Because this learning process is also contextualized within communities of practice, we see again that innovation as an expression of learning that occurs as a process of mutually dependent problem solving among members of diverse communities of practice.

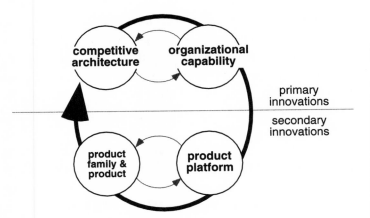

Figure 3.17 The Innovation Cycle. Architecture and capability development lead to innovations in product platforms and products. The use of those products and their impact in the marketplace creates new conditions, in which architecture and capability must then be reevaluated.

The complex Apollo system included many distinct and yet deeply overlapping communities—NASA, MIT, Grumman, North American, and hundreds of other subcontracting companies; analog designers, digital designers; control systems designers; rocketry designers; life support system designers, and so on.

Members of all of these communities work to advance the state of the art within their individual domains, and the interactions between them advance the system as a whole, and also inform and extend each individual community. Learning, the creation of new knowledge, and its application in the process of innovation, happens through individual work *that is therefore contextualized by the state of the knowledge in other communities.*

Hence, it would have been no use to have a rocketry system that could get to the moon and back if the astronauts had to be sacrificed along the way; and it would not have been to the point to keep the astronauts alive if the system couldn't get them to the moon and back.

One simply cannot apply new technologies as if they were functioning in a void. All technologies are part of larger systems that include the technology itself, its users, and all aspects of their reality. In this age of rapid change, managing the interdependencies among the communities of practice engaged in the process of technology fusion is one of the greatest management challenges in high-technology innovation.

We refer to this as the problem of "cognitive complexity," the critical challenge of developing cognitive skills to match the increasing complexity of the environment. To support the development of expanded cognition, tools and methods are needed to support memory, decision making, and effective collaborative effort in communities of practice. As the DocuTech story illustrates, the critical performance factor is the productivity of end users.

A documented architecture defines this broad context of cognitive complexity in explicit terms so that this understanding can be applied to purposeful innovation that will be of real benefit to users. This tells us that innovations must be introduced not just to communities of users, but within the entire context and infrastructure in which users exist and function.

An architecture, whether it is the competitive architecture of GM or the spacecraft architecture of Apollo, therefore spans multiple communities of practice that may also exist within diverse market segments.

Ken Cox's experience also highlights another great challenge facing those who would pursue the path of innovation, the resistance of others who are immersed in existing ways of thinking and working. Engineers at both Grumman and North American advised Ken to use the new digital capabilities only to do what prior analog systems had done, to "stick with the tried and true." Trapped within the boundaries of their existing models, they saw only the possibility for continuous innovation within the existing framework, and not the opportunity offered by the discontinuous application of new technology.

This shows that the potential of technology doesn't matter if the capability of your collaborators is not mature. More bluntly, collaborating with someone does not mean you are actually getting anything accomplished.

With the frightening benefit of hindsight, we see that if Ken had followed the advice he was given it was unlikely that the Apollo 13 crew would have made it back safely to the Earth. It takes someone with a vision of how the future could be better to make the intellectual leaps required to extend any existing architecture, particularly in the face of a majority who resist change.

This visionary's role as the embodiment of creative tension combines elements of the composer, who creates the score for the new symphony, and the conductor, who guides the orchestra in its performance. Both aspects of leadership are essential to a satisfying performance, and the orchestra team requires them even as the members remain the unquestioned experts in the use of their own instruments.

Thus, when we speak of competitive architecture and organizational capability we refer to this large set of models whose purpose is to help us understand how things are now, and how we would like for them to be different. The process of innovation is then the method of moving from the one to the other, and not coincidentally it is infused with a continuing search for new knowledge that is also the essence of adaptive change.

CHAPTER 4

The Knowledge Channel and Market Development

Models of competitive architecture and organizational capability guide the innovation process and the search for appropriate innovation targets. In reaching these targets, it is also critical to develop appropriate relationships between a company and its stakeholders. The shift from technology-driven to demand-driven markets is one manifestation of radical change in these relationships brought on by widespread and rapid change in the market environment.

Whereas in the past, companies simply sold their products into a few clearly defined distribution channels, today ongoing relationships between customers and companies are supported by ongoing dialogue, and these lead to intermittent sales transactions through a growing variety of channels.

The focus on relationships rather than on transactions creates the need for new methods of marketing, research and development, and customer support. As these relationships are also the basis on which mutually dependent learning between many different communities of practice among stakeholder groups takes place, they are central to 4th generation R&D. These new roles are explored in this chapter.

Market Research for Discontinuous Innovation

Customers are no longer passive recipients of the products and services a company chooses to make available, nor are other stakeholders including employees, stockholders, and neighbors content to be passive observers. This is as true in consumer markets as it is in business-to-business markets, and it calls for different ways of doing things.

Acts of consumption reflect lifestyle choices that are made, to a great extent, as part of each individual's tacit process of self-definition or self-creation. People choose products to complement their own identities and creative purposes, and driven by their own creativity, people will use products in ways that were never imagined by their makers. Therefore, customers need more than just the physical products and delivered services. They need knowledge to use these products and services effectively, more than they have ever required in the past.

Likewise, manufacturers and vendors need to understand the critical dimension of tacit knowledge to effectively create the new products and services to fulfill customer needs, but traditional market research has not been sufficient for obtaining that knowledge.

In 1983, for example, the consulting firm of McKinsey and Co. was commissioned by AT&T to assess the market potential for cellular telephones. McKinsey researchers concluded that the total worldwide cellular phone market would be 900,000 units by the year 2000. By 1994, there were already 17 million cellular users, with many more new ones every day (see Figure 4.1).[1]

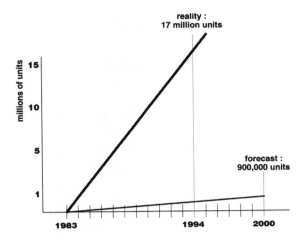

Figure 4.1 The Cellular Phone Market Forecast. Predicting future markets for new technologies is difficult to do accurately.

Traditional market research is likely to be misleading when assessing discontinuous innovation, as Glen Urban, Dean of MIT's Sloan School suggests: "Consumers are notorious for defying the rosy predictions of surveys when it comes to new technology products."[2]

The underlying problem is revealed when we recognize the critical role that tacit knowledge plays in the success of all products and services. Using dialogue and questionnaires, traditional market research is limited to identifying the explicit level of existing knowledge, existing needs, existing products, and existing services, which we call "marketing$_1$" (see Figure 4.2).

While useful in continuous innovation, traditional approaches are consistently misleading when applied to discontinuous innovations, where unexpressed and largely inexpressible tacit needs are tremendously important.

The focus of research for discontinuous innovation therefore shifts from explicit knowledge conveyed in dialogue to the much richer domain of tacit knowledge as created and conveyed through experience.

But for innovations that are new to the world, literally no one has any useful experience. Other than value frameworks that remain

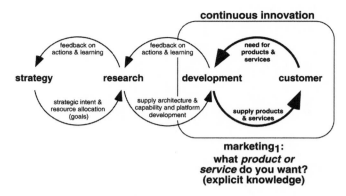

Figure 4.2 Marketing₁. Traditional marketing, marketing₁, uses dialogue and questionnaires to define the existing explicit needs of customers. Fulfilling these needs is done through continuous innovation in the product development process.

relatively stable, there is not yet any existing tacit knowledge to consider: "The problem with doing market research for the information highway [is that] it's like asking 19th century Americans their opinions on airline travel. The result has been contradictory and questionable findings."[3]

Where new technologies are emerging that no one has used, customers are forced to guess about the performance of future products and services in future product platforms and dominant designs. Likewise, manufacturers and service providers are forced to guess about customer demand for the new technologies that they are developing. This excessive guessing leads to wasted opportunities and wasted resources on both sides.

The development of the minivan shows how difficult it is for those who are immersed in an existing market to recognize new ones. Hal Sperlich led the development of the breakthrough Ford Mustang, and later he developed the minivan concept at Ford. But Ford's leaders did not grasp the minivan's market potential, and Sperlich took his idea to Chrysler, where, not surprisingly, he also met opposition. Sperlich later noted: "They lacked the confidence that a market existed because the product didn't exist. . . . We couldn't prove that there was a market for the minivan because there was no historical segment to cite. . . . In ten years of developing the minivan we never once got a letter from a housewife asking us to invent one. To the skeptics, this proved that there wasn't a market out there."[4]

Looking only at existing explicit knowledge, the minivan concept was incomprehensible. Only later, when Lee Iacocca became Chrysler's chairman did Sperlich gain top management support, and the two million minivans that Chrysler then sold in the late 1980s saved the company from bankruptcy. A decade later, Chrysler still had 50 percent of the U.S. minivan market, and thus derived a significant portion of its profits from Sperlich's tenacity.

To successfully develop and introduce discontinuous technologies, new ways of thinking are therefore required for recognizing and understanding tacit knowledge. The market research process for discontinuous innovation is based on *creating new, shared experiences* and therefore the new knowledge through which vendors and customers can make credible joint assessments about value.

One way to create these new experiences is through "expeditionary marketing," where vendors and customers work together to explore the uses and implications of new technologies, new capability, new products and services, and new markets. Expeditionary marketing is driven by complementary scenarios. For the customer, an application scenario describes how a technology can be used and what benefits may result. For a vendor, a technology scenario describes how technologies must be fused to achieve business purposes in fulfillment of the application scenario.

To undertake expeditionary marketing, a vendor will typically identify a small group of lead users who are themselves committed to understanding the implications of new technologies for their own use and their own capability development. Working together in the customer's actual work environment, they will define relevant application scenarios and then test technologies in real-world applications. Together, they will learn about the technologies as well as the critical underlying tacit dimensions that make technologies useful or not.

This form of learning is the core of the 4th generation R&D business process, and the detailed process for doing so is the subject of Chapter 8.

Even without using expeditionary marketing, vendors and customers have a persistent, mutual need to know about what is possible, and to know it earlier. Customers therefore reach deeply into the vendor's organization, effectively pulling research and development personnel into direct relationships on an ongoing basis.

This takes place before a sale, because customers need knowledge as much for making a decision as afterward when performing the necessary integration and use. Hence, R&D enables the advanced marketing and sales force to engage in useful interaction with customers, together defining how various application scenarios can be optimized.

In this new role as "marketing$_2$," R&D therefore supports customers using existing product platforms and architectures, and also has the responsibility for identifying latent customer needs that will create new business opportunities. By working together, vendors and customers do joint research as part of the customer's search for new capability, and the vendor's search for new product platforms and dominant designs.

In the end, customers think of "your" research as "their" research, which is one of the most significant changes from current practice (see Figure 4.3).

The marketing and R&D functions are merged in the front end, with research responsible for leading the development of new capability and architecture in the context of new technologies. Through this merger, science in the form of anthropology, ethnology, and video ethnography are among the tools used to expose the tacit dimension of technology use, just as science has also been applied to technology development.

Thus, when Honda creates a new trunk design, it is not based on explicit needs that customers have specifically articulated. Instead, this innovation is useful and notable precisely because it fulfills a previously unnoticed and unmet need that was only discovered through careful observation of tacit factors that had not been recognized before.

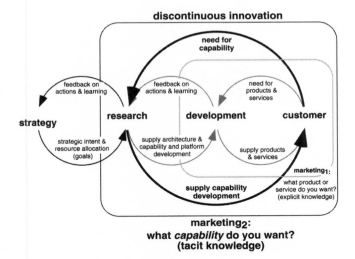

Figure 4.3 Marketing$_2$. The focus in marketing$_2$ shifts from identifying and satisfying existing needs for products and services to identifying and satisfying latent needs for new *capability*. This puts the research activity in direct communication with customers in a process of mutually dependent learning that supports discontinuous innovation.

Effective market research therefore applies science to go beyond the voice of the customer, to uncover the hidden needs and preferences that most customers are not aware of, and are consequently unable to express. Through such a process, tacit knowledge is externalized, made explicit in the evaluation of new capability enabled by technology. This knowledge thus becomes accessible to the design process and applicable to architecture development, capability development, and market development.

The process by which this happens can be visualized through Nonaka's model of knowledge creation (see Figure 4.4).

At Stage 2, the core function is building capability to supply products, services, and knowledge, whereas in Stage 3 it is building capability to use them. Both forms of learning are critical and necessarily concurrent to success at innovation.

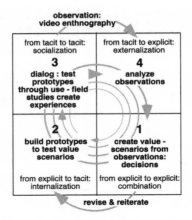

Figure 4.4 Knowledge Creation in Marketing$_2$. In Stage 1, dialogue, brainstorming, and discussion among diverse participants (who may be aware of different tacit factors) create value scenarios. In Stage 2, prototypes are built based on these value scenarios, and tests are designed for their validation. In Stage 3, prototypes are tested in use by real stakeholders, creating experiences that embody tacit knowledge. In Stage 4, observation, largely by video ethnography, is used to expose the tacit dimension and make this critical knowledge explicit through analysis. The process then returns again to Stage 1 for the revision of the value scenarios based on what has been learned. Decisions are then made about subsequent research and development activities.

This is the precise knowledge-building process, but since we know that information and knowledge are not the same, we have an indication here about the source of the productivity paradox. By assuming that information and knowledge are interchangable, the information technology industry has ignored the importance of the tacit dimension in knowledge building. Since information processing functions only at the explicit level, it is only in the first quadrant that information processing adds value to the process, while the critical functions of the other three do not lend themselves to automation as it has been done to date.

In Nonaka and Takeuchi's words, "Organizational knowledge creation is a spiral process, starting at the individual level and moving up through expanding communities of interaction, that crosses sectional, departmental, divisional, and organizational boundaries."[5]

Conducting this knowledge building process at the point of *use* is a way of testing customer experience in an ongoing way. Instead of waiting for product development cycles, testing can be done continuously, and with far wider participation than in formally run experiments. Using the Internet, data from use can be gathered in real time, remotely. Applying this model in conjunction with the Internet creates the knowledge channel and makes it an effective part of innovation. Marketing and product development will never be the same.

The Knowledge Channel

Particularly in business-to-business markets, there is a compelling need for productivity improvements at all levels of all organizations. With the widespread recognition that productivity increases come about through learning that extends existing knowledge[6] it is no longer sufficient for vendors to supply only products and services. Customers now select products and services as components of larger functional systems, and they often undertake the system integration, installation, and later reconfiguration functions themselves. This may be as true for the customer's computer systems as it is for the design and furnishing of workplaces, inventory and delivery systems, and telecommunications systems.

This new form of demand changes many traditional fixed products into "technology kits" that include the products themselves as well as the underlying knowledge about how they were designed, manufactured, and configured for use. Numerous communication channels provide this knowledge: toll-free phone lines, published product literature, advertising through many media, sales and customer service representatives, and direct sales forces, both multilevel and conventional.

The emergence of the Internet and the World Wide Web has provided a powerful new medium of communication with many compelling and useful qualities that other media do not provide.

Together, all these media have become the "Knowledge Channel" enabling customers to find the information and knowledge that they need to choose and make the most effective use of a company's products and services.

But unlike traditional distribution, the knowledge channel does not just carry one-way messages. It is bidirectional, providing a powerful means for suppliers to receive real-time feedback from customers and potential customers (see Figure 4.5).

The knowledge channel is not simply a medium of dialogue. It is, rather, a way of referring to many different forms of interaction between companies and their stakeholders. Hence, it includes traditional forms of research and communications, as well as elements such as

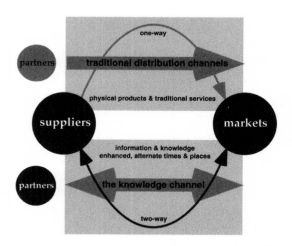

Figure 4.5 The Knowledge Channel. The knowledge channel shows the dyadic structure of today's parallel distribution channels, one for products and services, and the other for information and knowledge.

expeditionary marketing, field trials of new technologies, distribution strategies, customer service, sales, and advertising.

From the vendor's perspective, customers and other stakeholders using the knowledge channel become part of the learning system of an organization; viewed from the customer's side, vendors become part of the learning system of the customer's organization. From both perspectives, two communities of practice overlap to create new, shared experiences that lead to new knowledge.

Sometimes, the knowledge channel exists as an electronic linkage using computers or telecommunications, but often the knowledge channel comes about through face-to-face dialogue when one individual goes physically to meet with others.

Whether face to face or virtual, this two-way learning system supports continuous innovation in existing products and services, and their ongoing support in the customer's use. The knowledge channel can also expose new tacit knowledge that becomes the basis of discontinuous innovation.

Reflecting this shift, AT&T recently established a Customer Expectations Research Lab in Murray Hill, New Jersey, with 40 PhDs, including physicists, chemists, and biologists. But rather than studying the laws of nature, their focus is on how people adapt to new technologies, and hence their work is also part of the knowledge channel.[7]

Another example of the knowledge channel is NikeTown, the company's chain of retail stores. With only a small number of NikeTowns planned worldwide, the purpose of these stores is not to make a direct or significant impact on Nike's overall sales volume. Instead, these stores are flagships of the company's retail marketing and brand management efforts, intended to demonstrate better marketing methods to Nike's retailers and to enable the company to be in direct contact with individual customers in the immersive context of a richly detailed display environment.

Interviewed for this book, Nike Director of Design Gordon Thompson discusses these aspects of Nike's strategy, the issues that led to the creation of NikeTown, and some of the outcomes.[8]

NikeTown

We have a horizontal and a vertical strategy at Nike. The horizontal is brand and the vertical is category. It's important to do both great. We have to keep the Nike brand alive, and fresh, and vibrant, and young, and hip, and everything that it can be.

Vertically, in the product categories, we have to be extremely meaningful and make great products for the athletes who are playing sports.

We rely on both things 50-50. We want people to have brand loyalty, obviously, but we also know that we've got the responsibility to give them a great running product. It's a dual responsibility.

In the stores, it's the same thing. We've got the responsibility to keep the stores very brand-focused, but then, when you walk into a pavilion in a store, it's very category-driven, and it has the latest and greatest products.

On Retail

We want to be in retail, but we don't want to be in retail like a retailer is in retail. We want to make money, but we also have a lot of communication and storytelling and educating of consumers to do.

We're making money in retail, but that's only a part of the equation. The bigger thing is we're getting people interacting with the brand firsthand, instead of going through a magazine or going through another retail store.

We're really great at distribution with our retailers, and our relationship with them is pretty good. The sell-through is good, so there's not a financial need or a burning need to get involved in retail, like it's some big money-making thing for the company. We realize that we can do that through the normal distribution channels. What we need is a house for people to visit Nike. NikeTowns give us "regional houses of Nike."

We make them for people who like Nike, and people who are curious about Nike. We get a huge repeat business.

We're targeting them the same way we target our advertising, [to a] sort of young or young at heart audience that loves sports.

The Objectives of NikeTown

1. *To Inspire Our Retailers* Nike's problem in 1988–1989 was that the Jordan shoe had really taken off, a lot of our air technology had been bought and we were doing extremely well as a company, but merchandising in the sporting goods industry was not at the level of other retail merchandising, such as the fashion industry, the electronics industry, or anyone else. Sporting goods stores were still caught in the past.

We had, and still have, a very large line of apparel in footwear that was not presented well at retail. In frustration, we thought it would be good to open a retail store to help inspire retailers, our retailers specifically, that displayed our products correctly and communicated to the consumer. A superstore that could really represent Nike.

2. *Direct Communication with the Public* Another objective came out of our frustration at not being able to communicate directly with the public, except for advertising and some sports marketing.

I'm amazed at the consumers' response to NikeTown. It's a breath of fresh air to go to one of our retail stores and listen to what people say about it. That's very exciting. It gives you a real sense that you've created something for someone very special. The age span is wonderful too. Those stores have touched everyone from young children to very hip teenagers to my parents, and everyone in between. I think it's a testimony to the brand, and to the fact that the stores capture the brand.

I'm going to take all the design directors for footwear, apparel, accessories, and image, to New York after the store is open there and have them work in the store for a couple of days, interacting with people in what is going to be a good learning experience. The learning we get now is via a box or via report, it's not firsthand. Utilizing the stores as a place for us to work and really intermingle firsthand with people is a great asset and we need to take more advantage of it.

3. *Direct Feedback* And the third point was we didn't really get quality feedback from our retailers on what was selling, how it sold, what people had problems with, what the questions were about the product, all those sort of things.

Now the feedback from NikeTown is tenfold more than what we can get from our retailers.

We use comment cards, asking for input, and surprisingly a lot of those cards get back to us.

The store manager, the footwear manager, and the apparel manager make summary reports and we see what's selling every week, what the hot initiatives are, where we're down, what people aren't buying, what colors are selling. That information is invaluable for us.

We also get feedback at the emotional level, feedback on advertising, feedback on what the latest and greatest thing is, and because everyone from store manager to sales associate, to me, to Phil Knight, are all on E-mail, everyone sees the feedback.

Now we plan to open 20 stores worldwide in key markets where we are undistributed, or where we would like to get quality feedback from consumers.

NikeTown Imitators

We've been knocked off six ways from Sunday. And that's fine because we've gotten knocked off by our own retailers, which is outstanding. That's one of the reasons we built the stores. We have seen an incredible improvement in the product presentation in athletic stores.

Other industries have also picked it up. There was no such thing as a Warner Brothers store when NikeTown opened, and no such thing as a Disney store. After NikeTown, brand retailing started evolving quickly.

NikeTown has become a huge success; its locations in Chicago and Portland have become leading tourist attractions that also serve a strong base of local customers, showing that Nike customers, as with customers everywhere, want access to knowledge.

In addition to Warner Brothers Studio stores and Disney stores, many other manufacturers have followed Nike's lead into direct retail including Sony, Levi Strauss, Speedo, and others. In many of these stores, the knowledge gained by the company is probably far more important than the revenue generated.

As sources of critical feedback and new knowledge for both these companies and their customers, this approach to retail has become a focal point for the development of the market.

Market Development

When new products and services are ready to be marketed on a widespread basis, the focus shifts from joint development involving companies and selected customers to mass marketing on a larger scale. To be successful in the broader market, the *experiences* of new value that have been shared within a small development group must somehow be brought to the larger market.

In the classical literature of the diffusion of innovations as developed by Everett Rogers, this means expanding market penetration beyond innovators and early adopters and into mass markets.[9]

Many discontinuous innovations also require a parallel effort of building new infrastructure that will be required to make them salable or usable. Such infrastructure may simply provide the means to support sales and distribution, or it may be more extensive, involving new tooling and behavior on the part of suppliers of complementary products and services, and also new behavior by end users.

Both of these facets—the one involving marketing$_1$ and marketing$_2$, and the other involving the creation of new infrastructure—are the elements of market development. The early stages in the development of commercial aviation demonstrate both.

A few years after the Wright brothers' first powered flight, Marshall Ferdinand Foch, professor of strategy at the French Ecole Superieure de Guerre (War College) showed his mastery of an obsolete paradigm in his comment, "Airplanes are interesting toys, but of no military value." World War I proved him wrong, as the conflict was decided through the application of discontinuous innovations such as the tank and the very airplane whose utility Foch had not understood.

By 1918, however, hundreds of former military pilots had no future in aviation simply because there was no civilian aviation industry to employ them. The challenge of creating such an industry was soon undertaken by William Stout and Henry Ford. In the following story, Michael Maxtone-Graham describes their contributions to the commercial aviation industry through the development of one of the first commercial aircraft, the Ford Tri-Motor, which became a success in large part due to Ford's skill at *both* aspects of market development.[10]

The Ford Tri-Motor

Only 78 years ago, planes were made of wood, had open cockpits, and were noisy. The plane that single-wingedly changed all this was the Ford Tri-Motor or Tin Goose, proving that what was good for the goose was good for aviation.

Any traveler who steps aboard a sleek and comfortable jet airliner owes a debt of gratitude to what must seem by today's standards an ungainly, almost alien aircraft—the Ford Tri-Motor. Dubbed the Tin Goose because it was the first plane [built in North America] to have a metal skin, this amazing plane almost single-handedly launched commercial aviation.

When World War I ended on November 11, 1918, all of the world's major nations had hundreds of planes and trained pilots. But when peace came, the momentum of the embryonic technology that had produced these aircraft quickly faltered. The astonishing fact was that ordinary people could think of no possible peacetime use for airplanes. Cars, trains, and ships, they believed, would continue to fill all the transportation needs the world would ever have.

While this seems hard to believe today, a closer look back reveals some compelling reasons why people didn't take flight seriously 78 years ago. All aircraft, even the biggest, were biplanes made with wooden frames covered by stretched canvas. Anyone brave enough to hire a plane had to sit in an open, unheated cockpit while being assaulted by twin demons—wind and the horrific noise of a primitive engine.

Although regular airmail service had been inaugurated on August 12, 1918, the post office department's abysmal safety record over the years hardly inspired confidence. In 1920 alone, nine pilots were killed in daylight accidents.

By 1923, the situation hadn't improved much. Landing fields were scarce, bumpy, and primitively equipped; the guiding radio beam had yet to be invented; and no aircraft could carry a respectable load of passengers or freight for any meaningful distance.

To solve this last problem, enter William B. Stout, a brilliant engineer and promoter. Imbued with endless enthusiasm and a contagious faith in the future of aviation, he determined to build a plane that was large enough, comfortable enough, and safe enough to persuade people that flight could logically and successfully play a key role in the transportation future of the United States.

Raising more than $125,000 from Detroit businessmen, he formed the Stout Metal Airplane Company and started to design an aircraft that would meet his requirements. Another of his requirements was a good landing field in the Detroit area, and to help him achieve this he approached Edsel Ford, who was known to have a keen interest in flying. In summer of 1924, at a meeting with Edsel and his father, Henry, Stout was able to fire them with an enthusiasm equal to his own.

Offering him a 260-acre tract of land, the elder Ford insisted only that the airport should become "the finest landing field in the world."

It did. The finished airport had runways 300 feet wide by 3,400 and 3,700 feet long, generous hangar space for transient pilots, and an exemplary parts and service facility; 200-foot letters of crushed white stone that spelled out "FORD" were visible from a height of 10,000 feet.

Firmly bitten by the flying bug, Ford's next step was to build a factory, at his own expense, for the Stout company. It was here, while sitting on a pile of lumber as he listened to Stout expound about the future of aviation, that he decided to take an even bigger step.

"Stout," he said, rising to his feet, "this whole picture looks to me as if it was something that somebody has got to put a lot of money behind to make an industry out of it. I don't know why the Ford Motor Company shouldn't do just that."

Later, Stout would write, "In my opinion, the greatest single thing I accomplished for aviation was getting Mr. Ford into it." When news of the famed industrialist's participation became public, many people believed that aviation would now truly come of age.

Stout, now working with Ford engineers, continued to develop and test the new aircraft. Serendipitously, the Aluminum Company of America had just developed an alloy of aluminum and copper that was very strong and very light. It was decided to use this new "Duralumin" for the plane, corrugating it for even greater strength.

In a bold and innovative stroke, the engineers eliminated the lower wing and moved the pilot's controls in front of the remaining wing, enclosing the entire cockpit. The new monoplane had an unprecedented wingspan of 70 feet. Archives reveal that at 136 pounds, 19-year-old Vern Mundinger was small enough to crawl inside the wings to spray the tips with a protective coating.

Safety was the company's watchword from the beginning. The Ford Tri-Motor's three engines were more powerful and larger than anything then in use. The revolutionary aircraft could sustain flight on two engines or prolong it on just one. It could climb 900 feet a minute and cruise at over 100 miles an hour at 15,000 feet while 11 passengers seated comfortably in wicker chairs were served coffee by "flight escorts." There was even a separate cargo space for freight.

Additional refinements in subsequent models would include a kitchenette, folding berths, a radio cabinet, a writing desk with book case, card tables and a refrigerator. Most welcome of all, perhaps, was the introduction of a lavatory with toilet, running water, and towels.

As Ford had anticipated, the tri-motor was a phenomenal and instant success. Realizing that here at last was an aircraft that provided comfort, an efficient payload capability, and unique dependability, the country's fledgling airlines wasted no time in placing their orders. Many of them, in fact, started their business with just a single Ford Tri-Motor.

In 1928, Ford sold 36 aircraft; the following year, 86. Production problems had been quickly mastered, and before long, 1,600 workers were employed in the new factory. In one month alone, 18 planes rolled off the line.

Among the early customers were Juan Trippe, who launched Pan American Airlines, and World War I ace Eddie Rickenbacker, who headed Florida Airways Corporation. Transcontinental Air Transport, known as The Lindbergh Line and then experimenting with a combination of rail-plane transport from coast to coast, was also an early customer. Others were Boeing Air Transport, National Air Transport, Pacific, Stout, and Varney, which in 1931 decided to unite their routes and services to become United Airlines.

In spite of his aircraft's enthusiastic acceptance by the industry, Ford realized that he would soon have a problem. If the general public was not persuaded to travel by plane instead of train, he reasoned, the newly formed airlines would have no need of additional planes. In order to ensure that his aircraft division would continue to sell tri-motors, he decided to take on the job of persuading the public to fly.

He accomplished this with a remarkable advertising campaign consisting of 17 advertisements that appeared in 10 national magazines over an 18-month period starting in 1928. The campaign was remarkable because the advertisements described with rapturous prose and intriguing illustrations something that did not even exist at the time—commercial aviation.

Lift Up Your Eyes

How long ago did Orville Wright circle the drill field at Fort Myer while a few score of astonished witnesses stared open-mouthed at the sight of this first man to fly with wings for more than an hour? . . .

How long ago did the intrepid Bleriot hop in his flimsy, scorched monoplane from France to land precariously on the cliffs of Dover? . . .

How long ago did Graham-White circle the Statue of Liberty, struggling dexterously with his hands to maintain equilibrium? . . .

It seems only yesterday!

Yet in the few brief years since then man has learned a new technic in existence. He has explored the earth's atmosphere, his noble machine climbing on after human faculties had failed.... He has skimmed lightly over the impenetrable ice barriers of the polar regions.... He has taken in his flight not only the gray, fog-blanketed waters of the North Atlantic, but the empty blue seas of the South Atlantic—the Mediterranean—the Pacific—the Indian Ocean—the Gulf of Mexico.... He has soared confidently over the sands of Sahara and the Great Arabian Desert, where only the camel had dared venture before....

Created by Ford and the N.W. Ayer advertising agency and based largely on inspired conjecture, the ads imparted a sense of the extraordinary adventure and exhilaration of flight while always stressing safety and dependability. The brilliantly written ads showed airports, planes in flight, planes on the ground, and passengers enjoying the ministrations of an attentive cabin staff. (It was Henry Ford's idea to depict the pilots and flight escorts in uniforms.)

The advertising was wildly successful. Ticket sales for scheduled flights almost tripled. And across the country, more and more municipal governments approved the expenditures necessary to create the airports that would link America's cities and make the dream of commercial flight a reality.

But in July 1932, poised on the threshold of this exciting reality and just four years after launching his advertising campaign, Ford abruptly withdrew from the aircraft business. There were several reasons for this seemingly paradoxical departure.

Although, technically, the Ford Aircraft Division had made a profit during its seven-year existence, total expenditures (for factories, landing fields, and experimentation) more than canceled any gains. Now, the Great Depression that had started in 1929 began to affect all of the new airlines because fewer people could afford to fly, thus the demand for new planes fell off drastically.

On top of that, General Motors was making competitive inroads and starting to hurt Ford's automotive business. And finally, the Ford Motor Company's labor disputes were escalating. As the industrialist's problems mounted, his enthusiasm for aviation waned, and ultimately he decided to concentrate all his efforts on the manufacturing of cars.

The division's demise constituted a business failure, of course. But the advent of the Ford Tri-Motor had been an unprecedented success. In spite of a truncated production life, it was responsible for an important and badly needed aeronautical breakthrough at exactly the right time. The advent of commercial flight would have been considerably delayed without Henry Ford's visionary dream that gave American travelers this revolutionary plane. One of his advertisements describes both his dream and his tri-motor:

"Beautiful as a jewel, it spreads its wings like burnished silver, to fly with the smooth grace of an albatross over sea, over land, over deserts or Arctic wastes. Here, truly, is a yacht worthy of the modern man of spirit and imagination."[11]

The themes here are similar to the stories behind many discontinuous innovations that have significantly affected our lives. Somehow, somewhere, someone takes on the challenge of, in Ford's words, "making an industry out of it," or in our terms, market development. This means both developing the necessary infrastructure and the public's acceptance.

Many innovations, particularly those in transportation and communication require extensive infrastructures. Railroads need tracks and stations, airplanes need runways and terminals, cars need roads and gas stations, telephones need wired or wireless networks, and lacking any of these critical elements, there cannot be an industry.

Infrastructures typically span multiple markets and multiple industries, often leading to joint ventures and alliances among complementary companies. Road builders, oil companies, and auto companies are mutually dependent on the success of the others.

Other innovations are not particularly infrastructure-dependent, but must overcome considerable skepticism among development partners as well as customers. During the 1930s, for example, Chester Carlson invented xerography and then offered to sell his technology to North America's leading manufacturers of office equipment, including IBM, RCA, and GE. These companies and more than a dozen others turned him down, and only after six years of failed marketing did the Batelle Memorial research lab finally agree to license and develop the technology. Ten years later, a small firm called the Haloid Company took over from Batelle, perfected the technology, and went on to become one of the hottest stocks in Wall Street history under the name of Xerox Corporation.[12]

The development of the personal computer follows a similar story line. In the words of Steve Jobs, "We went to Atari and said, 'Hey, we got this amazing thing, even built with some of your parts, and what do you think about funding us? Or we'll give it to you. We just want to do it. Pay our salary, we'll come to work for you.' And they said, 'No.' So then we went to Hewlett-Packard, and they said, 'Hey, we don't need you. You haven't gotten through college yet.' " Forced to go it alone, Jobs and colleague Steve Wozniak went on to found Apple Computer and to undertake the development of the products and infrastructure to support the personal computer industry, as well as the education of the marketplace. Twenty years later, these and other founders of the industry have become some of the world's wealthiest individuals based on the value that they helped to create in the process of creating a new industry.

One of the most interesting uses of the PC is for connecting to the Internet, the rapidly growing global communications systems that links millions of people into a new metacommunity of practice, in which the creation and sharing of knowledge plays a key role.

Point of Use and the Internet

The customer's demand for information and knowledge will only increase, and consequently companies will have no choice but to make new information and knowledge services universally available. As this need becomes more pronounced, however, its character gradually changes, because while there is a great need to have more knowledge, there is also a limit to how much knowledge can be assimilated in advance.

Therefore, customers insist on receiving the information and knowledge that they require at two discrete times. First, while they are in the process of choosing what to buy, they need comparative information about performance, price, and the infrastructure that they will need to use a product or service. They may also require knowledge about how the product or service works.

Because of increasing the complexity of products, services, and the systems in which they function, customers will also require more detailed knowledge about how to actually use the product or service after they have made a purchase. In response to both needs, companies in all market sectors have found themselves establishing huge rooms full of telephone-based customer service and technical support staffs, but even so they are unable to meet the demands of customers.

In the personal computer industry, hardware and software companies are inundated with calls, and it is generally accepted that no more than 35 percent of all calls for technical support will be answered. Many who get answers to their questions do so only because of their willingness to spend hours on hold, waiting for their chance to learn what hundreds of pages of user manuals have not conveyed.

And it is not just the computer industry. At Federal Express, hundreds of customer service agents answer thousands of calls each day from customers, who are wondering where their packages are and when they will be (or were) delivered.

If you look on the labels of most common household products, you are likely to find a toll-free 800-number, and if you call that number, a customer service representative will talk to you. There are hundreds of thousands of people answering these calls, and specialized consulting firms to train them, set up their telecommunications systems and databases, and then improve their performance.

These examples suggest that customers require knowledge about the use of products and services not only before they are using the product or service, and not only after, but more precisely at the *point of use*.

Awareness of the importance of the point of use began in the pioneering automobile production system developed at Toyota, where two key point-of-use concepts have revolutionized manufacturing worldwide: just-in-time inventories and the *kanban* communication system. Just-in-time means, "In a flow process, the right parts needed in assembly reach the assembly line at the time they are needed and only in the amount needed,"[13] and kanban is the method of communicating between processes.

Similarly, what is now required in the marketplace is "just-in-time knowledge," which has also been referred to as "kanbrain" and "knowban."[14]

Prior to the 1990s, there was certainly a latent need for distributed point of use knowledge delivery, but the capacity to provide it was limited to the telephone. With high operating costs leading to a 65 percent failure rate in tech support, basic needs were not being satisfied.

However, the emergence of the Internet as a global medium of communication has fundamentally changed the situation, because the Internet can do things that have never been possible or practical before.[15] The Internet is therefore a new expression of the knowledge channel that supports a wide range of communications needs and has tremendous potential for point of use applications.

Compared with the telephone and other media that are more effective and commonly used for one-to-one and one-to-many communication, the Internet is uniquely a mass medium that enables a new form of interaction between many individuals and organizations at the same time (see Figure 4.6).

Internet communications can be rich with text, graphics, photos, video, and sound, all integrated and delivered via a single medium. And since users control the experience, it can be truly interactive. Both capabilities make the Internet effective as a medium for dealing with tacit knowledge as well as explicit.

These multidimensional capabilities are drawing more and more people to this new medium, and a critical mass of users will soon be achieved that will create thereby a new mass market. A 1995 study by Morgan Stanley indicated that there were about 10 million Internet

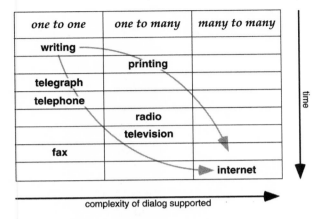

one to one	one to many	many to many
writing		
	printing	
telegraph		
telephone		
	radio	
	television	
fax		
		internet

time

complexity of dialog supported

Figure 4.6 The Evolution of Mass Media. Since the invention of printing turned the one-to-one medium of writing into the first one-to-many mass medium, new forms of communication have evolved with the advance of technology. The Internet, however, is the first mass medium that has the capacity to be used as a many-to-many medium, and this unique many-to-many capability offers significant potential for the knowledge channel.

users,[16] and estimates by others indicated that there were about 20 million users in 1996, and between 50 and 80 million by 1997.[17] Usage is more than doubling each year, and if it continues to grow at this rate there will be 300 to 400 million Internet users by year 2000. This group will constitute a significant and important market for information, knowledge, products, and services (see Figure 4.7).

In addition to its many-to-many capability, the Internet has many other compelling qualities. The Internet never sleeps, so Web pages can be accessed at any time, day or night. Customers can get much of the same information that was once provided only by a phone staff, and they can get unlimited detail in presentations that may include text, audio, and video.

Internet communications also support live interaction between people, so that customers who visit a company's Web site can also engage in written, spoken, and videoconferenced dialogue with support staff who can help them find exactly the information that they need.

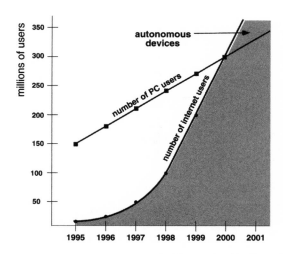

Figure 4.7 Growth of the Internet. The number of Internet users has increased exponentially since 1995. The number of PC users also grew strongly but not quite as quickly during the same period.

Since the Internet is accessible worldwide, a company can provide global support at a fraction of the cost needed to set up a worldwide telephone network.

And then there is the cost factor for end users. Once an individual has made the investment in a computer, a modem, and access to the Internet, the cost to send a message over the Internet is approximately nothing. Hence, the cost characteristics of Internet communications introduce a fundamental change in the way that telecommunications have been provided and priced for more than 100 years.

This is especially interesting when viewed in the context of the recent history of information-related industries. Beginning in the late 1970s, research by the Harvard University Program on Information Resources Policy led to the development of a matrix on which key information-related industries were plotted. This "Information Business" map showed how various industry sectors were related by association with other businesses and industries (see Figure 4.8).

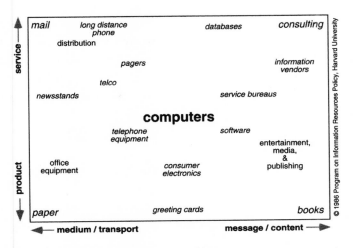

Figure 4.8   The Information Business Map.[18] The vertical axis shows the continuum from pure products at the bottom to pure services at the top. A piece of paper is a physical product at the bottom of the map, while its delivery by the post office is a service. The horizontal axis shows the continuum from value provided through the process of transport at the left to value provided by the content of what is transported on the right. Hence, paper is a medium at the left, and only when it is imprinted with words or images does it convey the value of content in book form at the right.

Although it is not quantifiably precise, the map is invaluable because it shows critical relationships between industries and industry sectors. For example, prior to the 20th century's development of computers, the entire information business consisted of companies that operated at the periphery of the map, and industry segments were quite distinct.

However, the development of electrical and then electronic communication created new industries at the core, including the computer industry itself just at the center, as well as applications in the telephone, consumer electronics, and significant portions of the entertainment industry.

The map was used to make forecasts about the future of the mapped industries, and many of them proved to be quite accurate. With the continuing decline in the cost of computing power, it was evident that any and everything that used computer technology would undergo radical change in the 1980s and 1990s, and beyond. Those who studied the map foresaw the gradual erosion of the boundaries between many industries, leading to new forms of competition as computers, consumer electronics, telephones, and office equipment gradually became interchangeable, a phenomenon that came to be called "convergence" (see Figure 4.9).

The map also shows that whereas the basic operating costs of most industries at the periphery of the map were bound by the law of diminishing returns and the limitations inherent to physical commodities, the cost structure emanating from the center of the map was quite different. As Intel cofounder Gordon Moore recognized as early as 1965, the power of computer chips was increasing exponentially with each generation even as the costs were in reciprocal decline due to the increased efficiencies of production and the increasing size of the market.

Hence, while costs at the periphery were necessarily increasing, those at the center were decreasing. The contrast between these two

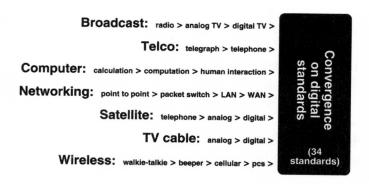

Figure 4.9 Convergence.[19] Broadcast, wired and wireless telecommunications, computer, satellite, and cable TV are all converging on a single set of standards. At least 34 standards must be negotiated before full interchangability is achieved, and as each standard comes about through a grueling negotiation involving many conflicting stakeholders, it does not happen quickly. Nevertheless, the increased utility that results from convergence means that it is inevitable.

cost vectors was largely responsible for the ongoing computerization of every information-related business and industry throughout the 1970s and 1980s.

In the late 1980s, however, something changed. In conjunction with the widespread profusion of inexpensive personal computers and modems, the development of the Internet and then its privatization brought the computer industry to the periphery of the map for the first time. Suddenly there was a new way to deliver the mail, one that did not require the transport of paper, but just electrons. The declining cost structure from the center of the map reached the increasing cost structure at the periphery, and caused a bubble at the top of the map (see Figure 4.10).

With the invention of the World Wide Web in 1990 and the Mosaic browser in 1993, Internet use began the phase of exponential growth shown in Figure 4.11. By 1996, 95 billion messages were sent and delivered over the Internet while 85 billion were carried by the U.S. Mail.

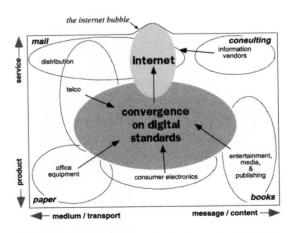

Figure 4.10   The Internet Bubble. The declining cost of computers reaches the periphery of the map with the use of the Internet for electronic mail, putting it in direct competition with the postal service.

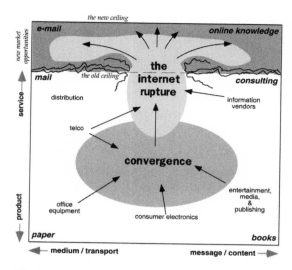

Figure 4.11 The Internet Rupture. As Internet use explodes and achieves a critical mass of users, it brings new forms of competition to all the businesses that were located anywhere near the top of the old map. The turbulence associated with this rupture can be expected to last well into the 21st century, as companies struggle to understand the implications for their markets. New competitors emerge without warning from nowhere in particular, as individuals with computers based on any continent can look just like the largest corporations, and suddenly and effectively enter into competition in local markets thousands of miles away.

The result is a fundamental change in the patterns of human communication, which we have elsewhere labeled as the "Internet rupture" (see Figure 4.11).[20]

Underlying its rapid growth and the new competition that it brings, the Internet is becoming a universal medium for communication using technology that is growing progressively less expensive to buy and use. Since it is scalable, new users can continue to join the Internet without affecting the performance that old users are accustomed to, and therefore there is no practical limit to how large the Internet can become.

Hence, the top of Figure 4.7 suggests an important phenomenon—beyond the intersection point of the curve of Internet users with PC users, forecasted to occur in the year 2000, the curve of users continues upward even though all PCs are by then assumed to be connected to the Internet.

These additional users will not be people using computers, but rather *devices* that will autonomously use the Internet as a medium of communication to interact with *other devices* and with people.

What kinds of devices will these be? Every kind. Conceivable application scenarios include houses connected to the Internet so that simple detection systems such as burglar alarms, smoke detectors, and video cameras can be monitored from a distance.

But it won't be just houses. In fact, any and every device will have the inherent capability to communicate using the Internet because simple computer chips that monitor and communicate the status of objects will soon be available for pennies.

These devices have been referred to as "things that think," and a project of the MIT Media Lab has been established to study and develop them. Some of them will be hardwired into existing telecommunications networks, but most of them will be connected via wireless networks. Your car will tell you how to get to your destinations, and your "smart dipstick" will tell you not only when an oil change is recommended, but when it is mandatory. The condition and performance of each system and subsystem will be monitored continuously, alerting you or your mechanic when necessary.

Your golf shirt will critique your swing, while your clubs will tell you how well or poorly you struck the ball. Together, they might be able to take ten strokes off your game so that you can play like Tiger Woods, almost. . . .

Perhaps your shoes or your belt will communicate with your home and office building so that your telephone calls can be routed to the phone nearest you.

Your washing machine will insert the correct amount of soap into your laundry, depending on how dirty your clothes are.

Industrial equipment will operate without human assistance and be monitored remotely, while even individual pieces of paper will have tiny chips embedded in the fibers so that when you lose track of them, they can be easily found.

"Knowledge at the point of use" and "knowledge on demand" take on new meaning when devices receive instructions in how they are designed and used, especially when those instructions can be delivered in a very specific context related to the conditions in which the use is to take place.

This specificity of each individual's context means that it becomes possible to effectively address small market segments, trending toward markets of one. This is a shift from knowledge and information that are broadcast to those that are "personal cast," or as the name of a new company in this new business implies, Point Cast. The emergence of personal or point cast technologies using the Internet is a knowledge channel strategy that supports optimum quality and relevance (see Figure 4.12).

Individuals communicating this way build new communities of practice in which important tacit knowledge is shared and refined. This applies to the use of the finished product, and also to the

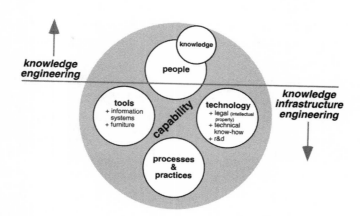

Figure 4.12 Knowledge Engineering and Knowlege Infrastructure Engineering.

development process itself. The concept of jointly developing new technologies side by side with customers also takes on new possibilities, as the feedback from the use of prototypes and finished products can be gathered continuously and remotely from any location.

Recognizing the knowledge channel as an important new means of communication with their products, diagnostic capabilities are built into CAT scanners and MRI machines from GE Medical Equipment to enable the company to monitor the performance of the machines remotely on a continual basis. Instead of waiting for the machines to break down, the company takes the opposite position and guarantees up time. This eliminates the conflict of interest associated with the sale of spare parts, and achieves higher profits for GE and its customers, who pay a premium for the guaranteed usability of their equipment.

Ultimately, the configuration and performance of many products will be "tunable" locally and from a distance, giving new meaning to the concept of "mass customization."

All of this capacity to communicate does not come without a price, however, as issues related to privacy will become even more important and more convoluted. Although many of these functions will prove to be tremendously valuable, new standards will be developed to govern their inevitable use. There will be new language to describe new concepts, new opportunities for investors and entrepreneurs to develop and market new technologies, new sources of tax revenues, and with it all new forms of employment, new markets to develop, and new forms of crime.

Together, the elements presented in this chapter are many of the tools necessary for bringing discontinuous innovations like these successfully to the relationship-oriented market. These include new approaches to expeditionary market research that are focused on creating shared experiences between customers and vendors, technology development driven by application scenarios, the use of the knowledge channel in many different forms, the delivery of knowledge at the point of use and the possibilities this offers for personal casting and mass customization, the necessity of considering infrastructure that enables new products and services to become useful, and the integration of R&D and marketing into the function we call marketing$_2$. All of this constitutes a revolution in the activities of marketing, and given the poor track record of traditional marketing, only a revolution will be sufficient. Henceforth, the science that drives marketing will not be the science of persuasion, but the science of understanding tacit needs.

CHAPTER 5

Managing Knowledge and Financial Assets

The role that innovation is expected to play for the future of any particular firm can be defined as a matter of policy and then executed as matter of leadership and management, but even when all three elements are present and there is a strong commitment to innovation, many obstacles may still beset the typical organization.

Most can be traced to a misfit between the required capabilities and those that are available, as the transition from the industrial economy to the knowledge economy creates new kinds of needs that are only now becoming fully understood. The emphasis has shifted from the focus on managing hard assets, labor, and technology, to managing tacit and explicit knowledge and business processes in a competitive architecture (see Figure 5.1).

The implications for management are significant, since managing processes and knowledge simply requires different skills and methods than have been used in the past, while applying old methods to these new asset classes leads to problems.

In particular, currently accepted methods of accounting, finance, and decision making, all now matured for the Industrial Age, can present enormous impediments to innovation. In this chapter, we explore

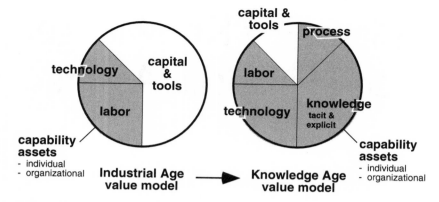

Figure 5.1 Capability Assets in Two Ages. The relative importance of capital and tools has diminished significantly in the Knowledge Age, while people with knowledge, technology, and businesses processes have become much more important.

alternatives to some of these practices, and in Chapter 6 we consider implications for the design of the organization itself.

Accounting

Together, tacit and explicit knowledge are often referred to as human capital, a term first used in the 1960s by Nobel Prize winning economist Gary Becker. He wrote, "The growth of physical capital, at least as conventionally measured, explains a relatively small part of the growth of income in most countries. The search for a better explanation has led to improved measures of physical capital and to an interest in less tangible entities, such as technological change and human capital. . . . it is fully in keeping with the capital concept as traditionally defined to say that expenditures on education, training, medical care, etc., are investments in capital. However, these produce human, not physical or financial, capital because you cannot separate a person from his or her knowledge, skills, health, or values the way it is possible to move financial and physical capital assets while the owner stays put."[1]

Investment in innovation is primarily investment in human capital, and particularly in learning undertaken by individual people, but for the most part it fails to appear on the balance sheet. This raises the question, then, of how useful or accurate can such a balance sheet be?

Consider that if you bought one share of each of the 30 stocks in the Dow Jones Industrial Average (DJIA) on January 2, 1997, you would have paid $1,632.85. However, your pro rata share of the book value of those same companies, their accounted-for hard assets, would have been only $558.31.

The difference between these two, $1,074.54, represents the value that investors believe to be the net present value of future earnings (see Figure 5.2).

This difference is a measurement of intangible assets in the form of knowledge that will result in future profitability. It is also called "intellectual capital" or, in the language of Chapter 3, organizational capability. A company with exceptional organizational capability that consistently transforms its capability into new stakeholder value will

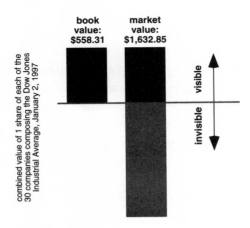

Figure 5.2   Invisible Assets.

legitimately expect to command a hefty premium above the value of its hard assets.

Beyond that, however, the proportion that is attributable to investor euphoria or that reflects a shortage of investment opportunities, and the proportion that represents the realistic future value of organizational capability cannot be calculated since there is no accepted measure of organizational capability (other than from the business results that it ultimately yields).

For the purposes of discussion, let us arbitrarily assume that the split is 50–50, yielding a value breakdown of:

$558.31 (34%)—Hard assets (book value).
$537.27 (33%)—Intangible assets, organizational capability.
$537.27 (33%)—Intangible assets, investor premium.

Naturally, the composition of intangible differs quite substantially from one company to another. Perhaps on January 2, 1997, you owned Coca-Cola stock, which had a book value of $3.05 per share, but a market value 16 times greater, the widest spread between book value and market value of the 30 DJIA stocks. Or perhaps you owned International Paper, with the smallest spread at a paltry 1.3. In between these extremes, the spread between Merck's book value and market price was a factor of 7.26.

In its current expansive frame of mind, the market places a high premium on companies that own significant knowledge assets, such as Coca-Cola with its strong brand name and distribution network, and Merck, which has both well-respected brands and significant intellectual capital emanating from its R&D and distribution systems. Companies like International Paper that own industrial assets, however, do not command much of a premium for today's investors.

This should have a significant impact on management, because although an abundance of internal effort goes toward managing hard assets, less effort is made to manage the intangible assets. In most organizations, in fact, many critical knowledge assets are not recognized as "manageable" at all, and no one does this task.

From the perspective of the industrial mind-set, this is understandable. In such a framework, assets in the ground, in a factory, and in a warehouse represent wealth. This is reflected in the Dow Jones Industrial Average of January 2, 1987, at which time the difference between book value and market value for the aggregate of the thirty companies was only 1.57, half of what it would be 10 years deeper into the Knowledge Age (see Figure 5.3).

In fact, the inflection point in the history of the Dow Jones Industrial Average was in 1980. Until then, book value composed most of market value, but since 1980 the value of intangible assets has been rising steadily (see Figure 5.4).

As the emphasis of economic value shifts away from hard assets toward knowledge assets, important managerial and accounting issues arise. As noted in the Introduction, if the purpose of management is to maximize shareholder value, then clearly the role of knowledge management takes on new importance, as this is by far the largest portion of the intangible asset base.

In this context, it is worth looking again at a figure presented in the Introduction, which shows the increasing investments by Japanese manufacturers in R&D during the 1980s (see Figure 5.5).

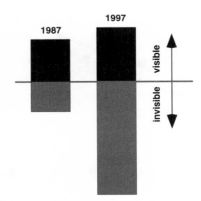

Figure 5.3 Invisible Assets, 1987 and 1997. Perhaps the definitive indication of the arrival of the Knowledge Age will come when the Dow Jones Industrial Average is renamed the Dow Jones Knowledge Average.

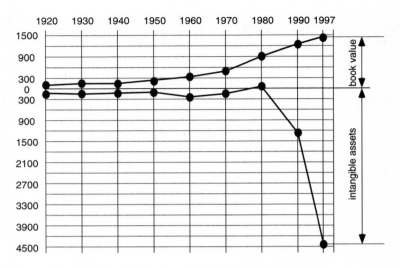

Figure 5.4 The Dow Jones Industrial Average, 1920–1997.[2]

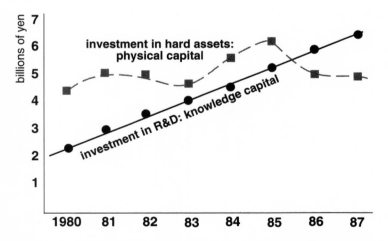

Figure 5.5 Japanese Manufacturing Investments, 1980–1987.[3] While investment by Japanese manufacturing companies in hard assets was consistent from 1980 to 1987, investment in R&D increased steadily, and by the 8th year had doubled from 62 percent to 126 percent of hard asset investment.

This suggests that the Japanese have shifted a considerable proportion of the investment and management effort to knowledge management. Reflecting this shift, during the first quarter of 1997 four new books were published on the topic of intellectual capital and its accounting, including three that shared the title of *Intellectual Capital*.[4] The interested reader, who before this publishing convergence had to work hard to piece together a limited picture of this emerging field, suddenly faced the opposite problem of having to choose which books to read.

The purpose of creating organizational capability or "intellectual capital," as well as the purpose for managing it, come down to a few issues, and among them innovation must be prominent. As we have said repeatedly, the purpose of innovation is to create new value for stakeholders, and the method for doing so is to create new capability in the form of knowledge, tools, processes, and technology, all accomplished through the learning process.

Following Gary Becker and others who have developed economic theory in the domain of human capital, the practice of intellectual capital accounting has reached its current stage of development largely due to the efforts of two Swedish executives, Leif Edvinsson and Karl Erik Sveiby. Not coincidentally, they are author and co-author of the two most insightful books on intellectual capital, *The New Organizational Wealth* by Sveiby and *Intellectual Capital* by Edvinsson and Michael Malone.[5]

Edvinsson seems to be the first person ever to hold the title of "Corporate Director of Intellectual Capital" a position he accepted in 1991 at Skandia AFS, Sweden's largest insurance and financial services company. Sveiby was chairman of a Swedish publishing company for many years where he practiced knowledge management, and is now an entrepreneur, consultant, and academic on the subject.

The terminology they use differs only slightly, and this description from Sveiby's book introduces the principal concepts:

"People in an organization direct their efforts in two directions primarily: outward working with customers or inward maintaining and building the organization. When they work with customers they create customer relationships and an image in the marketplace that is partly 'owned' by the corporation. I call this an external structure. When their efforts are directed inward they create an internal structure, which in management literature is called the organization. I regard both as structures of knowledge."

In addition to these two forms of structure, a third form of invisible asset is employee competence, and Sveiby suggests that they can be represented on a balance sheet like the one shown in Figure 5.6.

The visible portion is reflected in the audited accounts of the company as presented in official company reports, but the larger invisible portion is not reported except as ambiguous and arbitrarily defined "goodwill." However, our definition of organizational capability is well aligned with Sveiby's three categories of external structure, internal structure, and employee competence (see Figure 5.7).

In his work at Skandia, Edvinsson applied the same reasoning and developed a scheme to understand and describe the invisible portion in greater detail. He cites the following motivation: "I had long been

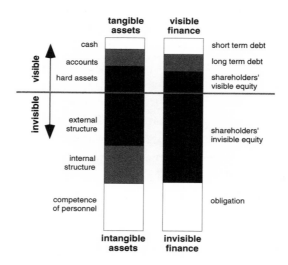

Figure 5.6 The New Balance Sheet.[6] As with stock values, the invisible elements of finance are now greater than the visible elements.

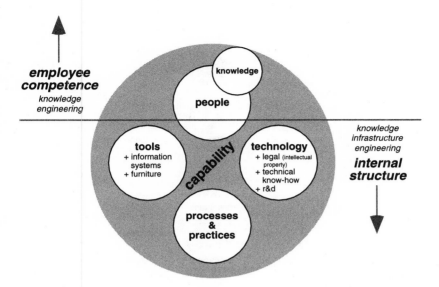

Figure 5.7 Organizational Capability and Intangible Assets. The concept of organizational capability maps closely onto the three classes of intangible assets as defined by Karl Erik Sveiby.

struck by the essential paradox of modern business investment: that if a company invests in those things that will make it competitive, like human capital and information technology, it will suffer a short-term deterioration of its profit and loss statement, which in turn reduces the value of the balance sheet, thereby reducing the book value of the organization. In other words, the more the modern company invests in its future, the less its book value. This is absurd. We needed another value-mapping system."[7]

In May 1995, Skandia presented the first formal statement of its Intellectual Capital in a supplement to its annual report, distributed to shareholders at the company's annual meeting (see Figure 5.8).

In addition, mapping the Skandia chart onto our model of organizational capability shows a significant degree of coherence (see Figures 5.9 and 5.10).

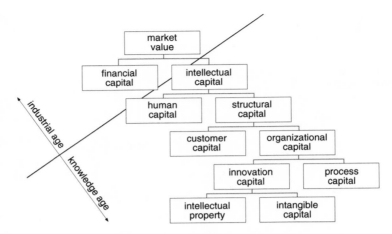

Figure 5.8 Skandia AFS Intellectual Capital Accounting Model.[8] Market value consists of financial capital and intellectual capital. Financial capital is predominantly the Industrial Age asset base, while intellectual capital is the Knowledge Age asset base that consists of many other forms of capital, all intangible.

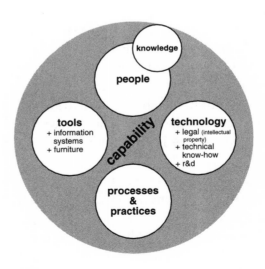

Figure 5.9 Capability.

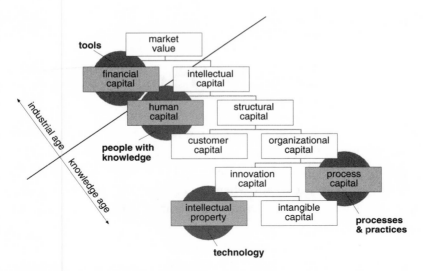

Figure 5.10 AFS Intellectual Capital Accounting Model Mapped to Organizational Capability. Of the five classes of intangible capital identified by Edvinsson, only customer capital and intangible capital do not have corresponding elements in the organizational capability model. Note that customer capital is a marketing asset, developed primarily through relationships established in the knowledge channel.

These concepts are the beginning of workable, effective models, and they begin to address the need for new practices that will provide effective support for innovation.

As with all accounting models, intellectual capital accounting is inherently a static view that fails to comprehend or represent the dynamic character of knowledge. And it is precisely the dynamism that makes knowledge so useful and so important.

Because of the additional insight that they offer, these models may nevertheless come to play a role in how investors and analysts look at the companies they invest in. By showing the linkage between investments in organizational capability, innovativeness, and business results, companies will be able to make the case for increased valuations based on demonstrated improvements to capability.

In addition to new forms of accounting, new practices are needed in finance and decision making to support effective innovation.

Finance and Decision Making

Questions, problems, ideas, visions, and needs are the seeds of innovations and initiate the search for new value. In each case, the development of an individual idea requires specific learning, while from the overall perspective it is only when the aggregate of all learning keeps up with the external change that an organization can remain competitive in the marketplace.

Past success at innovation may provide a feeling of security and the expectation of more success, but in fact no one knows at the outset exactly when or where the innovation journey will end, or what successes or failures will ultimately result. The quest for new knowledge that characterizes the innovation process is inherently a venture into the unknown.

Further, the pursuit of innovation often requires substantial capital investment, but in most cases a guaranteed rate of return cannot be calculated since the outcome of the innovation process cannot be predicted at the outset, or even in the middle of the journey.

The situation is further complicated by competitors who are pursuing their own innovations, which may change the dynamics of the market in ways that *they* hope are unforeseeable.

As the practice of accounting is evolving to meet the requirements of today's organizations, so the practices of corporate finance and decision making must also be adjusted to support the innovation process. With the background of accelerating change, this means balancing current requirements with an even more pressing need to prepare for a long-term future that—to paraphrase Yogi Berra—probably isn't as long-term as it used to be.

But there is risk here, as the practice of 3rd generation R&D has emphasized. Long before an idea reaches maturity in the form of a marketable product or service, the unknowability inherent in the innovation process can only be overcome through some form of investment in the search for new knowledge.

In contemporary management, the problem is compounded because although the future of the marketplace is characterized by a high degree of uncertainty, today's methods of making decisions are based on gathering and assessing explicit information and quantitative measurements. To the near-total neglect of the tacit dimension, these measurements are applied through techniques such as "bounded rationale" for decision making and "discounted cash flow" (DCF) or "net present value" (NPV) for finance.

The application of these concepts can cripple the search for innovation. As bounded rationale is an attempt to "engineer" the process of decision making by using only explicit knowledge derived from past experience, this can stifle the search for vision and innovation. Bounded rationale provides a structural bias against uncertainty, but uncertainty is inherent to the learning process that drives innovation. Further, the possibility of future learning is explicitly excluded since this approach is typically "all-or-nothing."

Discounted cash flow analysis is also based on predictions of how much cash flow a given product or project will yield, but since one can only guess about the cash performance of an innovation in the early stages of development, there is no legitimate way to prove that a particular innovation will be a good idea. As Joe Marone, Dean of Rensselaer Polytechnic Institute has commented, "Everybody pretty much engages in discount cash flow calculation to do their business cases, but nobody takes them very seriously. And everybody understands that this is more of a ritual you have got to go through in order to get the project through. One guy was really overt about it. He said, 'Well, we put together the numbers and we took it down to the corporate board and they didn't like the numbers, so we went back and we changed the numbers, and they still didn't like it.' "[9] The numbers, of course, had no basis in reality, and were a formality rather than a legitimate, reliable, or trusted projection of what was going to be accomplished.

Others have pointed out additional problems with this approach. "The traditional net present value rule, which is taught to virtually

every business school student of economics, can give very wrong answers. . . . It is based on some implicit assumptions that are often overlooked."[10] These assumptions are related to the timing of investments
and their uncertainty, as some investments that we might not make
today may become critically important in the future.

However, the reliance on discounted cash flow to support decision
making tends to filter out projects that have a high degree of uncertainty. In the long term, this can constrict the development of new
knowledge and suppress the creation of useful possibilities for the future, and in this light, it has been suggested, "It's almost impossible to
justify anything that has to do with innovation because you can't prove
it in a discounted cash flow argument."[11]

But you can *disprove* it, and if a management team is convinced
that an innovation might not yield the necessary return, they probably
will not make the investment and they will never know what return it
would have produced.

These decisions are also likely to be influenced by market research,
but as the story of the minivan showed, Ford's decision not to build the
minivan and Chrysler's subsequent decision to do so shifted billions of
dollars of revenue to Chrysler. As Terrence Faulker of Kodak has suggested, "It is becoming increasingly clear that an uncritical acceptance
of the sometimes subtle implications of discounted cash flow can lead
the way into strategic error."[12]

Compounding the problem, today's decision makers must place
their bets in an increasingly turbulent environment, and their capacity to predict with accuracy may be declining even as the stakes are
increasing.

How, then, can management make reasonable decisions about long-
term investment in innovation?

As with their appreciation of tacit knowledge in product design
and marketing, it seems to be widely accepted in Japan that there is
more to finance and decision making than just explicit knowledge.
"For Japanese managers, decisions to invest in certain R&D projects
are based on the best way to meet the technological requisites of global

competitiveness. In contrast, the overriding concern of U.S. firms is to maximize financial returns on investment. To this end, U.S. managers have adopted a variety of quantitative methods, including discounted cash flow, to assess risk and return. Although Japanese companies also subject their investments to financial analysis, their analytical tools are not as sophisticated as discounted cash flow. Instead, managers rely on in-depth discussions of the pros and cons of moving in certain technological directions, paying careful attention to the explicit and hidden assumptions underlying scenarios of likely outcomes. Rather than allowing financial considerations to dictate R&D decisions, Japanese managers place their emphasis on what it will take technologically to be world competitors and how to make the best use of their research talent to reach the company's R&D goals."[13]

The idea of focusing on the "requisites of global competitiveness" is synonymous with the need to develop new organizational capability, as discussed in Chapter 3. This is far different from simply maximizing return on investment, as it incorporates qualitative aspects related to the evolution of the marketplace that quantitative measures are incompetent to address.

If we extend this line of thinking, it becomes clear that relying on strictly quantitative measures is a strategy for continuous innovation only, for maximizing and optimizing within an existing market architecture and an established dominant design framework. But when a new competitive architecture takes hold through the emergence of a new generation dominant design, companies that have not considered the discontinuous, tacit implications of market competitiveness and new technologies will be left behind.

And indeed, this is precisely what has happened: "American companies have used Du Pont's system of return on investment (ROI) since the early 1900s. Some thoughtful academics and practitioners have argued that its emphasis prompts a short-term orientation and causes dysfunctional behavior, such as the failure to make strategic new product development expenditures and capital investments. . . . Japanese companies instead focus on ROS, return on sales, in combination with the manufacturing improvement efforts."[14] It is for this reason that it has been suggested that "ROI" actually stands for "restraint on innovation."[15]

Driven by the link between ROI and their own compensation, managers are systematically encouraged to forgo desirable and even necessary investments in new organizational capability that will enable them to remain current with evolving markets. It is, in Drucker's terms, "a near-complete bar to innovation"[16] because (as Edvinsson notes) innovation investments will reduce ROI for an indefinite period and therefore reduce the compensation of those whose pay is linked to ROI measures.

Thus, when managing for discontinuous innovation in a changing environment, it is not feasible to rely exclusively on explicit measurements or explicit forms of knowledge. The tacit dimension is critical to the development of both new knowledge and the innovations that will constitute a response to change, and this knowledge must be applied not only to technology and market development, but also to the financing of innovation.

There is an inherent conflict that must be resolved. Whereas finance is necessarily concerned with obtaining an acceptable rate of return, the uncertainty related to innovation does not provide such assurances. Furthermore, the methodology of finance tends to regard this uncertainty as a source of additional and undesirable cost.

What is needed is an approach to finance that accommodates uncertainty with the recognition that learning which takes place during research and development provides ample opportunities to change course, and the knowledge with which to do so intelligently if it becomes necessary. Thus, instead of committing up front to fund an entire program of research, development, manufacturing, and marketing for a particular innovation, the company may more appropriately commit a step at a time as new knowledge is developed. This enables future learning to be taken into consideration in the subsequent stages of decision making, as the search for new knowledge that is inherent in the innovation process will progressively impact on how we understand a problem, and even how we define it. Because uncertainty is reduced as the search progresses, progressively better decisions are possible.

Hence, the practice of options finance as developed for security trading is now being used successfully as a means of funding innovation projects that involve high levels of uncertainty.

When investing in an innovation option, a company commits to funding only the first iteration of the research process. At the end of this stage, newly developed knowledge and understanding of the evolved conditions in the market will make it apparent whether to pursue further investment or drop the project.

A second option continues the project to the next knowledge threshold, beyond which additional stages can also be undertaken if the results call for them. The actual stages of options investment may correspond with the stages of the innovation business process, described in Chapter 8 (see Figure 5.11).

This approach to finance also provides greater flexibility for projects that may show significant promise, but lack one or two vital components that are not yet available due to technological limitations. Such projects can be suspended until the missing technology is available, rather than being scrapped altogether.

Overall, options finance entails a different approach to both the management of innovation projects and to the thinking that underlies them: "The discounted cash flow (DCF) mindset encourages a manager to focus on the most likely sequence of outcomes that could flow from an initial R&D investment and then estimate the ultimate, bottom-line value of that series of outcomes. An options thinking mindset emphasizes the uncertainty of the future and encourages an adaptive approach that monitors the resolution of future uncertainties and anticipates that course adjustments will be required. . . . The DCF mindset tends to focus managerial attention on a specified goal, while the options thinking mindset directs managerial attention toward a continual redefinition of the opportunities that are created by the resolution of uncertainty. . . . There are situations where uncertainty is good, and helps us to understand that the larger the amount of uncertainty, the greater the opportunity for value creation."[17]

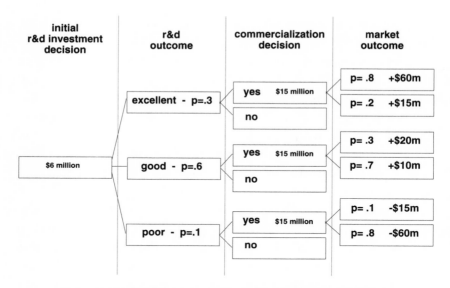

Valuation using Discounted Cash Flow: -$5.4m to -$11.4m
Valuation using Options model: $+2.2m

Figure 5.11 Options Finance.[18] Rather than a definitive go-no go decision at the outset based on guesswork and assumptions, options finance values a project in stages, with funding provided for only one stage at a time. This allows knowledge to be accumulated at each stage to clarify the real future value.

Using options finance, the creative tension that exists in the gap between existing reality and a vision may be channeled by investing in research options that systematically probe the domain of the vision, searching for specific ways to bring the vision toward reality. In this way, it becomes a significant factor in the design, development, and implementation of strategy throughout an organization.

Options finance helps to shift planning and implementing strategy from a rigidly deterministic vector in which plans are carried out with little regard for externalities, to flexible processes that are organized around learning. As Dwight Eisenhower commented, "Plans are nothing. Planning is everything."[19]

Still, there comes a point at which planning must give way to action. For companies such as Intel that compete in rapidly changing markets, the challenge of acting correctly involves taking risks that require years of work and billions of dollars of investment before the outcomes are known.

Investing in the Future at Intel

In 1965, computer scientist Gordon Moore suggested that the capacity of the most powerful computer chips could be expected to double every two years for the following decade because of continuing advances in science and technology. As long as chip manufacturers continued investing in the development of new generations of chips, Moore foresaw sustained exponential growth in chip performance. Moore went on to be cofounder and Chairman of Intel Corporation, now one of the world's leading chip manufacturers, and as noted in Chapter 4, his forecast came to be known as "Moore's Law."

As the decade from 1965 to 1975 passed, Moore's Law proved to be stunningly accurate save one detail—the actual rate of development was even faster than Moore had forecasted. He revised the trend line to reflect that the doubling of capacity was taking place every 18 months instead of every 2 years.

Remarkably, after more than 30 years, the rate of improvement suggested in Moore's forecast still continues, and because of the compounding of performance today's chips provide a 10-million-fold decrease in the cost of a transistor.[20] The desktop or laptop computer that costs $2,000 today deploys the power of a 1965 mainframe computer that may have cost $20 million or more (see Figure 5.12).

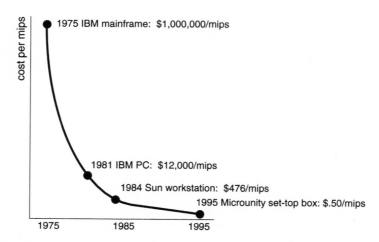

Figure 5.12 MIPS (Millions of Instructions per Second), 1975–1995.[21] As the capacity of computer has increased steadily, so has their speed. The cost has declined from $1 million per MIPS in 1975 to an astonishing 50 cents in 1995.

The computer industry has leveraged these advances in chip technology to become one of the most significant sources of economic development worldwide. It is estimated that 15 percent of the world's economy is now based on information technology, with trillions of dollars being spent on computer equipment and software every decade.

As discussed in Chapter 4, computer chips connected to the Internet are now or soon will be integral to all kinds of products in nearly every industry, from autos to consumer products in health, entertainment, and throughout the household in everything from smoke alarms to dishwashers and thermostats. In fact, many chips are used in cars, appliances, and other devices for every chip that is used in a stand-alone computer.[22]

But like any exponential growth curve, the boom in this technology may also carry the seeds of its own demise. Recently, Moore pointed out that the cost of building the specialized factories in which chips are made is also increasing with each new generation of chips. The cost of building new fabrication plants will inevitably continue to increase, and the return on investment to decrease, until it becomes nearly impossible to build new ones.[23] This trend is now known as "Moore's Second Law" (see Figure 5.13).

At a cost of $2 to $3 billion, today's fabs are huge investments, but new fabs will continue to be built as long as market demand remains strong. As of 1997, more than 200 of them were planned or under construction globally, some with price tags of $5 billion or more.[24]

As Moore points out, "Capital costs are rising far faster than revenue in the industry. We can no longer make up for the increasing costs by improving yields and equipment utilization. . . . I am increasingly of the opinion that the rate of technological progress is going to be controlled from financial realities. We just will not be able to go as fast as we like because we cannot afford it."[25]

At these prices, the industry is reaching the limits beyond which it is no longer economically feasible for individual companies to build new fabs. Hence, joint ventures have been announced between major American and Japanese chip makers: Texas Instruments with Hitachi, Advanced Micro Devices with Fujitsu, and Motorola with Toshiba.[26]

Further, the product development cycle and the sales cycle are consistently out of alignment. Intel president Craig Barrett points out that

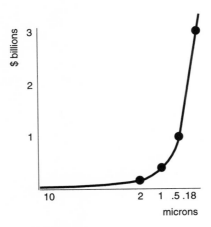

Figure 5.13 Moore's Second Law: The Cost of a Fabrication Plant.[27] The cost of a computer chip fabricating plant is now in the billions of dollars, and increasing significantly with each subsequent generation of chips.

the company builds new plants as much as two years in advance of when they are needed, and before the products that they will manufacture are designed.[28] And while it takes 2 to 3 years to develop a new Intel microprocessor chip, its life cycle in the marketplace will be shorter than that (see Figure 5.14).

Alternatively, if companies do not ride these product waves, they cannot sustain a position in the market. In Moore's words, "Each new generation of semiconductor products and technology completely wipes out the previous generation. . . . Because a recession in the industry or the economy as a whole lasts the length of a product generation, companies never recover in existing products. If they come out of a recession at all, it is on the back of new products. Clearly, then, a successful research and development program is essential for survival in the industry, and the industry routinely invests 10 to 15 percent of revenues in R&D. A plot of Intel's financial performance over the years would show revenues dipping here and there, earnings fluctuating wildly, and R&D expenses following a smooth, exponential growth curve" (see Figure 5.15).[29]

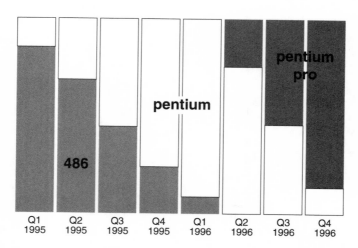

Figure 5.14 Pentium Life Cycle. The life cycle of a microprocessor is about 2 years. If it doesn't make money for its manufacturer in that time frame, it never will, and it may pull its maker down with it.

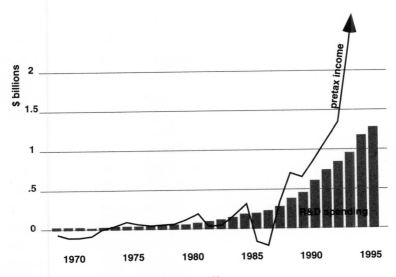

Figure 5.15 Investment in R&D at Intel.[30]

For Intel and its competitors in the chip business today, this situation makes the management of innovation perhaps the single most important factor affecting long-term success. To stay in business, it is necessary to keep up with each advancing generation of technology, even though the escalating cost of current technology appears to be heading rapidly toward business models that are unrecognizable in today's competitive architecture.

Although the scale of investment for most companies may not be as large as the investment issues facing Intel and its chip industry competitors, the inherent problem of balancing short- and long-term investments amidst a changing market architecture is not much different.

The chip industry, however, is unusual in that the shift from one generation platform to the next occurs with predictable regularity. This makes an interesting case study in the dynamics of large-scale change, and as the pace of change accelerates throughout the economy more companies and industries will be confronted with "regularized ruptures" that occur in ever shorter cycles.

It is even worse, however, when you know that ruptures are coming, but you don't know when. In these situations, many commonly accepted and intuitively sensible methods of decision making may not lead to the right conclusions, as we have noted with respect to discounted cash flows. The critical flaw is generally an overreliance on rational thinking, which tends to emphasize the past and to assume that the future will be similar to the past. In times of rapid change, this can be a disastrous assumption.

To a significant degree, this issue of how people think lies in the realm of cultural anthropology. As discussed in Chapter 3, the Western-trained mind is conditioned to rely on "rational" thought and planned actions, as the following comparison between European and Micronesian culture, taken from *American Anthropologist* describes: "Thomas Gladwin has written a brilliant article contrasting the method by which the Trukese navigate the open sea, with that by which Europeans navigate. He points out that the European navigator begins with a plan—a course—which he has charted according to certain universal principles, and he carries out his voyage by relating his every move to that plan. His effort throughout his voyage is directed to remaining 'on course.' If unexpected events occur, he must first alter the plan, then respond accordingly. The Trukese navigator begins with an objective rather than a plan. He sets off toward the objective and responds to conditions as they arise in an ad hoc fashion. He utilizes information provided by the wind, the waves, the tide and current, the fauna, the stars, the clouds, the sound of the water on the side of the boat, and he steers accordingly. His effort is directed to doing whatever is necessary to reach the objective. If asked, he can point to his objective at any moment, but he cannot describe his course."[31]

As this description shows so clearly, the Western approach to conceiving and solving complex problems is one among many possible ways of approaching difficult management issues. Working with chronically incomplete information does not lend itself to a deterministic approach, and this is precisely the situation of innovation.

The Trukese method of navigation has a lot in common with how the innovation process actually unfolds, both as a matter of learning that progressively reduces uncertainty, and of finance that is committed incrementally as learning takes place.

In conditions of high ambiguity, therefore, it is feasible and desirable to adopt a more process-oriented approach to management, while a more deterministic approach will still apply in many situations that are clear-cut.

However, the real insight is that shifting between the two modes can be very effective. This is a practical example of how complementary (or dyadic) concepts discussed in Chapter 2 can play a role in determining the competitive architecture and in managing as well.

Interestingly, it has been shown that alternating between complementary modes of thinking is also the key to creativity.[32] Switching back and forth between convergent thinking (going into more detail) and divergent thinking (pulling back to get the broader view) is the methodology that drives the creative process, because it allows one to see the possibilities in detail as well as the context in which they may be meaningful. Similarly, alternating between the possibilities of continuous and discontinuous innovation targets, and finding the correct applicability of each, drives the management of innovation.

By alternating between thinking modes in the creative process itself, ideas and concepts that were once seen as unrelated can be combined in an effective way that yields a new level of performance. This insight is the basis of Arthur Koestler's work on creativity, *The Act of Creation*.[33] "Koestler maintained that usual, normal thought proceeds from a single frame of reference, and that while a person may be familiar with many points of view, most of us operate from only one frame of reference at a time. Creativity occurs when a person can relate what are normally independent frames of mind."[34]

This explains why people who are working outside the field for which they were professionally trained can be so effective as innovators. Coming from the outside, they are not burdened by a detailed understanding of what cannot be done. Those inside are often victims of "trained incapacity," the conundrum in which "the more we know about how to do something, the harder it is to learn to do it differently." This also accounts for Kaplan's "Law of the Hammer," which states, "It comes as no particular surprise to discover that a scientist formulates problems in a way which requires for their solution just those techniques in which he himself is especially skilled."[35]

Outsiders, however, see instead new possibilities to apply what they learned elsewhere to problems in professions where this knowledge may now be applied for the first time, and with positive results.

Hence, innovation is an outcome of the creative process that usefully connects formerly unrelated things, and it is directed by a management process that effectively distinguishes between an appropriate context for either continuous or discontinuous approaches to the market.

However, while it may be obvious that dealing with discontinuous innovations requires different management approaches, it is usually far from obvious when a discontinuous change has actually arrived. Sorting one from the other is an exercise in perpetual ambiguity.

Underlying all these conceptual models concerning creative, investment, and managerial decisions in innovation is the critical process of deciding what is real. Determining which signals are important and how they are to be filtered from the background noise is vital to success at innovation, as with all aspects of management.

Signal and Noise

Companies that are doing well in any particular market architecture are particularly susceptible when a major change is imminent but not yet recognized. These companies have an incentive to resist change, to try to prolong the old structure and milk from it every last drop of profit. Andrew Grove, Moore's colleague and successor as Chairman of Intel, describes such a discontinuity as a "strategic inflection point," and he suggests that when a strategic inflection point sweeps through an industry, the companies that were most successful in the old structure are also the most threatened by change, and therefore the least likely to adapt.[36]

Chip Holt suggests, "The stronger the technology that you own is, the better you become at it and the more susceptible you are to blind side shifts as the technology changes."[37] Further, Harvard professor Clayton Christensen notes that this problem confronts successful companies that are too well attuned to the needs of *existing* customers. "The list of leading companies that failed when confronted with disruptive changes in technology and market structure is a long one. . . . One theme common to all of these failures . . . is that the decisions that led to failure were made when the leaders in question were widely regarded as among the best companies in the world. There are two ways to resolve this paradox. One might be to conclude that firms such as Digital, IBM, Apple, Sears, Xerox, and Bucyrus Erie must never have been well managed. Maybe they were successful because of good luck and fortuitous timing, rather than good management. Maybe they finally fell on hard times because their good fortune ran out. Maybe. An alternative explanation, however, is that these firms were as well managed as one could expect a firm managed by mortals to be—but that there is something about the way decisions get made in successful organizations that sows the seeds of eventual failure. . . . Precisely *because* these firms listened to their customers, invested aggressively in new technologies that would provide their customers more and better products of the sort they wanted, and because they carefully studied market trends and systematically allocated investment capital to innovations that promised the best returns, they lost their positions of leadership."[38]

This shows the importance of a strategic perspective on the difference between continuous and discontinuous change, and the differing management practices that they require. The underlying question is how to distinguish between the strong signals of continuous evolution in the marketplace, and the weak early signals of discontinuous change.

In the situation of continuous change, strong signals provide the necessary information to make incremental adjustments to strategies, capabilities, and architectures, whereas weak signals are noise to be filtered out. In the situation of discontinuous change, however, strong signals of continuous change mask discontinuous change, and make them difficult to recognize. Here the signal that appears to be noise is actually the most important, and the apparent signal itself must be filtered out.

In general, thinking this way is not comfortable for most managers, and they avoid it. Hence, McKinsey consultant Richard Foster points out three common errors that managers make when faced with a discontinuity. First, they believe that an evolutionary approach will be sufficient; second, they assume that there will be ample early warning when discontinuities come; and third, they believe that customers will want in the future what they want today.[39] None of these beliefs are valid.

Therefore, if you are confronted with continuous change that becomes evident in the marketplace and presumably emanates from a competitor, it is reasonable to assume that the strong signal is the important one. However, if it is the weaker signal that matters, then the stronger one must be filtered out, and this is precisely what is so difficult to do.

It can be done in the following way. The strong signal supporting continuous innovation reinforces an existing business model and existing relationships with customers and vendors. As long as the market continues along its existing vector, these relationships will provide appropriate guidance.

But when there is an indication, even a tiny indication, that a discontinuity is coming, then the appropriate response is to assume that existing business models, architectures, and relationships are false, and that they will *not* endure in the new architecture. This leaves a void, and the process of filtering *in* the weak signals will develop the new knowledge to fill that void with a new architecture.

As noted, innovation is primarily about intangible assets including knowledge, which is the pivotal asset in the new economy. New practices are therefore required in more than accounting and finance to effectively manage these assets.

One of these is simply the practical matter that people working in the day-to-day course of whatever they're doing continually encounter certain kinds of information, certain kinds of signals. They have the capacity to interpret and make use of some of them, but probably not all. This suggests that some degree of specialization may be appropriate so that critical messages do not slip through the cracks, particularly in the R&D functions.

Thus, as we have distinguished between marketing$_1$ and marketing$_2$, so now we distinguish between R&D$_1$ and R&D$_2$.

By R&D$_1$, we refer to activities needed to maintain existing lines of business through continuous innovation. This requires a superior capacity to interpret strong market signals. By R&D$_2$, we refer to activities more relevant to discontinuous innovation and the process of gathering and interpreting weak signals.

Gordon Moore, cofounder and Chairman Emeritus of Intel has described a facet of this problem in the computer chip industry. He notes that at Fairchild Semiconductor in the 1960s, it became increasingly difficult for the R&D lab to transfer knowledge to production even though spin-offs of Fairchild, and spin-offs of the spin-offs were successfully exploiting the same knowledge. From this experience Moore concluded that the not-invented-here mentality grew stronger at Fairchild as the production organization become more technically proficient. In establishing Intel shortly thereafter, "It was decided to forestall problems with technology transfer by establishing Intel without a separate R&D laboratory. At some cost to manufacturing and probably to R&D efficiency, development would be conducted in the manufacturing facility."[40]

Later a relatively small central research capability was established at Intel, but a significant portion of research was still in conjunction with manufacturing.

Hewlett-Packard has organized its research activities similarly, with a small central lab and most R&D distributed throughout business units.

This is a practical implementation of the R&D$_1$–R&D$_2$ concept. The organizational consequences of this approach are explored in more detail in Chapters 6 and 7.

CHAPTER 6

Organizational Architecture

In prior chapters, we have discussed the need for effective discontinuous innovation as well as many of the systems, methods, and concepts that are required to achieve it. These include the broader conceptual framework of the competitive architecture with dominant designs and product platforms; the internal framework of organizational capability and its underlying processes of learning, knowledge, and technology management; the issue of market development and the new knowledge channel; and new approaches to accounting, finance, and decision making.

This leaves three remaining topics. This chapter is concerned with issues related to the design of the organization, and Chapter 7 describes how this design supports ongoing capability development. Finally, Chapter 8 provides a complete description of the new innovation process itself.

Organization Design and Asset Management

As we have identified key differences between today's business environment and that of the past, we also recognize that it is not realistic to expect old organizational models to meet today's challenges. We must look for new models to enable effective performance in key areas.

One of these areas is knowledge management. When new assets of any kind are introduced into established organizations, new organizational architectures are often required to obtain the benefits that they offer. Now that knowledge is recognized as a major asset category, the design of the organization must reflect this not only in accounting and finance, but in the core organizational structure itself.

Historically, the first stage of use of a major new asset is marked by the creation of an asset management group. The emergence of computers as a key corporate asset, for example, led to the creation of a new department called MIS (management information system).

As computer technology then evolved from mainframes with centralized control to more distributed use at the personal level, a second stage of asset management developed with a different kind of responsibility. Layers were removed, enabling end users to plan and run their own applications, and to discuss applications directly with vendors. To implement the second stage, a user-based architecture was required as control shifted away from the centralized MIS department (see Figure 6.1).

Other kinds of assets have followed the same pattern. Copy machines used to be located only in centralized print shops, but now they are widely distributed. Even offices are following this pattern, as satellite "hoteling" offices and home offices enable many workers to avoid long commutes.

The emergence of knowledge itself as a critical organizational asset also requires change in the organization. In this case, we are making the transition from first stage practice to second stage practice. In the

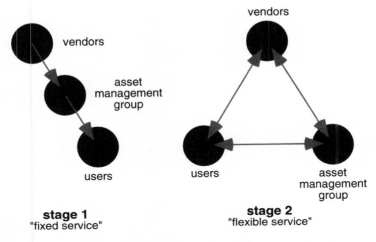

Figure 6.1 Stages of Asset Management. Whereas in Stage 1 the asset management group has considerable control over the use of the asset, in Stage 2 their role becomes the definition of an architecture to guide and support end users.

first stage, knowledge was concentrated for use primarily by senior executives, but now the creation and use of knowledge must be distributed throughout the organization. As we understand the linkage between learning, knowledge, and innovation, we recognize that only by distributing knowledge will effective innovation become widespread and enable mutually dependent learning between communities of practice.

To make this happen, we also must overcome many obstacles to innovation that pervade most existing organizational models.

Obstacles to Innovation

Innovation brings change within organizations and change in the external marketplace. Change, however, does not generally come easily in organizations, as resistance to it is one of the most significant factors that impedes innovation. Three different issues shape this resistance. First, the fear of change; second, the denial of its significance; and third, the lack of proper capability to respond to the changed environment, compounded by the lack of a means for its development.

Ed Schein shows clearly how bad experiences with internal change initiatives result in fear-based behavior patterns that block subsequent effort to adapt to external change.[1] Traumas from reorganizations and downsizing create the expectation that change is painful, so newly proposed changes are typically met with resistance, oversimplification, denial, rationalization, and ignoring of problems altogether.

To overcome this kind of obstacle, Schein shows that people must first be shown that the existing approach is not working, they must then be motivated to learn new things, and finally they must have a safe environment in which to move forward.

Another significant and prevalent obstacle to innovation is the widespread expectation that things in the future will be as they were in the past. This belief contradicts reality because the acceleration of change throughout the economy means that things are already considerably different, and they will become progressively more different as we move forward. Nevertheless, many people still believe that this external wave of change is not relevant to themselves or their companies.

This expectation becomes a persistent bias against innovation, which is therefore suppressed in the regular course of affairs simply as a result of what is considered normal corporate culture. Surprisingly, this happens even in companies that are young and apparently dynamic.

For example, Sun Microsystems was founded in 1984, and the young company grew rapidly because of the innovativeness, aggressive pricing, and high performance of its products, and the skill with which it defined and filled its market niche. In fact, the company was founded to establish an entirely new market niche, the computer workstation, of which Sun has consistently been a leading maker and seller. Only 11 years later in 1995, Sun introduced a breakthrough product, "Java," the new programming language for embedded and World Wide Web applications.

The development of Java began in 1990 at a facility located at some distance from Sun's main offices, a decision made specifically because it was recognized even then that the project must be protected from "corporate 'antibodies' " who were "well known for attacking innovative ideas."[2]

Here was a company whose products, services, and marketplace identity were all built around innovation, and yet even at the tender age of 6 years there was already significant internal resistance to innovation in the organization's social and operational fabric.

The idea that change is something to be resisted is an example of how paradigms of thought impact individual behavior, and thereby organizational performance. Kuhn has shown that when a dominant paradigm is brought into question, shifting from one to another is a traumatic process that raises many unsettling issues.[3] Much like the shift from one dominant design to the next, the shift from one dominant paradigm to the next creates tension that is resolved only when a new set of ideas becomes accepted.

A third barrier is related to the enormous complexity of dynamic sociotechnical systems. Further, people have false expectations about the usability of information, about the difficulty of translating information to knowledge and knowledge to action. As a result, people tend to wait for clarity of information, but as noted in the Introduction, with the achievement of full clarity, opportunity is gone.

To overcome this tendency, stochastic models of information such as those used in weather forecasting and scenario-based planning are needed. These tools are used in conjunction with capability development activities in the form of training and practice in individual and group decision making, with the emphasis on situations characterized by fuzzy options. Sports practice and military war games are examples of necessary investments in developing "situated" tacit knowledge linked to particular activities and environments.[4] Methods for practice are discussed in greater detail in Chapter 7.

Sustaining and Disruptive Innovations

Because these obstacles are primarily psychological, it is necessary to introduce another distinction concerning the psychological paradigms associated with innovation.

The concepts of continuous and discontinuous innovation describe value as perceived *externally*, through the eyes and experiences of customers in the perceived and tacit elements of value that result in the decision to purchase. Another pair of terms refers to the *internal* organizational and psychological impact brought on by changes in technology, in the marketplace, or in the organization itself. This distinction between "sustaining" and "disruptive" innovations pertains to the supplier's perspective, and has to do with the capability of an organization to create and deploy innovations.

Sustaining innovations may involve fundamental changes in technology, but they have little organizational impact. When the same people who dealt with the old technology are able to learn the new skills required to handle new technology, then their ability to shift as technology shifts is adaptive change that sustains existing organizational models.

On the other hand, some innovations cannot be developed or brought to market using existing organizational competences and structures. When new approaches to management, manufacturing, development, distribution, marketing, or sales are required, these are "disruptive innovations" because that is what they do to already established ways of working and methods of serving customer needs.

Although technology seems to be the critical factor, in reality it may play little if any role at all. Harvard business professor Clayton Christensen points out, "[E]stablished firms confronted with disruptive technology typically viewed their primary development challenge as a *technological* one: to improve the disruptive technology enough that it suits known markets. In contrast, the firms that were most success-ful in commercializing a disruptive technology were those framing their primary development challenge as a *marketing* one: to build or find a market where product competition occurred along dimensions that favored the disruptive attributes of the product."[5]

An example of disruptive change is the Saturn division of General Motors, which was established because resistance to change within GM and GM's dealer network was so great that *cultural and organizational innovations* were repeatedly suppressed. The culture itself was interfer-ing with the development of both new architectures and new capabilities. The Saturn subsidiary was formed specifically to develop managerial innovations that were disruptive to the established ways of working and that would enable the company to successfully address new market segments.

Consequently, few of Saturn's innovations pertain to its actual products—as the cars themselves are not all that much different from other GM products. By far, the majority of these innovations reflect new ways of manufacturing, selling, and servicing.

The difference between sustaining and disruptive innovations therefore has much to do with the ability of an organization's man-agement to adapt to new ways of working or to the requirements of new market segments, and little to do with changes in the underly-ing technologies that may be embedded in any particular product or service.

In the end, innovations are disruptive when the current organiza-tion lacks the necessary models of competitive architecture and orga-nizational capability, and is therefore unable in critical ways to do what must be done.

When a disruptive innovation is also a next generation dominant design, the challenge is obvious and the shift to new organizational models is a necessity. Rarely, however, is the situation so clear. More commonly, disruptive innovations are difficult to manage precisely be-cause it is not clear what value they may offer to existing customers in existing markets.[6] Further, the criteria by which disruptive innovations should be evaluated may not even be the same as those that apply to in-cremental ones.

To escape the limitations of known customers and known markets, it is necessary to understand how existing dominant designs are evolv-ing. It is also necessary to forecast possible combinations or aggrega-tions of new technologies that may provide new levels of performance in the critical categories of customer value, as these new applications of technology may become disruptive and discontinuous architectures. Overlaid on these two is the curve representing the evolving require-ments of customers (see Figure 6.2).

The curve of forecasted demand is relatively easy to determine in hindsight, but predicting it is a greater challenge. In this situation, the

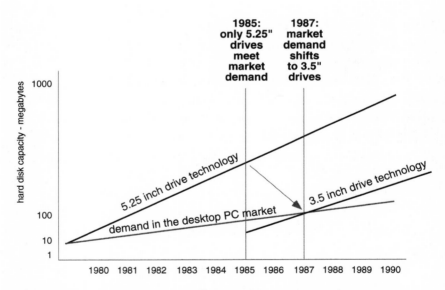

Figure 6.2 Disruptive Innovation.[7] Customers will not hesitate to switch to a new technology if it can better meet their needs. For suppliers who are not pre-pared to switch to the new technology, however, this is a significant source of disruption.

first step is to identify a population of buyers and to create application scenarios relating to their unmet needs. Second, determine how their currently defined needs are being met, what revenues are being generated, and how many units are sold per year. Third, a value analysis will suggest how much of this revenue can likely be displaced by the new technology, and at what average selling price. Fourth, estimate the duration of the market window by determining the historical cycle of dominant designs and extrapolating it forward. Finally, by putting all of this information together, an estimate of total units, units per year, revenues, ramp up, and the duration of the market opportunity can be represented in a curve of forecasted demand.

In addition, this curve will also suggest when to introduce competing solutions representing future dominant design and the critical performance factors they will have to achieve.

The relationships of the three curves make it clear which technologies are likely to meet the needs of customers, and they will not hesitate to switch if sufficient advantage is available.

In this context, a technological platform is simply and only a means of fulfilling customer requirements, so new technologies that are utterly disruptive to a supplier organization may be, to a customer, an easy and continuous transition.

From the supplier's perspective, the advent of disruptive innovation may call for the reinvention of the company itself, or at least part of it. Christensen suggests that the way to deal with disruptive technology is to set up separate business units to identify and serve the needs of customers who can benefit from it. On this basis, suppliers will then be able to expand into other customer segments and broaden the market base.

As with Saturn, this strategy may also be a way of dealing with internal resistance to change that is culturally induced, or a consequence of limiting factors such as labor agreements and fixed operational cost structures. This strategy led United Airlines to create its Shuttle subsidiary, established specifically to compete with disruptive management innovations introduced by competitor Southwest Airlines.

Learning and Unlearning

When Southwest was created major players within the airline industry viewed it with disdain, and only after many years of Southwest's consistent success that led to loss of market share did the established airlines begin to copy Southwest's innovations.

This shows how the words of Machiavelli, written nearly five hundred years ago, remain as true for us today as they were for the Florentine prince of 1525: "[T]here is nothing more difficult to carry out, nor more doubtful of success, nor more dangerous to handle than to initiate a new order of things. For the reformer has enemies from all those who profit by the old order, and only lukewarm defenders in all of those who would profit by the new order. . . . "[8]

The organizational status quo mind-set evaluates all events in terms of how they will impact the current structure of power. Whether it is the power of politics, management, or market incumbency, those who have it are loath to give it up.

In organizations, the people with power may not be the ones who can create the greatest value in the future. In the view of Nomura Research Institute scholars Teruyasu Murakami and Takashi Nishiwaki, organizations are populated by three kinds of people: Idea Generators, Idea Promoters, and Idea Killers:

"[T]he term idea generators (IG) refers to the individual personnel whose conceptions generate ideas that are the seeds of creation: the term idea killers (IK), to those personnel who try to suppress the idea, are opposed to the change it represents, or otherwise have a negative reaction to the prospect of its execution, and the term idea promoters (IP), to those personnel who support the idea, try to protect the IG from the IK, and attempt to foster the growth of the idea. . . . "[9]

An American perspective on this classification scheme is offered by former NASA scientist Dr. Michael Wiskerchen, who suggests, "85 percent of the people in an organization will be the status quo. Twelve percent will fight most changes because they have a well-defined reward system. In government organizations that percentage is probably a little bit higher. And 3 percent are innovators."[10]

As discussed in Chapter 1, after decades of research Everett Rogers and his colleagues have developed a clear model of how innovations are received in the marketplace. Rogers has defined a diffusion curve showing the process by which new paradigms come into widespread acceptance, regardless of whether they are new paradigms of scientific belief, new dominant designs for products and services, or new organizational mind-sets regarding the necessity of change (see Figure 6.3).

This difference between acceptance of and resistance to change can also be framed in terms of expectations for the future. Those who believe that success in the future will be a logical extrapolation of the trends of the past and present may resist innovations and the changes they bring. On the other hand, those who recognize that the only way to achieve or sustain success is through innovation understand that

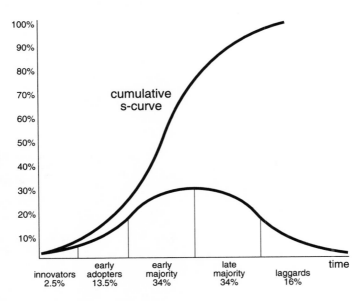

Figure 6.3 Diffusion of Innovations.[11]

this will necessarily bring change, and they are psychologically prepared to accept it, or even to welcome it.

Here the critical aspects are nearly always at the tacit level, as those who resist change may have been strongly influenced by negative experiences in the past that have never been fully analyzed and discussed.

Based on these ideas, we can now extend the learning model expressed in the path to wisdom by noting that in the decision-making process, knowledge leads to decisions, which lead to action. Just as there is a filter between data and information, there is also a filter between knowledge and subsequent action, the filter of models (see Figures 6.4 and 6.5).

The challenge in this process is to make explicit the decision-making models that serve as filters so that they can be evaluated and perhaps revised in the light of new knowledge. As long as they remain tacit, they will exert tremendous power even as they are inaccessible and perhaps dangerously obsolete.

Another situation arises when new data obtained through observation will not fit existing models. This is the situation described

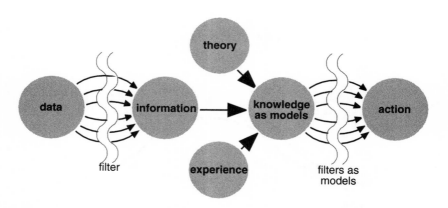

Figure 6.4 Knowledge to Action. The filter between data and information affects how we interpret the world, and that between knowledge and actions how we choose to act.

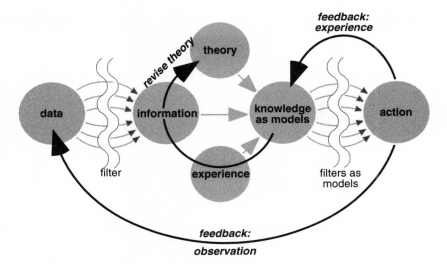

Figure 6.5 Feedback Loops in the Knowledge to Action Model. There are two forms of feedback from action. Feedback from observations provides data that must be filtered to obtain useful information. Feedback in the form of experience is knowledge; when integrated with theory and information, it provides the basis to evaluate and perhaps revise existing theory to reflect newly discovered realities.

in Chapter 5, where the difference between signal and noise must be reconsidered. In effect, innovation rarely offers clear-cut, either-or decisions, so at least two decision-making scenarios must be kept in mind at all times. One may describe market evolution as continuous, where signal is signal, or as discontinuous, where noise is signal. Constant evaluation and reevaluation of these criteria are required when, like today, change is rapid and unpredictable (see Figure 6.6).

When existing filters and models turn out to be unhelpful or counterproductive, a special kind of learning is required. As we have described the learning curve as the process by which continuing learning leads to new knowledge and improved performance, now we must utilize the *un*learning curve.

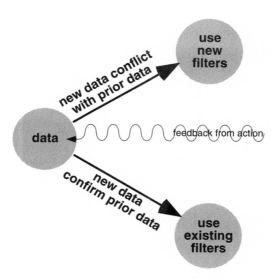

Figure 6.6 Knowledge to Action in Two Scenarios. When new data conflict with prior data, perhaps this means that a new set of filters is required to filter weak signals embedded in noise. When new data confirm prior data, existing filters are probably effective.

Unlearning is the difficult process of accepting that old realities, old mental models, old paradigms are no longer valid and must be replaced. In fact, when we are dealing with the tacit realms of beliefs and expectations, little if any learning can occur unless simultaneous unlearning occurs.

In Schein's model, unlearning is called "disconfirmation," the perception that current ways of doing things are not working.[12] Rather than the gradual development curve suggested in the learning curve model, unlearning is usually a steep plummet that typically bottoms out, finally, with a moment of insight that switches denial and resistance into exploration and commitment (see Figure 6.7).

In the context of the changing environment and the innovation process, unlearning is precisely the process of abandoning old filters and models that creates the space to develop and utilize new ones.

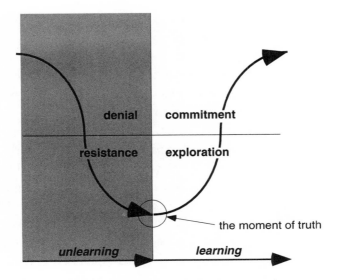

Figure 6.7 The Unlearning Curve.[13] This model was adapted by psychologists Dennis Jaffe and Cynthia Scott from Dr. Helen Kubler-Ross's seminal work, *On Death and Dying*.[14] When confronted with a significant change, the first reaction is commonly denial, followed by resistance. An individual reaches acceptance at the moment of truth, and switches to exploration and then commitment.

The Hierarchy

Yet another obstacle to innovation is the very structure of organizational hierarchies that separate knowledgeable individuals into different departments where they are frequently restrained from easy communication with one another. This inhibits the sharing of knowledge among diverse communities of practice and blocks the creation of new knowledge. In contrast, a great deal of learning might occur if people were expected to participate in group learning activities conducted concurrently with their core responsibilities.

In the words of Ken Cox, "I suppose that part of our problem today is that the bureaucratic process began to take over as we got into the Shuttle. It's a 30-year program, and any time you've got a 30- or 40-year program, bureaucracy just feeds on itself, people gradually develop turfs and stovepipe organizations. Today, 30 years later, NASA is also burdened by the traditional don't-ever-throw-anything-away mentality. 'We flight tested it, it works, keep it.' So NASA applied the HAL [programming language] to the early Space Shuttle, and today the Shuttle has something in it that's about 30 years behind the times. Even today, today! Today we fly with some of that compiler language that was developed for Apollo. This is not a good story. It's probably the wrong thing to do."[15]

Similar thinking has led the designers of the Space Station to build its control systems around the Intel 386 computer chip. Sadly, a project so vital for NASA's image and the future of the space program will rely on a computer that is painfully obsolete.[16]

When critical knowledge sets isolated into separate compartments of the tacit domains in various communities of practice, the integration of diverse perspectives is systematically prevented from occurring, which thus prevents the discovery of latent needs that are hidden in the interstices between disciplines.

Since the integration of diverse perspectives between individuals from different departments is one of the critical elements of knowledge creation and of innovation, the boundaries between departments must be curtailed as people cooperate in performing business processes. For example, there is now evidence that the shift to working in teams may account for two-thirds of the productivity gains in the United States in the 1990s.[17] As noted, Chrysler's shift to "platform teams" is an example of this focus on collaboration through new organizational models.

Although from a macroeconomic perspective, productivity gains have been insufficient, such gains as there have been deserve to be studied and supported. But it turns out that the movement toward teams is also a subject of controversy: ". . . work teams and employee involvement programs are coming under growing legal attack by

America's unions and the National Labor Relations Board, who believe some of these programs improperly usurp the place of unions in representing worker interests."[18]

How ironic that a movement which originated in response to industrial abuses would have a difficult time accepting the new rules of today's economy, as wages simply cannot increase without productivity improvements. Interesting, indeed are the dilemmas that our allegiances devise for us.

Specialization

Another manifestation of resistance to innovation arises in the technical disciplines. As knowledge becomes more and more specialized, it becomes increasingly difficult for specialists of different disciplines to communicate effectively with one another. For example, the convergence of broadcast media such as television, cable television, computer, and telephone technologies toward unified digital communication is an evolutionary outgrowth of advances in electronics that utilize knowledge from several disciplines. Early on, however, it was observed that although cable television engineers and telephone engineers had overcome many of the same technological hurdles in establishing their networks, the terminology that each group had used was similar, but different, with obvious duplication of effort. What a telephone engineer called a central office, a cable engineer called a head end. What a telephone engineer called a feeder, a cable engineer called a trunk. What a telephone engineer called an optical network unit, a cable engineer called a feeder. As a result, confusion and mutual distrust inhibited innovation until someone took the time to create a translating dictionary.[19]

Although advanced technology is critical to the success of many new products and services, the specialization of the people involved is an obstacle that must be countered, in part by new organizational practices. One of these practices is based on recognizing the relevant communities of practice, both in different projects and in different departments, and then supporting individuals to serve as bridges between communities. These people develop the linkages between different languages and cultures, enabling groups to better appreciate each other's needs and capabilities.

Once a basis of communication is established, maintaining these linkages does not always require face-to-face interaction. Project status information can be posted on story boards and bulletin boards in group spaces to support the exchange of information without requiring synchronous interaction or tedious replication of voice mail and e-mail messages. Information is maintained in context more easily, so less time is wasted in recreating the broader situation in which specific information may be relevant.

Another response to the problems brought on by increasing specialization is the use of new organizational models.

The New Organization: Delayering and Relayering

In the old command-and-control organizations, the CEO sat atop the pyramid. At the next level down, the senior management team consisted of the top managers in each of the major functional areas (see Figure 6.8).

Two critical shortcomings of this model are, on one hand, the lack of integration between the critical knowledge sets that are the responsibilities of the various departments, and on the other hand the difficulty of involving so many people in senior management discussions.

Figure 6.8 The Old Organization.

It has been shown that group sizes of four to seven people are most effective as a small team, but here we have at least ten. Furthermore, today's demanding travel schedules make it difficult to get everyone together unless meetings are arranged well in advance, which inhibits learning opportunities that arise spontaneously (as most do). Finally, this organization does not reflect the principles of competitive architecture, organizational capability development, knowledge management, and many other discoveries and principles pertaining to innovation management.

Hence, a new level of abstraction is needed in the design of the organization itself.

As suggested by Sveiby's model underlying intellectual capital accounting, there are three critical types or classes of knowledge, and these are central points around which the new organization may be oriented.

These are Employee Competence—knowledge and capability enabled by technology, and the basis for accomplishing all work; Internal Structure—the organization, processes and tools, and infrastructure that make a company flow; and External Structure—the valued services and artifacts that define customer perceptions, interactions, and relationships.[20]

As the three critical performance domains in the organization, each of these three areas becomes the responsibility of a senior manager, to whom report all the other functional heads (see Figure 6.9).

The advocates of delayering may not welcome the suggestion to add another organizational layer, and although their argument is compelling, it does not take into account increasing complexity and the very real systems problems that it causes. The necessity to define new levels of abstraction to deal with complexity cannot be avoided, and this necessity will inevitably be translated into new organizational responsibilities. Each of the three functional managers therefore has a primary and a secondary responsibility in the management of intangible assets (see Figure 6.10).

To some degree, the rush to delayer has missed the point, since the problem with layers is not the layers per se, but the separation that they cause between communities of practice with critical and complementary knowledge sets.

While a decade of delayering has removed obstacles in the functional bureaucracy, perhaps improved information flow, and given

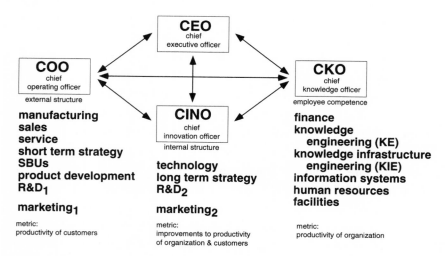

Figure 6.9 The New Organization. The organization consists of a senior officer in charge of each of the three major domains of intangible value.

	primary responsibility	secondary responsibility
COO chief operating officer	**external structure**	**internal structure**
CINO chief innovation officer	**internal structure**	**employee competence**
CKO chief knowledge officer	**employee competence**	**internal structure**

Figure 6.10 Distribution of Responsibility for the Management of Intangible Assets.

people at lower layers more autonomy (and a lot more work), the structure of an organization must at the same time maintain its competence to deal with increasing complexity.

Now that delayering has been accomplished, the ultimate solution to the problems of complexity involves two steps. First, the protocols for interaction between distributed individuals must be systematically changed so that there is much more useful, effective, and efficient interaction between communities of practice.

The movement toward cross-functional teams is an example of new interaction patterns. Since the critical factor is not from which layers of an organization the team members come, but rather what knowledge and capacity they bring to the team, we are back to issues of knowledge and knowledge management as far more important considerations than position in the hierarchy.

The second step is to follow up delayering with *re*layering. The new layers are middle managers whose specific role is to transform tacit knowledge into explicit knowledge that becomes the basis of business growth. In the words of Nonaka and Tekeuchi, "Middle managers serve as a bridge between the visionary ideals of the top and the often chaotic reality of those on the front line of business. Middle managers mediate between the 'what should be' mindset of the top and the 'what is' mindset of the front-line employees by creating mid-level business and product concepts."[21] The name they give this approach is "middle-up-down management," a function of creating new knowledge that is well established in Japan.

This is quite different from the role that middle managers have played in the past as filters of information and diffusers of commands. In contrast, the relayered organization is engaged in the creation of new knowledge and its application in innovation as it applies to all aspects of corporate life, including the creation of new products, services, processes, and organizations; new product platforms and dominant designs; and entirely new industries with new companies to compete in them.

Middle managers will be successful at this when they understand how learning occurs, and how to facilitate it, and they themselves will serve as links between different communities of practice who have complementary knowledge. As mobile, interacting centers of coordination, they will facilitate the aggregation of knowledge across disciplines and groups, and its application in practical terms.

However, the relayering of middle management is not enough. To reflect the new distribution of asset value and the importance of knowledge and knowledge management, there must also be a significant change in the structure of top management, or the senior team.

In both the old organization and the new, the Chief Operating Officer is responsible for the management of business operations, which in Sveiby's terms are the external structures. Sales, customer service, product development, applied R&D, or $R\&D_1$, and manufacturing are in this domain. Business units, divisions, sectors, and lines of business report here, and short-term strategy is developed as well.

Since employee competence consists of both the physical and knowledge assets of the company, managing these becomes the responsibility of a new officer whose responsibilities include finance (the Chief Financial Officer), facilities (typically, the VP of Real Estate and Facilities), people and processes (the Human Resources Director), and information system (the Chief Information Officer). Not coincidentally, these elements (excluding finance) together compose the disciplines of knowledge infrastructure engineering, while the new finance role has to learn and practice intellectual capital accounting and options finance when appropriate.

Although the title Chief Asset Officer might be used for this role, the awkwardness of such a title would soon become apparent. The title Chief Knowledge Officer seems more appropriate because knowledge is the critical differentiating asset in today's markets. It also reflects the role that facilities and information systems play in supporting knowledge creation and sharing.

In Sveiby's model, the third major element is internal structure, but since we emphasize the role of architecture and capability development as enablers of internal structure, here the model does not map perfectly onto our schema. Key aspects of capability are employee competence managed as human resources issues, which belong in the employee competence category.

Hence, our view is that the third critical element is innovation itself, reflecting the intimate relationship between competence, innovation, and learning. We suggest that the Chief Innovation Officer (CINO), the final member of the senior team, is responsible for and leader of the capability and architecture development processes, and for the practices of discontinuous innovation incorporating fundamental R&D ($R\&D_2$), marketing$_2$, and the mastery of new technology. Product development, however, remains focused on continuous innovation and is managed as an activity within the various business entities.

The Chief Innovation Officer

As noted, one of the reasons for the widespread failure of discontinuous innovation is that no one individual is responsible for ensuring that it happens. Hence, it is this officer's responsibility to oversee the integration of all the elements that constitute the innovation process (which we will present in full in Chapter 8). In Drucker's words, "There has to be a special locus for the venture within the organization, and it has to be pretty high up. . . . Innovative efforts, especially those aimed at developing new businesses, products, or services, should normally report directly to the 'executive in charge of innovation' rather than to managers further down the hierarchy. They should never report to line managers charged with responsibility for ongoing operations. . . . The best, and perhaps the only, way to avoid killing off the new by sheer neglect is to set up the innovative project from the start as a separate business."[22]

From the broadest perspective, the Chief Innovation Officer (or CINO) has three major concerns. The first is technology and fundamental as $R\&D_2$, under the leadership of the Chief Technology Officer who may also be the Director of Research and Business Development. Second is the development of long-term strategy, which often has its own managers, and the third is marketing$_2$, expeditionary marketing. Marketing$_2$ will focus on identifying the latent needs that will drive the next generations of dominant designs in each line of business and major business process.

With the description of innovation as the fusion of R&D and marketing, we have created an organizational model to support this convergence.

Thus, it becomes the chief innovation officer's responsibility to manage both the radical and the evolutionary development of the organization's models relating to the new terminology presented in Chapters 2 and 3, including the competitive architecture, dominant designs, product and distribution platforms, and the learning that drives organizational capability.

We have already described the innovation process as one driven by forced questioning, and we can therefore define four critical questions that any CINO should be asking:

1. Given the company's existing situation, what is today's competitive architecture?

2. What organizational capabilities do we apply to address it?
3. How will technology change the market, and how therefore can we leverage new technology to improve our position in the marketplace?
4. What new capabilities must be developed to accomplish this?

Answers to these questions are reflected in the output of the innovation group, which is then directed toward the support of the internal and external structures. For the internal, the management of innovation is focused on improving the tools, processes, and new products and services used inside the organization, while support for external structure stresses new relationships, partnerships, and distribution channels including the knowledge channel.

Each of the three segments of the organization measures its results differently. For the managers of employee competence, success is primarily a function of *increasing productivity and effectiveness within the organization,* which can be assessed in financial terms with conventional productivity measurements. It will also be reflected as increases in the value of the company's existing tangible and intangible assets, and in the creation of new ones. This, by the way, suggests an entirely new definition of the role of human resources management.

Success for operations is primarily a function of the *productivity of customers,* whereas success at the innovation function defined as internal structure must be measured according to *new value* provided to both internal and external customers as seen in productivity increases derived from the group's innovations.

For all three new senior managers, and indeed for people throughout the organization, identifying and overcoming the obstacles to innovation through new organizational practices and organizational models requires consistent effort. Whether it is in the ongoing course of business or in response to significant external change, these issues are ultimately related to human needs and human behavior, so they will inevitably arise and must be dealt with frequently.

The story of the turnaround of Hewlett-Packard's Test and Measurement Organization (TMO) illustrates many of these issues and frames them in the real-world context of large-scale economic change.

The Story of HP's TMO Turnaround

In 1970, Hewlett-Packard Company was 31 years old, its revenues were $365 million, and its products were mostly analog test and measurement instruments used primarily by other companies, not consumers.

During the 1970s, however, new applications of digital technology were rapidly being developed by innovators such as those at Xerox PARC and NASA. Analog instruments were gradually being displaced by digital instruments that were generally more precise, more reliable, more flexible, and less expensive.

Just to stay viable as an instrument company, therefore, HP was forced to develop extensive capabilities in digital electronics, which meant that the company had develop many of the same capabilities as computer companies.

HP did not resist the change, and in fact the company's leaders recognized the opportunity to make a fundamental switch to digital technology. Only 10 years later, HP was primarily a computer company, and its revenues had grown tenfold, to $3 billion.

Even more remarkable than this growth is that this happened at the same time that many other companies were exiting the computer business. The leaders at Hewlett-Packard understood the larger pattern of change driven by the consequences of Moore's Law, and they successfully exploited it.

As a computer company during the 1980s, HP saw the advance of the PC and reasoned that there was a significant opportunity to sell printers to growing numbers of PC users. At the time, it was a very risky and disproportionate investment, but by 1990 HP's printer division was tremendously profitable, with sales of more than $3 billion, while HP's total sales had climbed to $13.2 billion.

Continuing to follow the continuing distribution of computing infrastructure in the computer business, many HP printers were sold for use in homes. HP expanded on this success in 1995 by establishing a new division to sell computers to the home market through low-profit, high-volume, mass market retailers such as Costco.

To succeed in this competitive and fast-moving market, HP's products had to be closely adapted to short-term demand conditions that changed constantly. Therefore, each product was introduced with the expectation that it would be upgraded to a new version in 120 days, and upgraded again in another 120 days. This ensured that there was nearly always an HP product available with the newest, hottest features.

This strategy required HP to develop close relationships with its retailers so that designers could learn what was in demand in the market, but it was a worst-case situation for the engineering and manufacturing organizations.

Product design decisions were made at the latest possible time, and sometimes even later, to take full account of emerging trends in the marketplace. This left the engineering and manufacturing groups only a few weeks to turn out a new product. The retailers, of course, loved this, because their feedback showed up in new products almost immediately.

HP used this strategy to capture a significant share of the home market, and the HP Home Products division achieved profitability in only its second month of shipping products.

In marked contrast, HP's direct competitor, Apple Computer, suffered steady declines in market share and huge operating losses while HP's sales and profits were growing steadily. Apple, like IBM, had created a market shift but had failed to understand the underlying architectural changes that were the consequences of its own actions.

This demonstrates that the time for change in the competitive arena of business is when it is least apparent. Chip Holt of Xerox points out, "The time to invest in a new technology is when you are at your most productive point in the technology you're using, but if you're managing the denominator of the productivity equation that is a very difficult thing to do."[23]

One of the key differences between the strategies of the HP and Apple was that at Apple, product generation development cycles were measured in months rather than weeks. "At Apple, the engineers would just laugh at you if you wanted to get out a new product in less than 4 months."[24] There can be no effective discontinuous innovation without comparable innovation in the productivity of operations, including product development (or $R\&D_1$).

Apple's organizational pattern had carried over from the early days of the industry when things changed much more slowly, and this resulted a severe penalty in the more demanding marketplace of the early 1990s. Although few companies perform at the consistently high level of HP, it is clear that HP's willingness to undertake organizational innovation is key to its extraordinary capacity to successfully market and sell innovative products (see Figure 6.11).

By 1995, HP's total sales approached $30 billion on the strength of its consistent product and organizational innovation cycles.[25]

Meanwhile, the test and measurement portion of HP's business, the original company (now called the TMO division), had continued to grow even as the rest of the company grew even faster. By 1995, the

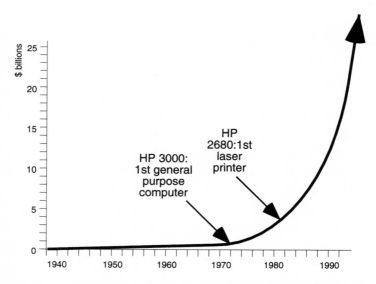

Figure 6.11 Hewlett-Packard Sales History, 1938–1994.[26] By becoming a computer company and then developing consumer-based computer printers, HP's revenues grew exponentially from 1970 onward.

revenues of the TMO had topped $3.5 billion, it consisted of 23 divisions, and had about 18,000 employees. If it had been a separate company, it would have ranked about 350 on the listing of the Fortune 500.[27]

Five years earlier in 1990, however, the prospects for the TMO had not seemed so bright. After the peak of the Reagan administration's Cold War spending spree in 1984, the aerospace and defense market went into a steady decline. This had been the largest customer sector for the TMO, and over the following decade the TMO's aerospace and defense market business fell off at the rate of 20 percent to 30 percent each year.

In 1990, in the midst of this decline, Ned Barnholt took over as senior vice president and general manager of the Test and Measurement Organization, not yet realizing that the unit was heading straight into a crisis.

By May 1992, the TMO suffered the first monthly loss in its history, and Barnholt initiated a fundamental change process that he called "Project TMO." In the following story, he describes some of the major elements and discoveries of Project TMO, as the unit turned itself around to become one of HP's most profitable in only three years.[28]

Project TMO

At the time I took over the TMO things were not so bad. When I went into the job I didn't realize what was coming, but shortly after I took over things started going sour. Towards the middle of 1991 things started getting really bad.

Although our profits were declining, some people thought it was just another business cycle and we would tighten our belts and get through it. But as we started looking under the surface at the changes in our customer base, it was clear that aerospace and defense was going away, and we realized that this was a lot more, a structural change that required much more dramatic action.

We saw increasingly complex market forces at work, but we couldn't stand back from the business long enough to see how those forces applied to us, and we had clearly run out of big ideas. We were preoccupied with evolving our old product lines instead of moving in new directions. We had all the characteristics of a technological dinosaur, slow and lumbering to the tar pits.

So we surveyed the market, trying to understand the underlying dynamics in the industry, what businesses were hot, where we could invest to grow the business. We concluded that we needed to realign our investments. We needed to get more focused in the communications test business and the semiconductor test business, and we needed to provide more complete solutions and services to our customers. Instead of just selling boxes, we needed to provide more value to our customers.

So we made some organization changes. We took all the divisions that had traditionally been aligned around product lines and we realigned them around systems and solutions.

When we started, we had about 19,000 people. We went through a 20 percent to 25 percent downsizing of our workforce to align our cost structure. It was very painful to go through that and at the same time we were trying to redirect the business.

The downsizing didn't just happen because of changes in the customer base. There was also a great reduction in the number of components in TMO's instruments, as electronic parts shrunk and more functions were put on integrated circuits. At the time, for example, an oscilloscope had about 1,000 components, but today it has about 100.

It turned out, though, that reorganizing was actually the easy part. About 3 months later I went to a number of these divisions and asked how it was going, and I discovered that most of them were struggling to understand what their new charters really meant. It became clear to me that there was a lot more to change than just changing the organization chart.

So we convened a meeting of 60 of our top managers, and discovered that everything known to man was wrong with our organization, including the fact that we had reorganized wrong and had to do it again. This is what led us to start Project TMO.

We began a more detailed study of our problems, and one thing we discovered was that we were missing important skill sets that our managers needed to be able to lead change in their organizations. We found that we needed to work in five different areas, and we had a study team look at each of them.

One was to sharpen our strategy to win, to make sure it was clear and well articulated and communicated to our people what we were trying to accomplish.

Two, we needed to work on our decision-making processes, particularly the speed at which we made decisions.

Three, we needed to work on our leadership skills.

And finally we needed to work on things like accountability and communications.

Scenario planning helped us get a lot of the issues on the table, facilitate the dialogue. It helped us identify some of the implicit, under-the-surface assumptions that we had made but never written down about growth in the aerospace and defense business, and growth in the communications business. It helped us to explore different ways that the businesses might unfold and to build common views of the future.

We just spent a lot of time on those kinds of issues, and we came up with a clear strategy for our business, and then we worked hard to articulate that clearly to our team. We also worked on defining the mission and purpose of our business. We used to be internally focused, thinking we wanted to be the leading supplier of test and measurement equipment. Now our mission is externally focused, to use our core competencies to help our customers improve their business results. We're only in business if we help our customers be successful.

It also became very clear that if you're going to make the organization change, we had to groom our people through that change process. How do you change the culture of the whole organization? So we created a sixth task force on people and culture.

We went through 2 or 3 years of task forces and learning exercises that opened people's eyes to a different way of looking at their business.

A couple of key learnings for me through all this, the bottom line, is first of all the importance of empowerment and really engaging your team in this change process. The notion of having task forces and learning forums has really helped our organization grow.

We also learned the importance of having a facilitator, a coach who does this full-time and brings the right resources to help us keep on track.

From an overall process standpoint, one of the biggest discoveries for us was the importance of alignment. In the past we would identify a strategy, decide what we want to do and then jump right into action. We'd miss the middle step of alignment.

Now we say, "Okay, here's our strategy. What are some of the key success factors that we need to be successful with that strategy? What are the barriers to success within our organization? What do we think we need to change in our business processes, our management processes, our skills, behaviors, organization, compensation, cost structures to be successful in this new business?"

For example, the division that we asked to get into the systems solutions business was struggling after 3 or 4 months trying to understand what that meant. They finally asked, "What are the skills we need to have to be successful in this business?" Identifying what's different about a business and understanding the gap between where you are today versus the skills and the processes that you need to be successful is critical. Gap analysis is really crucial to alignment and we spent a lot of time on it.

They discovered that we needed project management skills, but as an instrument company we didn't need those. We also needed program management skills, cost-estimation skills, and a project costing system as opposed to our traditional costing system. We needed a way to track deals over different stages of the process.

These things were not in place, so they started systematically putting them in, and low and behold, a year-and-a-half later they were booming, and they're still booming.

That middle step of alignment was one of the key ah-hahs for us to the whole change management process.

How We Got into the Video Server Market

As part of our scanning exercise in the early '90s we went to the Telecom '91 Trade Show to look at what was happening in the telecommunications industry. It became clear that video was going to be a very big growth market.

At that time we had very little going in the area of video test. So we went to a number of our divisions and asked them to investigate the area of video test. Everybody came back and said, "That's really great, but we're too busy building spectrum analyzers, network analyzers, signal generators, so we don't have time."

We realized the only way we were ever going to free up resources to work in new areas like video test was to reduce our investment in some of our more traditional businesses. So we took all of our traditional instrument product lines and put them in one big division, and took the other divisions and changed their jobs.

One group had responsibility for microwave signal generators and microwave power meters, one of our oldest, most traditional divisions. All of a sudden one morning we told them that they were our video test division. This was a gigantic shock. Even though this wasn't necessarily something they thought they wanted to do, we assigned the business to them.

Six months later they said, "You know there's actually a bigger opportunity out there in video servers." At that time HP wasn't doing any work in that area, but they told us we should. So they became HP's Video Server Division. It was a major change. They had to find people who had the right skill sets, learn a new set of customers, a different set of industry standards committees.... There was some work going on in HP Labs, so we transferred that technology to the division and they productized it. They were generating revenue in less than a year.

Unfortunately the video server business hasn't taken off the way we had hoped. The good news is we became the market leader and we've won a large share of the deals in the last few years. The bad news is that it's going to be several more years before there's really major demand for video servers. But we've taken the same technology and we've brought it to the broadcast industry to replace analog tape in the newsroom and to do ad insertions digitally. Now we're into news editing, tape delay, broadcasting, and we're doing quite well.

Partnering with Customers

While we were working on our product strategy and business strategy, it also became clear to me we needed an organizational strategy. What kind of organization do we need? We could change business today to be successful, but what about the next turn in the road? How are we going to be successful then?

I kept saying over and over was that we had to build an organization that was inherently flexible, responsive, that valued change as opposed to resisted change, and was really customer centric and didn't lose sight of where customers were going in *their* businesses. One of the ways we implement the customer focus is through customer partnerships.

We team a lot more now with our customers, and very often with third parties to be able to deliver solutions. We bring customers in earlier into the development cycle—not all customers, but a few leading edge customers even in the product definition stage.

We also get involved in developing specific solutions for specific customers, and we literally sit in their plants as part of their business teams.

When I go out and challenge the team to get a project out in a year, they'll say, "No way, we can't do it." But you send the R&D team out and meet face to face with a customer who tells them if you don't have it in a year, you're going to miss the business, miss the window, they say, "We can do that." It's amazing what can happen when you get the team directly in front of customers.

Now engineers from the Labs often accompany us to customer calls to better understand market needs, and how we might apply new technology to solve customer problems.

In the operating units, this was later translated as the need to, "get marketing out from between R&D and the customers" so that engineers would learn about customers needs directly.[29]

On one project, the customer came to work directly with HP engineers. What ended up happening was that the product developed as the customer's desires evolved. The box we were originally going to build for the customer is not the box we will build now. It has features the customer didn't ask for in the beginning. So the team and the customer locked in at the right time, just as the customer's vision was jelling.[30]

Even in our more traditional box business we do that today. It's a different paradigm of design. We don't do anything that doesn't have some customer and development partner with it.

We have also entered the consulting and education business as another way to add value to our customers. [Susan Curtis, TMO's Manager of Strategic Programs, adds, "Customers want us for our knowledge. Consulting is a major growth area for us. They are asking for integrated solutions, and companies like Ford have told us that they want to outsource their testing to us."]

Managing Change

We talk a lot about being continually scanning, being out there looking for the next turns in the road, being willing to kill some of your current programs in order to move on to better opportunities. We talk a lot about the traditional S-curve model of businesses and identifying some of the newer emerging businesses early, having some overlapping investment, even though it may be not neat and tidy. We'd rather have the second best product come from another HP division, and if that's a new S-curve then we want to get on it early.

Individuals have to know that in the course of a 30-year career, they're not going to be able to do the same job day in and day out. A lot of our people had gotten into that mode, had been growing and successful for so long that they just assumed they could stay in their same work group, do the same job forever. We're saying, "No, that isn't the real world. The world of today in the electronics industry is that cycles come and go very quickly. You have windows of opportunity. You either hit that window or miss it. And, if you're going to hit it you've got to be early and you've got to be willing to change."

Part of the change management process was getting people, including our managers, to recognize that change is a way of life in this business, and that the organizations that recognize it and structure themselves and have the right skills and behaviors to respond quickly to those changes are going to be the ones that succeed.

Just getting people to understand the realities of the business is part of the cultural change. Our business isn't quite as bad as the PC business, but it is certainly moving that way, where every morning you read the *Wall Street Journal* to find out what your challenge is for the day based on what somebody else did yesterday. In the past, particularly 15 or 20 years ago, we could invent a product and chances were it would last 10 years. We could forget about it and go invent another product. Those days are gone.

To be successful means not just innovation in the products, but also innovation in your organization. It means being willing to change your organization to respond to whatever businesses you choose to be in. It's important to get alignment of your organization, getting yourself aligned with where your customers are going, and getting your employees to support and understand what that is.

People have done this in different ways. Some people use TQC or TQM as a way to drive change, some people drive change in other ways. We've tended to drive it through self-discovery, by becoming a learning organization and learning together the skills and the processes that we need to be successful, and learning how to manage change itself as a process. I don't think this is the only formula that works. Obviously there are different ways to bring about change. It just happened that this worked for us, and it was very consistent within our culture.

By 1995, aerospace and defense was only 10 percent of the TMO's business, while the information industry had become the largest customer segment. From 1993 through early 1996, the TMO achieved record orders in 11 consecutive quarters, showing clearly just how successful Project TMO was.

New Processes and New Leadership

In the language of 4th generation R&D, the story of TMO highlights a number of key elements. First and foremost are the critical roles of architecture and capability development, evident as the core of the change process.

The first stage in Project TMO was focused simply on understanding how the competitive architecture was changing and the impact that this was having on TMO. Changes to the TMO organization were then made to reflect the new architecture, but these were not sufficient.

It turned out to be tremendously difficult to understand the new organizational model because people lacked the required capabilities and therefore the second stage of the project was focused precisely on developing new organizational capability to implement the new architecture.

The story of the video server business also illustrates how primary innovations in architecture and capability development must be accompanied by secondary innovations in platforms, products, and services. The innovation in organizational architecture of assigning the video server project to an existing group, and reassigning their former responsibility elsewhere, created the means to develop a new product platform and then derivative products based on it.

As the innovation cycle shows, management practices define the framework through which products and services are developed and delivered to market. The constitution and adaptability of those organizations is as important over the long term as that of the products and services themselves, for they are necessary complements to one another. Without alternating iterations of innovation in architecture and capability and in platforms, products, and services, innovation is not sustainable in either (see Figure 6.12).

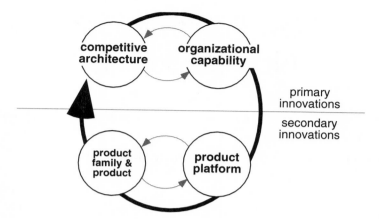

Figure 6.12 The Innovation Cycle. Innovation begins with architecture and capability development, which creates the foundation for innovation in platforms, products, services, and distribution systems.

The sustaining linkage between primary innovations in architecture and capability development, and secondary innovations in products, services and platforms, is evident in the story of the TMO, and in every other case that we are aware of. It may even be a general rule. Repeatedly, we observe the secondary feedback as well, when innovations in products and services call for innovations in architecture, capability, and management, following which these innovations create the conditions in which the development of further product and service innovations becomes both possible and necessary. Companies that hesitate or fail entirely to pursue subsequent iterations of the cycle also fail to benefit fully from their R&D investments.

The story also shows how the direct relationship between R&D and customers that we call marketing$_2$ leads to the development of the market and unanticipated new products by enabling R&D to have a direct experience of customer needs, at the same time enabling customers to have direct knowledge of emerging technical capabilities.

Without knowing about 4th generation R&D and without using its language, the TMO is nevertheless practicing an advanced form of it under Ned Barnholt's leadership.

The new leaders in the organization must look broadly rather than narrowly. They must have a solid technical foundation, but also understand people, business, learning, information technology, and marketing. As a result, they advance by ensuring that knowledge aggregation occurs in individuals and team at all levels.

The new leaders guide organizational systems through the creation of new knowledge and new infrastructures to support knowledge development, the twin disciplines of knowledge engineering and knowledge infrastructure engineering, rather than through industrial engineering that relies on centralized structures driven by command and control (see Figure 6.13).

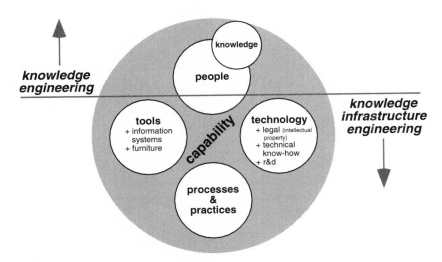

Figure 6.13 Knowldge Engineering and Knowledge Infrastructure Engineering. Two critical new disciplines for organizational leaders are knowledge engineering and knowledge infrastructure engineering, through which new organizational capabilities are developed and applied to the competitive architecture for competitive advantage.

Peter Drucker points out, "Innovation, rather than holding on to what already exists, must be made attractive and beneficial to managers. There must be a clear understanding throughout the organization that innovation is the best means to preserve and perpetuate that organization, and that it is the foundation for the individual manager's job security and success."[31]

CHAPTER 7

Organizational Capability Development

The key standards of success for today's organizations are competitive productivity improvements. To support all the required improvements, it is essential that a process for developing and enhancing individual and organizational capabilities be an integral part of every organization, which includes suppliers and customers as part of the system. Hence, to complement the organizational architecture presented in Chapter 6, we describe the model for mutually dependent capability development in this chapter.

The key to effective capability development is recognizing the distinction between three very different modes of thinking and working. In the most common mode, we engage in the day-to-day work that is before us. We apply existing knowledge in the context of groups, tools, processes, and practices to get the work done.

It is a different mode, however, to think about and enact improvements in the way that we work today, and yet a third to consider what future discoveries will be needed, and how to make improvements to

231

the way we improve. Although the difference between the second and third modes is not widely understood, this distinction is critical to implementing capability development.

Improving operations, which we call improving$_1$, is what we do when, for example, we refine our skill in the existing processes and practices of any particular discipline. We improve our work as managers, or researchers, or writers, by studying and changing our approach to reflect new needs or new possibilities. However, the decisions we make concerning what methods of improvement to utilize take place at a different level of thinking, and these are a function of what we call improving$_2$.

When managers consider how to improve their capabilities they may choose, for example, to focus on discussions in peer groups, to study for an MBA degree, to accept an assignment overseas, or perhaps to transfer to a department in which they have not yet worked. This choice, made at the level of improving$_2$, then becomes the basis of work at the level of improving$_1$, which in turn becomes manifested in better performance at basic day-to-day work. Organizing these three levels and linking them in an integrated approach is the heart of the capability development model, and an important enabling aspect of the process for continuous and discontinuous innovation.

The key linkage is people themselves. Since knowledge exists only in people's heads, knowledge flows when people move around and participate in different activities on all three levels. This combination of breadth and depth is a key difference between industrial engineering with its division of labor, and knowledge infrastructure engineering to support the aggregation of knowledge and the creation of new knowledge (see Figure 7.1).

The need for these three different stages seems to be invariant in all kinds of systems, as the same basic dynamics seem to pertain to all aspects of life, including work, sports, education and leisure.

A particularly strong description of this pattern has been developed by computer industry pioneer Douglas Engelbart, who is also responsible for developing numerous innovations in computing that are now taken entirely for granted, including the mouse (on which he holds the patent), text editing, multiple on-screen windows, and the earliest

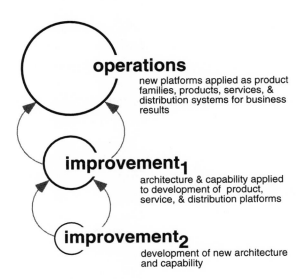

operations
new platforms applied as product
families, products, services, &
distribution systems for business
results

improvement₁
architecture & capability applied
to development of product,
service, & distribution platforms

improvement₂
development of new architecture
and capability

Figure 7.1 Capability Development. For every core business activity, the role of improving₁ is to better the performance of that activity, and the role of improving₂ is to make improving₁ more effective. Improving₁ would therefore focus on reducing product-cycle time that would make smarter, faster, and higher quality core operations activities, while improving₂ focuses on reducing the cycle time for improving₁, which includes discovering the types and content of cycles that will occur in future iterations.

working hypertext systems. Engelbart was also a member of the original design team for the Internet (then Arpanet), and is certainly one of the most honored individuals contributing to the development of the computer industry.

But Engelbart's interests are broader than just technical innovations. Since the early 1960s, he has studied the enormous impact of massive technological change on organizations, and he has recognized that the parallel development of human capabilities and the tools we use holds the key to sustainable success for organizations and for society as a whole.[1]

Hence, Engelbart has described how to improve both kinds of systems based on the insight that operating a system is not the same as improving it, nor is improving a system the same as improving the *capability to improve* a system.

This is critical because a truly adaptive organization must contain the knowledge *and* the knowledge infrastructure for its own development, and also for that of its suppliers, customers, and other stakeholders as well.

The pivotal insight is that although anyone may both operate within a system and make improvements to it, the processes for doing so are necessarily different.

In the context of business, these core functions are the processes and their management, based on both tacit and explicit knowledge. The business focus is on agility and performance in the here and now, and the continuing dynamic of change in the marketplace creates a compelling urgency in the day-to-day responsibilities that leaves little or no time to work on improving or replacing today's products and services. Improving today's capabilities typically is a lower priority.

Improving the productivity of operations is an entirely different matter that requires a completely different set of interests, understandings, and skills. The focus here is in developing new processes and tools through analysis, experimentation, simulation, and practice, improvements that will be relevant in the short to medium term.

The skills to do this will involve testing existing business processes, experimenting with alternative processes, and learning about both human cognitive and behavioral processes and the tools that support them. Improving$_1$ activities are the development of new capabilities and tools that will be tested and applied in the immediate future, even as soon as this afternoon. This is, therefore, the improvement of doing that which is based on knowing what we need to accomplish.

Improving$_1$ activities include human resources management, information systems design and implementation, work process design and redesign, and the design of the work environment, including technical specialties such as diagrammatic reasoning, interaction analysis, spatial cognition, and ergonomics. Most management consulting, whether sourced internally or externally, is also an improvement$_1$ activity.

But what about the things that we don't know about, but should? These pertain to the improvement of improvement, which is a third function that requires an entirely different context and process of thinking and working. Improving$_2$ activities are concerned with determining latent needs in future years, and how to develop improving$_1$ methods that will be effective in those environments.

It is these improving$_2$ activities, and how they provide leverage for improving$_1$ activities, that is not generally well understood. In most organizations, improving$_1$ and $_2$ activities are mixed together, and not sufficiently differentiated. As a result, fundamental architecture questions are handled side by side with incremental improvements, and the gap is just too great to allow for effective and systematic results. The intermediate improving$_1$ step facilitates the shared discovery of tacit knowledge pertaining to continuous and discontinuous innovations while allowing the improving$_2$ activities to explore the full range of future possibilities, which may be too abstract and far-reaching to be useful or comprehensible in the improving$_1$ and operations communities.

By analogy, we can look to the steerage of a large ship such as an oil tanker as a model of agility. The ship itself is the core activity, carrying oil from Alaska to California or Japan. To steer the ship and make it more agile, we have a rudder, an improving$_1$ activity. But the ship is so massive that were a helmsman to turn this rudder directly (with the help of a massive engine), the ship would still be very difficult to control. Hence, the rudder itself has a smaller rudder, called a "trim tab," which is attached to the trailing edge and enables the helm to maintain a finer control over the ship's course. The trim tab also creates a compounding effect for large course adjustments. The helmsman nudges the trim tab slightly to create a small eddy that induces the current to help move the rudder itself, which then turns the boat. The trim tab, used in conjunction with a global positioning system (GPS) for navigation, is an improvement$_2$ activity, a leverage strategy that "creates the capability to create."

Trim tabs are also used on airplane wings to help maintain stability amidst the turbulent winds of flight. Adjusting a small trim tab allows fine and efficient adjustments of large control surfaces.

Just as the trim tab is a leverage strategy for steering a ship or an aircraft, the three-level capability development model is a leverage strategy for steering the organization. Improving$_1$ provides the leverage to improve core activity, while improving$_2$ leverages improving$_1$ to achieve a compound improvement return with less effort.

In the language of learning theory, we would say that the three functions of operations, improving$_1$ and improving$_2$ are separate communities of practice, and Engelbart recognized that in the context of accelerating change, a strong capacity in each of these three communities is critical to successful adaptation.

In Engelbart's terminology, capability development is part of a broader process that he calls "bootstrapping," the progressive and systematic development of new capabilities that enable individuals, groups, and companies to succeed in markets even as they change.[2] In 4th generation R&D, we would call bootstrapping simply innovation, and note that while improving$_1$ is a strategy for continuous innovation, improving$_2$ is the method for discontinuous innovation. Improving$_2$ includes activities like the creation of new technical disciplines; for example, aeronautical engineering is a new capability that in turn creates new dominant designs (architectures) such as airplanes and the air travel industry.

Improving$_2$ is a way to discover that most valuable of gems, the things you don't know that you don't know, but need to know; these represent strategic capabilities: including scenarios you missed, hidden systems dynamics, and new rules for performance and value.

Note, also, that an improving$_2$ community group need not be a large number of people to effectively perform the "improvement of improvement." It is the process that matters.

Improving Productivity on Many Levels

Since productivity improvements are a fundamental concern throughout the organization, this three-stage leverage model can be applied not only to how individuals work, but also to how businesses are organized.

Defining the initial framework of the model makes it apparent that there are applications on four different levels: the individual; the department; the organization as a whole; and in the larger aggregations of industries with their supplier and customers, as well as communities, nations, and global society (see Figure 7.2).

Since productivity improvements begin with individuals, applying the three-level model is simultaneously a path of organization development and career development.

It would not be unreasonable to link improvements to compensation, although this must be done carefully to avoid creating unintended consequences. People will consistently respond in the context of how they are measured and compensated, and attempts to motivate them frequently backfire with unforeseen, counterproductive behaviors. At Sears, for example, linking the pay of auto mechanics to the

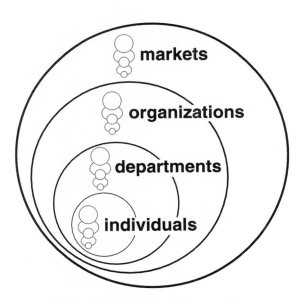

Figure 7.2 Capability Development on Many Levels. People working at the same functions at different levels are part of the same extended community, so the matrix function here pertains not to managerial oversight, but to the development and management of knowledge and capability.

replacement parts they installed led to—surprise!—unethical practices such as deliberate incorrect diagnoses and installation of unneeded parts.

HP cofounder David Packard observed the same dynamic by comparing his Japanese and American operations. "I had often seen the people in our operations at YHP [Yokogawa Hewlett-Packard, now Hewlett-Packard Japan] spend considerable time making sure that every adjustment was done just as accurately as possible. The same adjustments were done at HP in Palo Alto as quickly as possible to get them just barely within the limits specified. This came about because the people in Palo Alto were on profit sharing and people in Japan were not."[3]

While an individual may work in any of the three modes at any given time, significant progress at improving$_1$ or improving$_2$ comes about from the sustained application of effort. The questions, modes, and styles of thinking and working that are appropriate to improving$_1$ and $_2$ are quite different from that of day-to-day management, so while one can simultaneously think about and *observe* explicit activities in all three domains, one can effectively think about and *participate* at the critical tacit levels only by immersion in one or another at any point in time. Nevertheless, all three levels can be mixed, even on a daily basis, and this often happens with people who physically and mentally move between different communities of practice.

To develop substantial performance improvements, however, individuals need to remain in one role or another long enough to master the dialogue in that community and then contribute to it. How long varies from individual to individual, but the time frame can be managed as a function of improvements targeted both qualitatively and quantitatively. Annual intervals seem to work well for projects, since the aggregated tacit learning curves are substantial over such a period.

The need for immersion is also why a considerable portion of improvement$_1$ and $_2$ activities must occur in the same space and time as operations.

Whatever the time frame, leveraged improvement can be distributed, with each core operations function having its own improving$_1$ and improving$_2$ communities. Thus, there must be people specialized in improving$_1$ and others specialized in improving$_2$ within marketing, sales, manufacturing, finance, accounting, and even research and development itself, as well as all the other groups and subgroups that compose the organization.

The character of the improvement activities, however, will depend on where in the organization they are occurring. Improvement$_2$ activities that occur within the operations units are necessarily focused on the short term, and are incremental and continuous in nature.

Improvement$_2$ activities that originate with R&D$_2$ function under the chief innovation officer may be discontinuous innovation being developed in a much longer time frame. While the methods and processes used in both activities may be the same, the outcomes should be applicable at much different levels of the competitive architecture. Both, certainly, are necessary to maintain competitiveness (see Figure 7.3).

Regardless of the organizational level on which they are working, people engaged in improving$_1$ and improving$_2$ activities must have a detailed understanding of what the relevant core business activities are all about, how they are measured, and the tangible and intangible assets that result. To ensure a thorough mutual understanding, to develop their own capabilities, and to share their accumulated knowledge more widely within the organization, individuals move daily, weekly, or monthly among the three different communities to work for months or years on concurrent projects in each of them (see Figure 7.4).

Through people participating in different communities of practice and then moving to other communities, knowledge aggregation occurs between communities, supporting innovation and at the same time institutionalizing the fluidity and flexibility that helps resist the "bureaucratic imperative,"[4] the tendency of organizational structures to become rigid. Trust also builds through the mobility of people and their coparticipation as tacit knowledge is built and shared.

The language of core business activity, improving$_1$ and improving$_2$ can also be linked to Sveiby's concept of external structure, internal structure, and employee competence. While internal and external structure correspond to core activities, employee competence is the

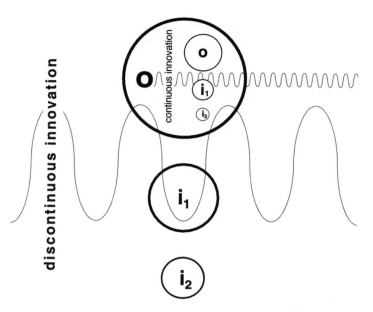

Figure 7.3 Continuous and Discontinuous Innovation. Innovation within operational units is necessarily continuous, while innovation sourced from the core improvement$_2$ community should be long-term in nature and concern the broadest levels of competitive architecture and the evolution of the marketplace, the domain of discontinuous innovation. Their methods, however, may be the same.

focus of improving$_1$ and technology and process are the focus of improving$_2$.

Thus, while the COO works on improving the internal and external structure of operations, the chief knowledge officer (CKO) is focused on improving employee competence using the tools that are balance sheet assets at the level of improving$_1$. The chief innovation officer is focused on providing leverage to the COO and the CKO through improving$_2$.

By harnessing the logic of the model, the concept of the three-level approach becomes a comprehensive strategy for developing organizational capability at many levels simultaneously, including the individual, the

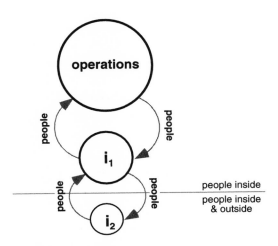

Figure 7.4 People Move between Communities. Applying the capability development model to the organization as a whole implies specialization, but not permanence. People move between communities, and by interacting with others in activities such as storytelling and the completion of actual business processes, they share tacit knowledge to build mutual understanding and new capabilities.

project team, teams of teams (development of the Boeing 777 was managed as more than 250 separate team projects), departments, core competencies, and the organization as a whole. The capability development model combines with architecture development for the implementation of 4th generation R&D.

Strategies for Improving$_2$

While the operations and improvement$_1$ functions are well understood, the role of improvement$_2$ has become clear only recently, and is therefore described in greater detail here.

Whereas the members of the improving$_1$ community must immerse themselves in the detailed specifics of operational realities, the members of the improving$_2$ community are more concerned with the broader long-term patterns and enabling capabilities in fields such as science, technology, learning, psychology, and sociology. Further, because new technologies and new competitors from converging industries arrive so unexpectedly into the marketplace, successful adaptation to exponential change requires a broader view of external trends. But since these trends may be far too vague to affect the near-term roles of operations management and improvement$_1$, the improving$_2$ community must concern itself with understanding the long-term issues that drive change in dominant design and strategic capabilities.

The improving$_2$ community is therefore focused on developing and refining plausible *and* implausible scenarios for the longer term, and on dealing with the high degrees of uncertainty and ambiguity that these scenarios will necessarily invoke. In conjunction with the evolving technologies that underlie the competitive architecture, these scenarios provide an early view of new capabilities that the organization may soon require.

Improving$_2$ work is concerned with exploring the limits of existing knowledge, technology, tools, structures, and processes, and then on prototyping extensions aggregated from relevant, diverse sources that are hypothesized to represent new value for customers. Because people working exclusively within the organization cannot do this effectively, their efforts must be supplemented by external viewpoints that can go beyond the tacit limits of experience that every organization imposes on its members.

Different kinds of external relationships enable the improving$_2$ community to transcend the supplier's organizational and mental boundaries to do effective research with stakeholders. Alliances between corporations, between companies and universities, and between companies and their customers down to the level of point-of-use dialogue with individuals are the three predominant methods to extend the reach of an internal improving$_2$ community.

Alliances between corporations enable them to share their research or to conduct joint research. Research consortia have proliferated in the United States since changes in government rules and regulations regarding collaboration were first made in 1984. Much of the impetus for changing the regulations has been led by Bruce Merrifield,[5] while Deb Chatterji recently published useful guidelines for alliances and other forms of partnership.[6]

Sometimes, even direct competitors will conduct research together when they cannot afford to do it on their own. The term "co-opetition" describes what happens when direct competitors work together, and it is detailed in a book by that title.[7] The three underlying pressures that lead to co-opetition are money, time, and intellectual property. It is expensive and time consuming to develop new technology, and those who do own critical intellectual property may nevertheless lack sufficient time and money to bring their valuable property to market. They team with competitors whose needs and capabilities are complementary, and find themselves cooperating in some markets and competing directly in others.

An excellent example of large company co-opetition is the relationship between HP and Canon. The two companies are development partners in the laser printer business, where HP's market share dominance is based on Canon's laser engine, even as they are direct competitors in the substantial ink jet printer business.

There are also compelling reasons to establish research and development relationships between large corporations and smaller companies, and even start-ups, where leveraged investments may give access to knowledge and increase options for the future.

Some small companies are pioneers in new markets and new technologies, and frequently their knowledge is also valuable to established firms. At Motorola, for example, Steven D. Leeke is Director and General Manager for Internet Content & Service Businesses of the company's New Enterprises group, which has invested $17.5 million in small companies during the past five years. Here he describes why Motorola is involved in making these deals, and some of the impact that it has on the company's strategic development activities.[8]

Making Deals at Motorola

To complement Motorola's R&D and business development efforts, we look into new businesses, new industries, new business models, new markets, new technologies where we can get in and invest in start-up companies, and where we can develop our own internal start-ups in these new areas.

Our organization has evolved over time, moving from more of a traditional M&A group to now much more focus on entrepreneurship, intrapreneurship to grow new businesses. This is really a small effort at gaining the know-how to enable us to go into new markets in a very big way later on if it turns out to makes sense.

The only way to get this know-how is to establish relationships with the people who have it. Many of the things that my group is responsible for are sufficiently new that there just aren't a large number of those experts available. If they're really good then they're fully occupied.

So we take minority stakes in start-up companies. We are on their boards and helping them, and in turn they're helping us learn and understand. We try to initiate complementary business strategies, we try to form business relationships across Motorola as well as across the companies we invest in. And we expect a big return on our investment in financial terms.

The single biggest challenge we have is fitting what could be a very aggressive deal-making capability in with the strategy concerns of a large corporation. Because of the nature of what we are trying to do, we are getting in to be in, not to get out fairly soon as a traditional venture capitalist might.

Impacts on Strategy Development

A lot of what we do is involved in transforming our company and transforming how people think. When we put together an Internet strategy, for example, the best thing that could happen is that we quickly lose the ability to count the impact of our particular group within Motorola. We know that it's big, but we can't totally identify it because people are taking on this new way of thinking and this new strategy as their own.

We certainly go through the accounting process once a year to look at what business revenues we can count as something that had a connection back to us. But if I had to look at the totality of our impact, that may actually turn out to be the minority because of the nature of what we are trying to do. We are trying to constantly be on the cutting edge of new markets, new opportunities, seeing the synergy between these new things with what we are already doing.

We go to Motorola's large, existing businesses and ask, "Have you guys thought about this?" When a multibillion dollar business suddenly turns in the direction of a new opportunity, it becomes very difficult to figure out our group's specific contribution, and not very important as well.

At Motorola, a natural question is, "What are the paging and cellular groups going to do about the Internet?" Our CEO set up a task force to examine the Internet, and I got concerned, so I simply said "Here is a list of questions that I think you should be asking." We routinely work with them both individually and in formal committees and task forces addressing those questions.

That is a large part how Motorola operates. The people at the top ask a lot of thorny questions about the critical issues, and provide guidance and an environment in which your business can thrive.

The focus of Leeke's work is on developing new capability for Motorola by playing the role of developer and facilitator of an improvement$_2$ community. In addition to accessing critical know-how and also achieving a satisfactory rate of financial return, one of the key capability benefits the group provides is improving the ability of senior managers to ask tough and relevant questions. In previous chapters, we have described "forced questioning" as one of the critical practices of managing for discontinuous innovation, and here the same method is applied in the development of new ventures, and in refining corporate strategy for established ones.

Having differentiated between a core activity, improving$_1$, and improving$_2$, we now recognize that "thorny" questions exemplify the improving$_2$ thinking process. They are a high-leverage method of ensuring that people are thinking about ideas that will extend existing knowledge toward the identification and creation of new value.

New knowledge is also a focus of colleges, universities, and other research organizations that have historically been engaged to perform research on contract for government and corporate sponsors. These agreements take many forms, including specific contracts for specific projects, and larger alliances for more complex activities. The MIT Media Lab, for example, is sponsored by dozens of corporations that pay an annual fee to have access to the knowledge that it generates.

When Media Lab research is used by corporate sponsors, the path is nearly always through the window of the sponsor's improvement$_2$ function, which (although these distinctions are not explicitly recognized) is intuitively where new knowledge is translated into a form that the organization can understand and apply.

Some management consultants also function as improvement$_2$ community members. Conferences that focus on long-term issues also play this role, as do formal and informal business networks that encourage interaction between diverse participants who may have useful and interesting surprises for one another based on the different perspectives that they bring to the dialogue.

As described extensively throughout the book, research relationships between companies and their customers are also critically important improvement$_2$ activities for both, particularly for discovering the tacit knowledge that is critical for improving products and creating new ones.

For example, during the development phase of the Lexus automobile, 3M adhesives engineers worked directly with Toyota engineers at the Toyota R&D facility in Japan to develop new methods of joining seals to body panels. When the design work was completed, the new methods and materials that resulted from the research helped both companies in the market. Risks and costs were reduced for both parties, and Toyota's decision on its vendor was made in favor of 3M during this joint research, far in advance of when suppliers are traditionally selected.[9]

This aspect of the three-level capability development model extends our description of the marketing$_2$ function presented in Chapter 4. When the customer and the supplier are working and learning together to define what is needed and what is possible, they are jointly applying the logic of improvement$_2$ to define targets for improvement$_1$ solutions that will impact core activities in both organizations (see Figure 7.5).

As long as their agreement allows it, either the customer or the vendor (or both) can also apply this new capability internally, to product platforms, products, and services that are not directly related to their partnership, and even to their own organizations (see Figure 7.6).

From the perspective of the core operations functions and improving$_1$ communities, the improving$_2$ community presents some challenges. To them, improving$_2$ is sometimes a dangerous realm of wild

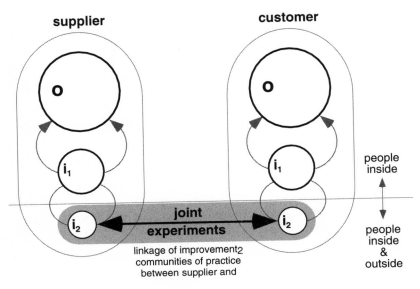

Figure 7.5 Mutually Dependent Learning in the Improvement$_1$ Communities of Supplier and Customer. Mutually dependent learning occurs by jointly defining the problem and the potential solutions. This leads to new capability for both parties.

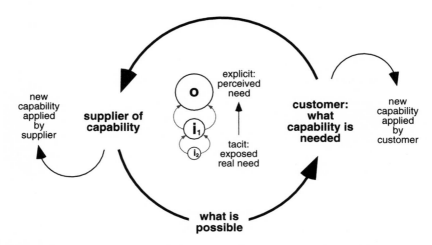

Figure 7.6 Mutually Dependent Learning with Customers Applied by Supplier and Customer. New organizational capability developed through mutually dependent learning can be effectively applied by the supplier and the customer to their own unique situations.

and threatening ideas that seem to belong in the distant future and have no apparent place in the real world of daily operations.

Whereas operations management and the improvement$_1$ communities work to distinguish between reality and illusion, and to apply performance improvements, the improving$_2$ community engages in creating and testing precisely the kinds of illusions and distractions that the others are diligently working to filter out. These illusions include new technologies and new markets that might or more likely might not come to be (see Figure 7.7).

To build trust between communities, travelers called Marco Polos move among the knowledge channels of all communities to share and build knowledge. These are some of the new leaders, working like composers and conductors in an orchestra, because specialized teams of multidisciplinary members, the musicians, are not enough by themselves to make the music sound right. They require the guidance and influence of the new leadership.

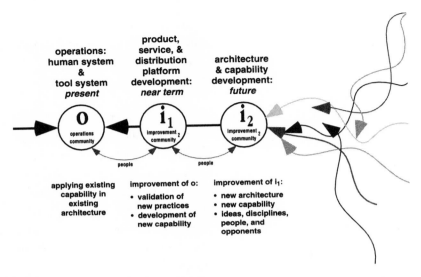

Figure 7.7 Capability Development. A conceptual straight line leads from the past to the current moment, now. This is our history, clearly illuminated and thoroughly comprehensible in the 20/20 perspective of hindsight. The moment of now is less thoroughly clear, but nevertheless things are happening and we can track those that stand out as important. Looking toward the future, however, we see a dramatically different image. For lurching toward us from the right is not a single, straight line, but rather an assortment of arcs and curves that converge toward the present from all different directions. The mastery of the particular forms of knowledge in each of the three communities of practice requires understanding of three different contexts. Moving between these communities therefore requires context switching.

From the perspective of now, Marco Polos see a future that is merely a collection of possibilities, some perhaps more likely than others, but a great many of them highly plausible and therefore requiring careful study. It is the responsibility of the improving$_2$ community to study these various vectors, to grasp in each one its unique character, and to understand the requirements that it might place on the organization were it to become reality.

The emphasis is on "might," for instead of one reality, the improving$_2$ community is constantly grappling with any number of possibilities and seeking to discern which one or ones will eventually converge into the now.

These differences are reflected in the different languages used by the members of the two communities. While members of the core business community speak in terms of performance ratios, cash flows, manufacturing capacity, transactions, and who did what today, improving$_2$ community members speak of likelihoods, of investments in new technologies and new markets as yet unproved, perhaps yet nonexistent, and worse still, perhaps never to come!

As noted in the Introduction, it has been shown in the realm of continuous innovation that it takes about 3,000 ideas to yield one substantially new and commercially successful product.[10] Research on patent submissions shows that of every 150 patent applications, approximately 112 patents are issued, but on average only 9 of those issued are considered to be of sufficient value that the owners are willing to defend their patent rights. Of these 9, less than one will ultimately be considered to be a significant knowledge asset to its owners, a strategic jewel.

The problem is that only time will tell which is the jewel and which 8 others to defend among the 112. Faced with these difficult dynamics and the necessity of getting it right on the first try, the members of the improving$_2$ community must attain at least a minimum of competence in perhaps 5 or 10 emerging technologies for each one that will eventually have significant impact in the marketplace.

Learning theory suggests that to grasp the critical tacit dimensions in any domain of knowledge, one must have actual experience of practice in the field. New competences cannot be developed simply by reading instruction manuals. Thus, new knowledge that is discovered in the improving$_2$ community will initially be conceptual and perhaps sketchy, but as more effort is invested, the knowledge and clarity of understanding grows. Time and money must be spent to understand new technologies, even though most of them will ultimately have no relevance.

The improving$_2$ community often appears to be the domain of lost causes, hopeless idealists, and fantasies. But it is also the domain of those individuals who foresee the future with astonishing clarity, and those who, remarkably, understand technologies that do not yet exist.

To add to the confusion, the person who fails one day may be the clairvoyant the next, and in any case it is nearly impossible to tell one from the other in the short term. Thus, it is the specific responsibility of the improving$_2$ community to explore many possible futures, knowing full well that among them all, only one or a few will ever manifest into significant business opportunities.

If it takes years to develop meaningful competence in a new technology—to master it to the extent that it can be applied in the development of marketable products and services—then waiting for new technologies to be introduced into the market by competitors is a dangerous strategy.

Tire companies that did not have the capacity to manufacture radial tires saw their market share plummet, but who could have foreseen the necessity to invest in radial tire technology in 1977 when it accounted for only 20 percent of the market (see Figure 7.8)?

Portfolio management as practiced in 3rd generation R&D,[11] when used with technology road maps,[12] improves the effectiveness of technology management when confronting the problem of many possible futures. The gaps that 4th generation R&D attempts to fill concern aggregations of technology and process platforms for existing and new dominant designs in each line of business. Establishing an improving$_2$ community is an effective way of dealing with this vital form of thinking, and giving it a place where it is always in context.

In the automotive industry, the research and engineering for new products can take decades, and as noted, a cadre of 700 Honda engineers is already working to develop more fuel-efficient gasoline engines and electric vehicles specifically intended to enable the company to be competitive in the market of year 2015.[13]

The unique character of this kind of development work can make discussions among improving$_2$ community members nearly incomprehensible to everyone else because almost everything that even

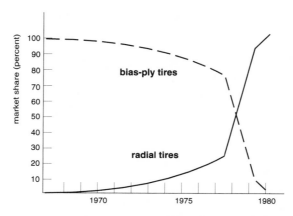

Figure 7.8 The U.S. Tire Market, 1970–1980.[14] A bias-ply tire manufacturer that waited too long to develop its competence in radial tires, incurred disastrous results. But who would have been willing to invest the necessary sums in new knowledge and production capacity when the market share in the existing market was **80** percent? Discontinuities present severe challenges to strategy formulation.

interests the improving$_2$ community represents some kind of threat to the core operation's current ways of working. These two groups are constantly in semantic opposition with operational differences lurking in the background in the form of changes that the improving$_2$ community will propose and the operations community may resist. While they need to communicate with one another effectively to be successful, communication is likely to be superficial if they are left to themselves.

Consequently, ensuring a steady flow of Marco Polos between and among these three communities is also a strategy for bridging the language barriers while building individual capabilities that become organizational capability. People engaged in learning through gaining direct experience of new ways of thinking and working gradually comprehend the key tacit knowledge that drives the innovation process at all levels.

Thus, managing the learning curve requires the understanding that just supplying information to people is insufficient, and information technology has its limits. Knowledge infrastructure engineering applies information technology differently from industrial engineering because it uses technology to augment people, not to replace them. People can, however, be replaced with new capability and new architectures that redefine markets and the means of providing value to them. Dominant design shifts frequently displace workers whose skills in now-obsolete paradigms no longer apply. The laid-off buggy-whip maker is a frequently cited example.

Thus, the distinction between the three communities does not impede the flow of ideas, but rather enables ideas to make the greatest possible contribution.

Overall, systematic use of the capability development model creates an appropriate context for distinguishing between three vital activities of improving organizational capability: refining existing organizational capability; developing new organizational capability, typically in the context of new architecture; and acquiring new knowledge that will help plan and direct future activities.

Measuring and Managing the Maturity of Capability

Since 1984, the Software Engineering Institute of Carnegie Mellon University has progressively refined a model that shows five stages in the maturity of individuals and organizational capabilities, defining the steps as Initial, Repeatable, Defined, Managed, and Optimizing. This model is now widely used to guide software development projects in hundreds of organizations (see Figure 7.9).

At companies such as Raytheon, Motorola, and Hughes Aircraft, application of the Capability Maturity Model is resulting in significant costs savings and productivity improvements.[15] Raytheon saved about $4.5 million in 1990 alone, and over a period of 4½ years, eliminated

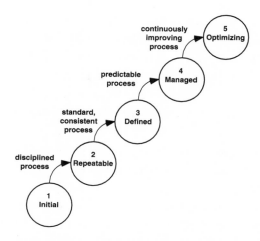

Figure 7.9 The Carnegie Mellon Capability Maturity Model.[16] Beyond Initial capability are Repeatable capabilities, wherein basic disciplines are part of an organization's function. Defined capabilities are those around which improvement processes have been defined, while Managed capabilities introduce more advanced qualitative measurements and management, and teams built around competencies. Finally, Optimizing capabilities reflect methods for continuous improvement of personal and organizational competence.

$15.8 million in rework costs. Hughes has reported a 5:1 return ratio on process changes implemented according to the model.

Motorola has found that advancing each level on the scale results in the reduction of cycle time by a factor of two (except from Step 2 to Step 3).

In the 4th generation R&D language of capability development, advancing from initial to optimizing capability occurs as unknown tacit factors become recognized, understood, and developed. The capability development model is both an expression of an optimizing competence, and a method for achieving optimization, and senior managers must be involved in all of these processes.

Whether they use this terminology or not, the three functions of operations, improvement$_1$, and improvement$_2$ are evident in all learning models, because each of these levels of learning must be present. Defining these three communities and assigning people to work within their guidelines is therefore a method of institutionalizing learning and the development of new capabilities not just in operations, but at the level of entire industries, communities, nations, and on a worldwide basis.

This problem has occurred in a most perplexing form in the semiconductor industry, where each subsequent generation of products and technology completely wipes out the previous generation, but due to the acceleration of technological development, each new generation does not last very long.

In our communities, the leadership and discovery centered at the great research institutions such as universities and institutes distinguishes robust economies from backwaters. Thus, Silicon Valley springs from Stanford and the University of California—Berkeley and, complemented by dozens of other educational institutions, becomes a source of tremendous economic strength for the region and the entire nation. Likewise, Harvard and MIT provide the intellectual spark for Boston's high-tech sector clustered on Route 128, and great universities worldwide are vital to the present and future well-being of the communities in which they are located.

Governments and intergovernment institutions such as the United Nations, NATO, the World Bank, UNESCO, UNICEF, and the Red Cross all represent still larger spheres of organization that function within the same capability development framework, just as the internal and external performance of all these organizations is improved, or could be, by adopting the model.

As they progress from the initial stage toward optimization, capabilities may also become an organization's core competences. These have been defined by Gary Hamel and C.K. Prahalad as areas of specialized expertise that are "the result of harmonizing complex streams of technology and work activity."[17] These are not simple knowledge sets, nor are they confined to individual disciplines. Core competences, rather, are aggregates of other capabilities, which as synergistic units provide unique capabilities in technologies, marketing, or operations.[18]

Defining any organization's core competences is essential to successfully choosing how new investment in learning should be focused, and in defining what knowledge should be developed internally and what should be obtained through relationships with other firms, customers, and universities through improvement₂ relationships.

Executive Time

Among the most important decisions that managers make are those related to the allocation of their own time. The oft-lamented tendency is to get drawn into the urgency of day-to-day affairs, neglecting by default important long-term issues. Ed Roberts has shown managers prefer consistent emphasis on problem solving in the core operations of manufacturing, marketing, and sales (see Figure 7.10).

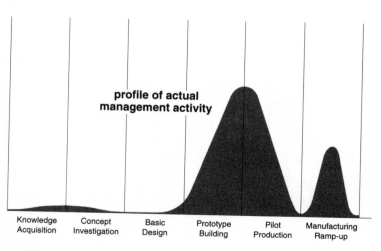

| Knowledge Acquisition | Concept Investigation | Basic Design | Prototype Building | Pilot Production | Manufacturing Ramp-up |

Figure 7.10 Management Activity.[19] A study of how managers spend their time shows a Consistent emphasis in prototype building, pilot production, and manufacturing ramp-up.

Unfortunately, Roberts also shows that the efforts of managers are most effective when applied in the improving$_1$ and improving$_2$ functions of research, design, and development (see Figure 7.11).

The time spent in research, design, and development has a high degree of influence on the future. Decisions made at these stages will shape the ability to create and deal with discontinuous change, and therefore with real future prospects. But when too much senior management time is spent on the downstream stages of manufacturing, marketing, and sales, their impact is only on incremental short-term results. Today, it has been suggested that only 3 percent of executive time is focused on the future.[20]

Managers generally prefer downstream activities because it is here that their efforts are tangible and measurable. As the majority of assets are now intangible, the misfit is glaring.

Behavior focused exclusively on operations is marginally effective, while efforts made upstream can provide leverage and compound benefits to long-term results. The time management agendas of senior managers must include the innovation-supporting processes of

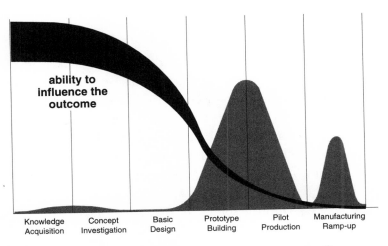

Figure 7.11 Effectiveness of Management Effort. Management efforts are most effective when concentrated in knowledge acquisition, concept investigation, and basic design, where their efforts have the greatest influence on the future.

defining competitive architecture and developing organizational capability through active participation in improvement$_1$ and improvement$_2$ communities.

If we compare the emphasis on latter-stage processes of corporate management with the normal conduct of sports, we see a surprising difference. In the corporation, little time is given to preparation and almost all the time is spent in the game. A typical manager may be lucky to spend an hour a week studying, reading, or otherwise preparing for the future.

In contrast, it is recognized in sports that the only way to win is by developing superior capability, and the only way to do that is to practice. From Little League to the pros, individuals and teams spend many hours in practice for every hour of game time.

But with little or no time invested in "corporate practice," learning is on-the-job training, with many attendant risks. Without conditioning, study, and strategy development, performance stagnates while pressure accumulates, often leading to organizational and personal problems, and medical problems as well: "The American Medical Association estimates that up to 70 percent of all patients seen by general-practice physicians come with symptoms directly related to unrelieved stress."[21]

Quantifying the risks of little practice, venture capitalist Judy Ross estimates that it costs $5 million to $8 million to educate a venture capitalist because that is how much money a novice is likely to lose in failed investments before learning how to make effective decisions.[22]

This is all compounded by accelerating change, which reduces the time frame in which managers must make decisions, and reduces the time available to make course corrections afterward.

But who would have thought that sports has realized a more progressive learning model than the corporation? And how has this come about? Part of the reason is surely the triumph of financial metrics in decision making, with the subtle but inexorable pressure to eliminate expenses that do not become assets.

All this suggests that a radical reallocation may be necessary for effective support of innovation, and the capability development model provides a useful framework here. While around 50 percent of every senior manager's effort must go into the playing of the game in the day-to-day operations, we suggest that as much as 30 percent of a senior manager's time can be well allocated to improvement$_1$ community practice activities that are focused on developing organizational capability. The remaining 20 percent or so is then invested in improvement$_2$ community activities that focus on identifying exactly what *new* capabilities an organization will require in the future, or in other words, designing the practice sessions for tomorrow and next season (see Figure 7.12). These activities include reading, study-oriented travel, continuing education, conferences, time in the company's own research labs and those of its partners, dialogue with customers, walking in the park . . .

For improving performance, the effective learning curve activities occur in improving$_1$ and improving$_2$ communities. The operations function is simply too busy getting work done to seek complex learning opportunities, or apply them in day-to-day work. Without improving$_1$ and improving$_2$, the curve remains nearly flat (see Figure 7.13).

Although the day-to-day pressures are severe, the number of people who are involved in operations work has been steadily declining for many decades. Partially as a result of delayering and of successful

Figure 7.12 Allocation of Management Effort in Building Knowledge and Doing Work.

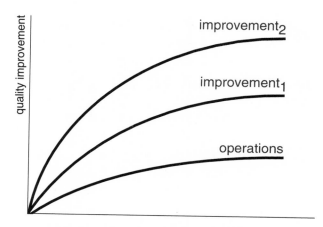

Figure 7.13 Learning Curves. Systematic use of the improvement$_2$ function yields the best learning curve, whereas operations alone achieves the worst.

automation in manufacturing and distribution, less people are now required for the same work. At the same time, more and more people are needed in other, knowledge-intensive aspects of the business.

Researchers at the Nomura Research Institute observed a significant realignment of effort from 1960 to the year 2000 and beyond, as more people become involved in development and management activities while fewer are required in manufacturing and distribution (see Figure 7.14).

To go along with the relayering of the organization to support more effective creation and management of knowledge, there is a general shifting of the effort required to sustain competitiveness. The capability development model suggests that as with the allocation of management time, the proportions of organizational effort may be in the range of 50 percent in operations, 30 percent in improvement$_1$, and 20 percent in improvement$_2$ (see Figures 7.15 and 7.16).

As people shift from operations roles to improvement functions, and as change continues to accelerate, the learning methods used become more diverse to reflect the many kinds of issues that have become critical to an organization's performance. Compressing the time for

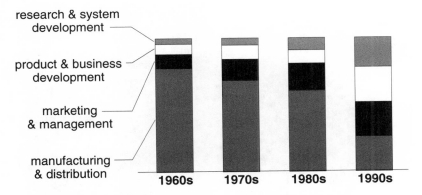

research & system development

product & business development

marketing & management

manufacturing & distribution

1960s   1970s   1980s   1990s

Figure 7.14   The Reallocation of People's Work.[23] From the 1960s through the 1990s, the distribution of people throughout the organization has shifted decisively away from manufacturing and distribution and towards many different kinds of knowledge work. This is one of the compelling sources of evidence for the shift from the industrial economy to the knowledge economy.

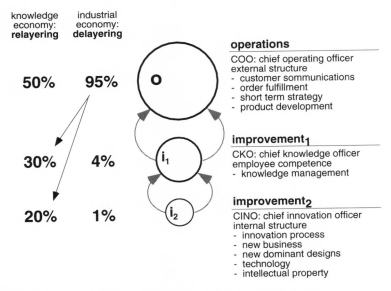

knowledge economy: **relayering**

industrial economy: **delayering**

50%   95%   O

30%   4% i_1

20%   1% i_2

operations

COO: chief operating officer
external structure
- customer sommunications
- order fulfillment
- short term strategy
- product development

improvement₁

CKO: chief knowledge officer
employee competence
- knowledge management

improvement₂

CINO: chief innovation officer
internal structure
- innovation process
- new business
- new dominant designs
- technology
- intellectual property

Figure 7.15   The Reallocation of People's Time. Just as we have relayered the structure of the organization to improve its capacity to deal with knowledge, so we also "relayer" the allocation of time to reflect the increased importance of learning in both the improving₁ and improving₂ modes.

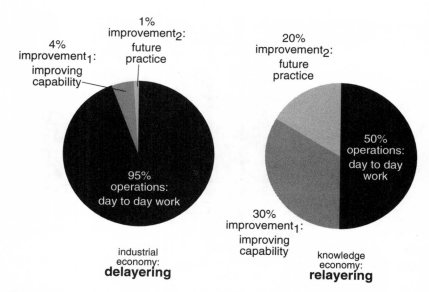

Figure 7.16 Reallocation of People through Delayering and Relayering. Relayering can also be described on a pie chart.

learning to occur is an important leverage strategy that can be provided through exercises in "future enacting."

Future Enacting

Besides the large investment that is required to educate a novice venture capitalist, another problem inherent in venture capital investing, as with all investing, is the long time it may take to find out whether an investment is good or bad. The problem is compounded because while waiting for the results from one investment to become evident, it is usually necessary to make additional investments based on an original set of as-yet unproved assumptions.

As both investment and innovation decisions are necessarily predictions about the future, studying that future through simulations, scenarios, and games is a way to "enact the future," to create knowledge in advance of when it would otherwise be developed, thereby compressing the time required for learning and improving the value of available knowledge.

Some future-enacting exercises are conducted through computer-based simulations, in which 5 or 10 years of activity may be compressed into a few hours. While the depth of experience certainly will not be comparable to 5 or 10 real years, many have found the practice extremely valuable because it helps them understand the behavior of dynamic, complex systems, and helps prepare them for the difficult decisions that they will eventually face. By getting quick feedback while testing differing strategies in realistic situations, a manager's experience base can be rapidly expanded.

"You can see steam venting from its tangle of pipes, two red flames burning off unwanted gasses, a tanker pulling into a nearby wharf with a load of crude oil. It's a complicated piece of hardware, this Chevron Corp. oil refinery, and you've just been appointed manager. Your first bright idea is to economize by feeding the refinery the lowest-quality crude on the market. Ouch. Your production reports tell you that the result of your decision is lots of low-margin oil products, including a huge load of asphalt which sells for even less than the crude used to make it. You have just created a loss on the refinery's books. Fortunately, you won't bankrupt the place and your career before you get things right, because the refinery is an electronic simulation, operating in full-color animation on personal computer screens at Chevron offices, . . . familiarizing Chevron employees with just what an intellectually challenging business they're in."[24]

Scenario planning is another simulation method for compressing time in the learning process, and as Ned Barnholt of HP noted in Chapter 6, it helped the members of the TMO to expose hidden assumptions and discover better ways to look at the changes in their industry.

Shell Oil also has a well-documented history of using scenario planning to accelerate the learning process. Sometimes using computer simulations and sometimes using dialogue, Shell managers developed skills at managing in a very complex market, and these skills contributed enormously to Shell's successful handling of the 1986 plunge in oil prices.[25]

Advanced forms of simulation are also practiced in the military, where the real learning happens in the life-and-death situations of full combat, and there are no second chances because wrong choices definitively terminate the learning process for the individual soldier. The only sensible way to practice, therefore, is in war games where you hold a real weapon and someone is really shooting at you, but where you can nevertheless "die" today and live to fight again tomorrow having learned from your mistakes.

War games and simulations are also effective for senior leaders to explore strategies without risking lives. With nearly two centuries of experience in being prepared to fight only the *previous* war, and being therefore consistently underprepared for the *current* war, the military has learned that it must find other ways to learn. (Not surprisingly, this problem also describes the classic behavior of corporations and other institutions.)

For this reason, the War Games Division of the Joint Chiefs of Staff organized an exercise in 1964 called Sigma II—an attempt to predict how the Viet Cong would react to a three-part American military strategy of border control, followed by retaliation for enemy aggression, and leading finally to overt military actions. "The result, in retrospect, proved uncannily accurate: 'Frustration in the air campaign compelled the introduction of U.S. ground combat units in South Vietnam. . . . Ultimately Sigma II predicted that the escalation of the American military involvement would erode public support for the war in the United States." [26] The results of the game, however, were ignored by the policy makers, and the military and societal debacle that resulted lasted a full decade, and still echoes today.

Having learned this and many other difficult lessons from its experiences in Vietnam, the U.S. Army now conducts large-scale battle simulations at the 100-square-mile National Training Center (NTC) in the Mojave Desert of California, where grueling war games follow a repeated daily cycle of planning, fighting, and reviewing what happened in order to learn from it.

For 14 straight days, a brigade of 3,000 to 5,000 soldiers fight mock battles against the NTC's resident brigade, and almost always loses. Every member of the "learning" brigade who has command responsibility, some 600 in all, are accompanied by an instructor who provides coaching and who also facilitates the review sessions at the end of each day, as the soldiers struggle to understand what went wrong and how they can avoid the same problems in the future.[27]

Simulations such as war games and computer games are powerful tools for developing capability, and in the language of learning theory they accelerate the process of accumulating useful experience. By integrating that experience with information and theory, individuals create useful knowledge that improves and leverages the dynamics of the learning curve. Hence, Major General Leon Laporte remarks, "I learned more at the NTC in 14 days than I learned in the previous 14 years of my career." [28]

Similar approaches are being used more frequently outside the military in all kinds of management situations, including hiring and training. At a new BMW factory in South Carolina, prospective employees work for 90 minutes on a simulated assembly line to see if they have the skills and team attitude that the company is looking for.[29]

At a new Cessna aircraft plant, prospective managers spend 12 hours simulating a day in the life of a busy executive who must deal with phones, faxes, and a bloated in box to show that they can handle the kinds of problems that will come up in the real plant.[30]

Simulations are even used in auto racing, where graphics software and computer-aided design programs are regularly included alongside fat tires and racing fuel. The Newman Haas racing team has spent as much time in computer labs as it has on the track, and using highly refined simulations, the team can predict how a car will perform under

20 different scenarios. All of this happens without using the car or the driver, leading team members to conclude that if you don't use computers to compress the learning process, then you have a serious disadvantage in competitive racing.[31]

Protocols: Learning How to Learn

The key to the effectiveness of the Army's NTC desert training ground is a process called the After Action Review. This process that makes the learning experience work, because it is here that decision making is analyzed and diagnosed so that tacit knowledge can be exposed.

Reviews are carefully facilitated to focus on identifying the mistaken underlying assumptions that led to errors, and on what can be learned for the future, rather than on assessing blame for what was done wrong.

Imagine sitting on a patch of parched desert with a group of hot, sweaty, dirty, and very tired soldiers at the end of another long battle day as they discuss why they lost in the last "battle" and what they will do differently next time (perhaps tomorrow). By discussing the factors that led them to take the actions they did, their unspoken assumptions are exposed, tested, and often corrected.

Hence, there is more than learning taking place in After Action Reviews. While the learning itself is critically important, even more important is that the NTC experience models the practice of "learning how to learn." By accurately reconstructing a sequence of actions taken under extreme stress, diagnosing the tacit assumptions and deductions that led to those actions, and then developing a new, better set of explicit models, soldiers learn how to learn in any kind of environment.

Only when you can self-diagnose your thinking process, explore your own tacit knowledge, discuss it with your collaborators, adopt new models, and then test them successfully in the real world can it be said that you know how to adapt to change. This is the very core of the capability development model as an organizational practice that may involve dozens or hundreds of people. The outcome is new architecture for competitive advantage, as well as the capability to achieve success in that architecture. The fact that the Army has developed a systematic practice that reaches to this profound depth of individual and team work models is fascinating, and it demonstrates an important quality that corporations and government agencies would do well to emulate.

The powerful leverage in learning how to learn is the same as the leverage in improving$_2$. This is the vital process of adaptation, and it is these methods and practices used at the NTC that are applicable in all aspects of military life, and outside it as well. The only way to adapt to a rapidly changing environment is to master the skill of learning how to learn, and this is precisely what is at the root of the NTC method. In the words of retired Col. James McDonough, "The National Training Center and the After Action Review are probably the two biggest changes in the Army since Vietnam. Everything follows from that." [32]

The effective discontinuous innovation practice will also consistently achieve a high level of success at learning how to learn because, after all, these two are really the same thing. When practiced in an environment of effective, open communication, the capability development model is an effective method of supporting both.

In the end, it is the openness of these dialogues that is an expression of the Army's commitment to learning, an openness based on interaction protocols that have specifically been established to support effective communication. It is more than a little bit ironic that the institution most associated with top-down command and control management has discovered that sincere, open-ended dialogue is the only way to be successful in unpredictable environments.

In some organizations dialogue covers everything *except* what is important, assumptions are scrupulously *not* exposed, differences of rank are used as weapons, and systematic learning does not take place.

Ed Schein's diagnosis of corporate resistance to change shows that when past experiences with change have been predominantly negative, people simply resist change. The reinforcement of negative patterns is much stronger at shaping beliefs than positive experiences, and a huge and sophisticated effort is needed to overcome entrenched resistance.[33] Safe environments must be created for positive learning experiences to occur, whose essential elements include, "(1) opportunities for training and practice, (2) support and encouragement to overcome the fear and shame associated with making errors, (3) coaching and rewards for efforts in the right direction, (4) norms that legitimize the making of errors, and (5) norms that reward innovative thinking and experimentation." [34]

Similarly, Chris Argyris has described the debilitating effects of defensive routines, and shows how they inhibit adaptation to external change. "One of the most powerful ways people deal with potential embarrassment is to create organizational defensive routines. I define these as any action or policy that prevents human beings from experiencing negative surprises, embarrassment, or threat, and simultaneously prevents the organization from reducing or eliminating the causes of the surprises, embarrassment, and threat. Organizational defensive routines are anti-learning and overprotective." [35]

Since external change is probably the number one cause of surprises, defensive routines that prevent organizations from recognizing and responding to these events and trends are leading causes of premature corporate demise.

Resistance and defensive routines must be overcome both as a matter of organizational structure as described in Chapter 6 and as seen in this chapter, focused management effort using appropriate methods such as the capability development model practiced in an open environment. Interaction protocols that transcend defensiveness are the equivalent of preventive healthcare.

Whether applied in music, sports, governance, or management, positive interaction protocols enable people to work together effectively by defining the rules for successful interaction, and these are necessary to accomplish anything of significance.

As mentioned, Boeing used more than 250 project teams to create its breakthrough 777 aircraft, which at an estimated development cost of $6.3 billion, is "the world's most expensive privately funded commercial venture." [36] To enable the teams to work together effectively over a period of many years, a meeting of everyone of the 5,000 people involved on the project was held once a week. But the biggest meeting hall that could be found held only 2,500 people. So the meeting was held twice, so that everyone could participate. The meetings were in fact highly structured interaction protocols, and the time invested in them was considered effective throughout the project.

We see the same dynamic clearly in the symphony, where the music is written by a composer while a conductor regulates the interaction of the members of the orchestra who actually play the music. Similarly, a highway is safe only when there are rules of the road that everyone knows. You drive on the right (or the left), and you stop at red lights and octagonal red signs. In contrast, if all drivers had to decide for themselves which side of the road to drive on and when to stop, the "system" would soon collapse into an impassible quagmire of collisions, which is occasionally what happens when the power fails and the signal lights go off.

Even hotly contested sporting events are played according to clearly defined rules that shape the character of the competition, and the opposing teams cooperate in following those rules even as they may compete ferociously for the title of victor.

In a sovereign nation, a constitution specifies who has which powers and which responsibilities, while among nations, the United Nations charter describes the protocols the nations observe in the international community. Such protocols work only because people know the rules, and they know that everyone else knows the same rules as well, and that all benefit from following them.

At the corporate level, designing effective interaction protocols is an important aspect of corporate culture, for even simple positive rules of human interaction, sincerely followed, distinguish organizations in which learning is embraced from those that are learning disabled. Openness, candor, and respect are among the critical qualities that sustain learning, and which sooner or later will lead to both continuous and discontinuous innovation.

CHAPTER 8

The Innovation Business Process

In the previous chapters, we have discussed many aspects of the innovation process as it is currently practiced, and as we believe it should be practiced to enable much more effective continuous and discontinuous innovation. Our prescription calls for 4th generation R&D and a new innovation business process to join already established businesses processes including product and service development, order fulfillment through the chain of supply, manufacturing, distribution, and customer communications. This new process supports innovation with the correct methods, activities, and allocation of resources.

Critical to success is the selection of appropriate targets for innovation, which requires identifying stakeholder requirements throughout the existing value chain of products and services and the new value chain of the knowledge channel. But as many of these requirements may be unclear and some will be conflicting, the way to resolve these conflicts is through mutually dependent learning involving participants from all relevant groups, including R&D, suppliers, and customers, plus distribution partners and other internal functional departments such as marketing, manufacturing, and finance.

Together, these participants must learn through iterations of design and testing which new capabilities will satisfy existing needs as well as latent, unmet needs among existing and potential customers, and in markets that do not presently exist. This is participatory research, in which stakeholders test product and service prototypes to define new competitive architectures, infrastructures, capabilities, dominant designs, and platforms for technologies, processes, and product families. And this kind of research forms the core of the new 4th generation R&D practice, the subject of Chapter 8, the final chapter of this book.

From 3rd to 4th Generation Practice

In 3rd generation R&D practice, the core processes are explicit customer feedback, corporate strategy, and discovery research in technology. Technology portfolios and road maps attempt to extrapolate the future performance of existing dominant designs, and together they constitute the input to product development activities (see Figure 8.1).

Since the primary customer feedback comes from sales data that reflect purchase decisions rather than use experiences, vendors remain considerably ignorant about latent needs arising from the performance of their products and services. And since the 3rd generation worldview is based on explicit needs, innovation is bounded within existing dominant designs. Existing competitive models are assumed to be true, and noise that is mixed with market signals is assumed to be unnecessary and is filtered out.

This drives a greater focus on the perceptions of need in existing markets, and the phrase "stick to your knitting" is often used to summarize its underlying strategic philosophy. The accompanying bounded rationale decision making and discounted cash flow finance models

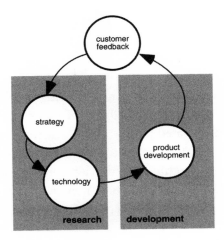

Figure 8.1 3rd Generation R&D Practice. Customer feedback is collected by the marketing staff in the form of surveys. The CEO then defines strategy, while R&D focuses on the development of new technologies, as driven by technology road maps. Together, these three become the basis of new product and service development.

lead to convergent thinking and at best, incremental, continuous innovation.

Under these constraints, this method has been consistently incapable of devising broad-reaching, discontinuous innovation, and today's innovation practice as a whole is in crisis. There is neither sufficient context nor sufficient conceptual development for knowledge aggregation at the theoretical level concerning the economy and the marketplace, nor at the practical level concerning the future of a specific firm.

But discontinuous innovation is precisely what is needed for survival in today's competitive markets, which are themselves characterized by discontinuities of many kinds. To accommodate rapid change while achieving discontinuous innovation, 4th generation practice adds key activities that were missing in the 3rd generation approach.

Prominent among these is one, mutually dependent learning, which we labeled in Chapter 3 as "marketing$_2$," (see Figure 8.2).

The method of marketing$_2$ is expressed in the knowledge creation spiral (see Figure 8.3).

Two, the delivery of knowledge to marketing people is done through the knowledge channel, also described in Chapter 3 (see Figure 8.4).

Third is the aggregated process of architecture, and fourth, capability development, which has been described in several chapters (see Figures 8.5 and 8.6). Architecture development is based on the identification of the relatively stable customer values and categories of value (Chapter 2); capability is the integration of people with knowledge, tools, technology, and business processes (Chapter 3); and capability development is the operations-improvement$_1$ improvement$_2$ process (Chapter 7).

The fifth practice is the shift from simple product development to the development of product, service, and distribution platforms and families, as derivative products can be developed from a common platform for as little as 10 percent of the cost of developing products when

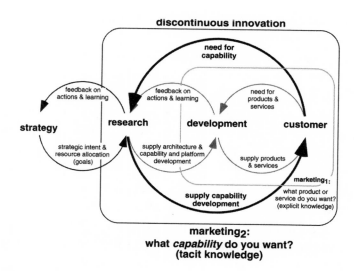

Figure 8.2 Marketing$_2$.

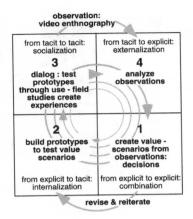

Figure 8.3 Knowledge Creation in Marketing$_2$.

not using the platform approach (Chapter 2). Cost savings of this magnitude are critical competitive factors, and therefore it is imperative to fully integrate the principle of platforms in the development process (see Figure 8.7).

Another is organization development achieved through the innovation cycle, in which development of architecture and capability is

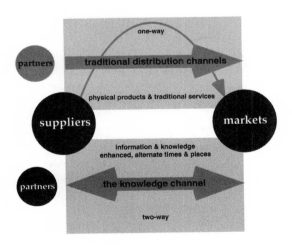

Figure 8.4 The Knowledge Channel.

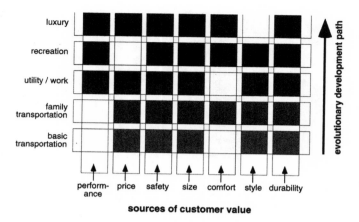

Figure 8.5 Architecture Development: The Value Matrix.

followed by a secondary cycle of platform, product, and service development (Chapter 2), which leads in turn to new consequences for architecture and capability, and the cycle continues (see Figure 8.8).

With the possible exception of the knowledge channel, these are all elements of what is sometimes called the "fuzzy front end" of the innovation process, which takes place prior to the more focused efforts

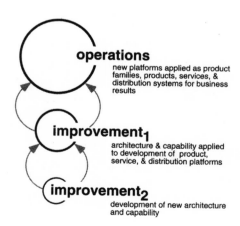

Figure 8.6 Capability Development.

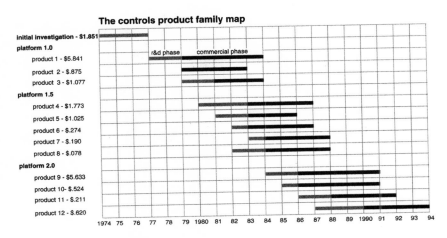

Figure 8.7   Product Platforms.[1]

of product development. It is here at the front end that the game of innovation is generally won and lost, because while most firms can competently execute product development, the correct *targeting* for development is more difficult and challenging. In this respect, the knowledge channel is part of the front end, as feedback from the marketplace received via the knowledge channel is an important part of the targeting process.

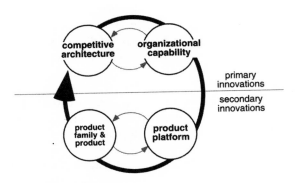

Figure 8.8   The Innovation Cycle.

The 4th generation calls for a considerable investment in knowledge aggregation and concept development to derive the proper context for effective innovation and effective decision making. Figure 8.9 shows the 4th generation R&D process.

Because this approach is based on tacit *and* explicit needs discovered through the knowledge channel *plus* tacit *and* explicit needs exposed in research, innovation is enabled to discover and define new dominant designs.

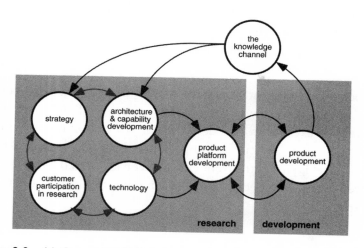

Figure 8.9 4th Generation R&D. Stakeholder participation (including customers) occurs in two places. Continuous feedback from ongoing use is channeled through the knowledge channel to support continuous and discontinuous innovation. Lead customers and other stakeholders also participate in research, where they experience prototypes of new technologies in new user scenarios, system architectures, and dominant designs, all in the context of real-world infrastructures. This method of mutually dependent learning exposes unmet, tacit needs, which then feed back to technology development. Exposed tacit needs also are inputs to strategy formulation. These converge to define the context of competitive architecture, organizational capability, and organization development. This synthesis becomes the basis of product, service, and distribution platform development, from which product families, products, and services then flow in existing and new dominant designs for each line of business.

Further, the knowledge channel provides customer feedback from both purchase and use, enabling a better understanding of tacit and explicit needs and expectations before, during, and after the sale, and throughout the life of the product.

Consequently, the top-level dialogue to target innovation is based not on technologies, but on end-user experiences and on application scenarios *enabled* by technology. Technology itself is understood to be the means of fulfilling latent needs rather than the means of creating and defining needs. As noted, it is the use of technology that matters now more than the technology itself.

The bidirectional linkage between strategy and the architecture, capability, and organization development process supports both a broader focus and at the same time better identification of suitable targets.

The approach assumes a discontinuous marketplace in which important signals are hidden in the background noise. Hence, existing models are assumed to be incorrect and evidence for new dominant designs is assumed to be present but as yet unrecognized. By looking outside existing dominant designs, the scope of innovation is unbounded, and divergent thinking becomes organizationally relevant. A broader scope of knowledge concerning both old and new technologies is aggregated within and outside the organization.

The difference, then, between R&D practices of the 3rd and 4th generations is predominantly in how innovations are identified and conceptualized. 4th generation practice recognizes that latent needs are expressed in tacit knowledge, and that dominant designs and platforms are the keys to targeting and developing successful continuous and discontinuous innovations. The innovation business process described here is a systematic method of dealing with these critically important abstractions.

With this new approach to the fuzzy front end in mind, we have now established the context in which to present the new business process for continuous and discontinuous innovation. To present the innovation business process as clearly as possible, the next section offers a concise introduction, which is then followed by a more detailed description that makes up the rest of the chapter.

The Innovation Business Process Map

From the first, faint glimmers of an invention or discovery that sparks the search for innovation, through its development, and finally in its full expression as a new dominant design or a new platform for technology, products, services, or distribution systems, the management of the innovation process must balance conflicting demands, contradictory data, complex requirements, and time pressure. While ideas may come from anywhere inside or outside, the dual goals of innovation consistency, and productivity mean that once recognized, they must be developed according to a defined series of steps that offers coherence and rigor while supporting discovery, creativity, and originality. Variation must come only according to the inherent requirements of an idea's potential, but not as a matter of serendipity or lack of management oversight and leadership.

Specific new knowledge must be created at each step, which means that certain kinds of questions must be considered and answered. Many of these questions are categorized and listed on the following pages.

The vital importance of identifying tacit knowledge and developing new knowledge (through learning) throughout the innovation process has significant organizational implications, as discussed in Chapters 5, 6, and 7. To support this on a widespread basis, the importance of cross-functional organization design is now well established, and Bob Cooper has shown that multidisciplinary inputs are critical to the success of new products.[2] Although his research refers specifically to product innovation, it can be applied to all phases of innovation, including architecture, dominant design, platform, product, service, process, and management. The participants in the process should therefore include a broad range of internal and external stakeholders whose diverse perspectives will be vital to success. They will include vendors, customers, technology partners, and members of the operations, improvement$_1$, and improvement$_2$ communities from all levels throughout the organization.

Their work will be organized by a process map that begins in Phase I with ongoing activity in the conceptual work of architecture, capability, and organization development, undertaken by the chief innovation officer leading the improvement$_2$ community. These models describe the organization as a whole, and as a competitor in markets that are likely to be characterized by rapid and discontinuous change (see Figure 8.10).

When a new event, fact, or idea emerges in Phase I that seems to embody the possibility of a new dominant design or platform, then a specific project begins to manage the development of this initial "seed." The specific output from Phase I is the transformation of this initial idea into the conceptual definition of a family of applications, driven

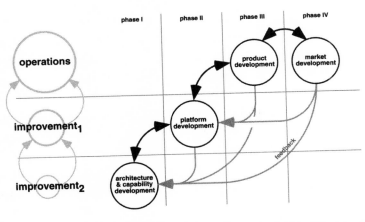

Figure 8.10 The Innovation Business Process, Summary View. The ongoing development of architecture and capability in Phase I leads to Phase II—development of platforms for technology, products, services, and distribution systems. Product development occurs in Phase III, followed by Market Development (Phase IV). As a project develops, the new knowledge created will also impact on the organization's overall models. Hence, a rich feedback between the phases is necessary to ensure coherence in a turbulent environment.

by a technology, product, service, or distribution platform, or combinations of platforms.

In Phase II, the improvement$_1$ community takes responsibility for the project, although many of the same team members may stay with it through this phase and the two subsequent ones. The R&D$_2$ and R&D$_1$ functions overlap as concept definition and development transitions to developing and testing real prototypes in laboratory and real-use environments.

Through progressive iterations of prototyping and testing among multiple stakeholder communities, the goal is the definition of a validated dominant design for new platforms, or new platforms for existing dominant designs.

From fully defined platforms, new products, services, and distribution families and methods are developed in Phase III by the R&D$_1$ communities in operational business units. At this point, the project shifts to focus on the development of product families and products following a more conventional path in a stage-gate process.

While the product family is being defined and expressed in specific products, services, and processes, the market development activities of Phase IV begin. This phase is an interconnected group of activities that includes revising the architecture framework to reflect whatever the product platform, families, and products have turned out to be, plus the ramp-up of full distribution, plus initiation of the knowledge channel for this particular project.

This structured process for innovation does not mean that you should follow this model with rigidity or invariance. The management of innovation requires considerable sensitivity, and one cannot expect to be successful by rigidly adhering to an organizational process or model because any model is necessarily a simplification of external realities. It may be far more appropriate, for example, to provide subtle support to a stealth project than to suffocate it in the name of corporate practice and policy.

As Chris Craft showed with his quiet support of the changes that Ken Cox proposed for the Apollo computer system, a public rebuke is not so bad when it is followed by private encouragement, and this can be a useful way to get important work accomplished in a complex management environment.

Since it is a principle of the capability development model that people should move between the operations, improvement$_1$, and improvement$_2$ communities to further develop their own capabilities, it is also reasonable to move people whose stealth projects originate in operations to the improvement$_2$ community for a time to afford them the proper support to explore new concepts and architectures.

In addition to the emphasis on concept and context development in the form of architecture and capability development, the innovation business process shows how responsibilities are distributed in each of the three different communities as described in the capability development model. This is also a break with the 3rd generation approach, which lacks the intermediate improvement$_1$ step between improvement$_2$ and operations (see Figure 8.11).

The jump from pure technology straight to product is too great. The language of the technologists is so different from that of product development that there is a critical lack of context in product development, opportunities for platform development are missed entirely, and critical feedback loops are disabled.

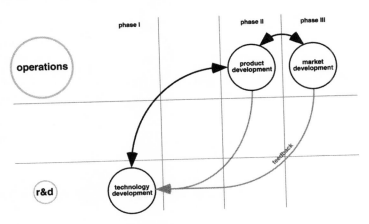

Figure 8.11 3rd Generation R&D. In the 3rd generation R&D process, technology leaps directly to product development, omitting conceptual development from the improvement$_2$ community, and platform development at improvement$_1$.

Each phase of 4th generation R&D plays an important role in the overall process, and each requires different capabilities and core activities. Phase I is primarily conceptual and requires the ability to see the overview, to profoundly grasp the essence of strategy, and to develop an view of the future. Phase II relies on the ability to apply platform thinking and to facilitate the definition and development of organizational capability, including knowledge, while Phase III requires strong skills in product development and Phase IV is focused on marketing, operations, and education, both internal and external.

These phases also require different approaches to finance and decision making (see Figure 8.12).

While ongoing activities in Phase I to maintain the architecture, capability, and organizational models are funded as ongoing research, Phase II is a specific project that is financed using staged options so that appropriate, incremental commitments can be made that reflect the development of validated capability and the discovery of latent market needs.

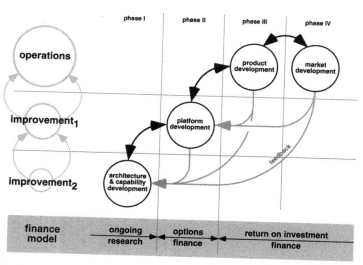

Figure 8.12 Investment and the Innovation Business Process. Phase I is funded as ongoing research, Phase II is based on options finance, and Phases III and IV are conventional ROI finance.

Phases III and IV are funded according to conventional return on sales and return on investment criteria, as innovations at this stage must survive on their own merits as providers of value to stakeholders and a sufficient return on the capital employed.

In each phase and each step, specific kinds of questions must be asked, and many of these are presented in the following detailed description.

The Innovation Business Process— Detailed Description

PHASE I AND STEP I. ARCHITECTURE, CAPABILITY, AND ORGANIZATION DEVELOPMENT

Fumio Kodama notes that most organizations do a poor job of what he calls, "gathering intelligence." Companies, he suggests, "typically focus on immediate competition and rely on a limited number of channels for collecting information. They lack the breadth of knowledge necessary for a technology fusion strategy. . . . The visible competitor is a known quantity. . . . Invisible competitors, on the other hand, are unfamiliar and unknown. They are companies from outside the industry that possess a technological capability that could be a threat if turned to new markets. . . . Of course, monitoring invisible competitors is not only a good defensive strategy but also a way for companies to spot innovations worthy of investment. [Note the role of Motorola's New Enterprises group, mentioned in Chapter 7.] But keeping tabs on an ever-growing diversity of technologies demands sophisticated intelligence gathering that includes both a formal and an informal capability. The formal capability includes such things as a network of offices around the world to monitor patent applications, a process for sifting through volumes of published information, and a system for finding innovative companies and technologists. Informal systems are based on tacit understanding by employees, from senior managers to research assistants, that they have a responsibility to the company for gathering and disseminating technical information, wherever it may reside."[3]

By defining the role of the improvement$_2$ community under the chief innovation officer to include responsibility for development of architecture, capability, and organizational models to feed platform development, and by including fundamental technology (as R&D$_2$) and expeditionary marketing (as marketing$_2$), the ongoing integration of these critical knowledge streams in the pursuit of innovation is thus reflected in the design of the organization itself.

With the participation of people from the improvement$_1$ and operations communities, the improvement$_2$ community maintains a continuous scanning and analysis activity, systematically surveying both previously specified and interesting but perhaps unspecified domains in search of new knowledge that may have impact on the future of the organization and its industry. New ideas percolating in the ongoing communication with customers via the knowledge channel are also monitored continuously.

Sometimes platform development can be stimulated by the call for new ideas at the corporate level. Since 1927, the perceived need for new ideas at Du Pont has been repeated in four consistent cycles of research, discovery, and development of about 17 years each.[4] At the beginning of each cycle, a formal request for new ideas brought forth an abundance of possibilities that led to breakthrough products in many areas.

The goal that guides the filtering of new ideas is the integration of new discoveries with defined corporate strategies and strategic intents, and existing and new tacit customer needs. When any of these or any combination suggests the possibility of a new dominant design

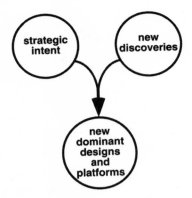

Figure 8.13 Interacting Knowledge Sets. Innovation projects begin when strategic intent and new discoveries intersect and suggest the possibility of new dominant designs or technology, product, service, or distribution platforms.

or product platform, focused concept development is initiated to assess and develop its potential (see Figure 8.13).

There are many different ways to approach the problem of intelligence gathering, and what is critical is not the one you choose, but that you choose one that consistently brings you a diverse mix of data that do and don't fit your models, that force you to reevaluate, to rethink, to doubt, and to redouble your efforts at concept building and testing.

In his important *Innovation and Entrepreneurship*, Peter Drucker suggests 12 different sources that may offer challenging data, and each of them can be systematically examined for clues about the emerging future:[5]

1. The unexpected success.
2. The unexpected failure.
3. The unexpected outside event.
4. Incongruous economic realities.
5. Incongruity between reality and assumptions about it.

6. Incongruity between perceived and actual customer values and expectations.
7. Incongruity within the rhythm or logic of a process.
8. Process need.
9. Industry and market structures.
10. Demographics.
11. Changes in perception.
12. New knowledge.

The first six of these sources present opportunities to learn about assumptions or sets of assumptions that may have been erroneous. The sooner such assumptions are exposed the better, although as Drucker notes, it may not be easy to accept unexpected successes if they indicate errors in management thinking. On the other hand, they usually offer abundant opportunities for successful innovation.

Unexpected and incongruous occurrences are frequently caused by changes in customer need or customer expectations. These, in turn, are often caused by the psychological and sociological impact of new products and services in the marketplace, whose very existence changes how customers feel about older products and services. Products and services that were highly desirable in the recent past may be displaced at any time by newer ones that offer a better value proposition.

Frequently, a new value proposition results from new capabilities enabled by new technology, but it can also result from new forms of architecture including distribution (or distribution platforms). Wal-Mart, now the largest retailer in the United States, exemplifies this attribute. As Amazon.com has shown, it can also result from new channels of communication such as the knowledge channel.

The success of any new product or service that, from the customer's perspective, is continuous with what has been available before is likely to be based on improvements along known performance parameters. However, products and services that are discontinuous and represent a break with the past will be successful when they address previously unrecognized and unmet needs. Such needs originate with the unexpected or incongruous when the perspective of customers or vendors concerning what was and was not possible is radically reformulated due to unforeseen events and technologies.

The seventh, eighth, and ninth sources—incongruity within the rhythm or logic of a process, process need, and industry and market structures—frequently arise in relation to the evolution of technologies and their impact on competitive architectures.

They also come about due to the uneven pace at which various technologies develop and then impact on each other and the marketplace. In general, new technology is the predominant driver of structural change because it creates new performance possibilities that change the value proposition in a marketplace, often by leading to new dominant designs.

Demographics and changes in perception (items 10 and 11) are factors of human interactions and the evolution of human culture. Due to increasing pressures as economic activity shifts from industrial practices to knowledge practices, dislocations become progressively more common, creating a turbulent environment and also creating new kinds of opportunities.

Drucker lists new knowledge last because although this is in his words the "superstar" of entrepreneurship and the topic that receives the attention, the money, and the publicity, the other 11 areas offer equal or greater potential. He suggests that the new scientific knowledge that comes from fundamental breakthroughs is "temperamental, capricious, and hard to manage," and although this is certainly true, it is also true that new knowledge about tacit customer needs and expectations may be just as valuable and far easier to utilize effectively. All innovation is a learning process through which people create the relevant new tacit and explicit knowledge that will enable them to coax ideas to maturity.

Drucker goes beyond his list of 12 sources to describe a concept that has been applied on a widespread basis. He advocates a policy he calls "systematic abandonment," through which "whatever is outworn, obsolete, no longer productive, as well as the mistakes, failures, and misdirections of effort" are abandoned. "The enterprise must put every single product, process, technology, market, distributive channel, not to mention every single internal staff activity, on trial for its life. It must ask: Would we now go into this product, this market, this distributive channel, this technology today? If the answer is 'No,' one does not respond with, 'Let's make another study.' One asks, 'What do we have to do to stop wasting resources?' "[6]

The research activities involved in investigating these 12 areas constitute fundamental activity that must be done systematically. The new discipline of knowledge infrastructure engineering suggests that a great deal of this work and the models developed in this process should be made accessible to everyone in the organization, and may be effectively presented in a learning center where data, information, and knowledge can be displayed so that useful connections between disparate items can be easily explored. In another book, we have referred to this as a "Management Center," a place where conceptual development and ongoing management activities coexist and support each other effectively.[7]

In the ongoing assessment, three aspects of discovery and conceptual development are linked and concurrent. The implications of an idea are explored in terms of the competitive architecture, in terms of organizational capability, and in terms of its potential as the basis of a new dominant design or platform. Many possibilities will be entertained in this way, as much of this is done informally by people pursuing various research threads. For ideas that possess significant potential after being examined informally, there also comes a time for a formal evaluation that must be based on a comprehensive business framework.

THE FORMAL INQUIRY

Formal inquiry for selected ideas covers many factors, including customer application; market size; competitive architecture; organizational capability; platforms for product, service, technology, process, and distribution; and impact on stakeholders. Questions and issues pertaining to each of these factors are listed in this section.

Defined categories of customer value help drive the process. There may be 5 to 10 broad categories of value, with each category consisting of 10 to 50 or more value attributes. In addition, there may be as many latent needs as there are perceived needs, or more.

Technology road maps and technology portfolios also provide useful reference points. In each line of business, the functional components in current products can be identified and mapped to the evolution of the technologies that enable these functions. Portfolio managers can perform competitive and life-cycle analyses of these technologies to predict future developments, setting the stage for the filing of patent applications as early as possible.

Targeting for the development of technology is based on defining what new technologies can be developed or acquired that will substantially add value in existing or new categories. Generally, attributes fall into broad categories that directly or indirectly affect human performance and the supporting infrastructure. These categories are the candidate dimensions of an architecture for technology platforms. Hence, a key question is, What categories of product attributes have to change to drive value?

The formal assessment of ideas within this framework is a detailed process that requires the participation of many individuals who are brought together specifically for this exercise. Their perspectives must represent the many different viewpoints that will have to come into alignment if an idea is to make it through the long development process and become successful in the market. Here are some of the questions that they must ask.

Customer Application

What is the scenario that describes how customers would use the innovation?

How would they feel about it?

Would it be perceived by them as continuous or discontinuous?

How would it be installed, and what infrastructure would be required?

What functional changes would be required of customers?

What would the emotive factors be?

What degree of market development will be required to make it a success?

Market Size

How big is the market?

Does it consist of new market segments that must be hypothesized, or existing segments whose behavior is known and can be studied and referenced?

How large is the upside opportunity if the idea were to become successful in the marketplace?

When customers have already experienced the same kinds of products and services that the innovation proposes, market research can be used to assess the size of the market, and thereby scale the investment that would be required for its development and diffusion. On the other hand, if an innovation is something that will be new to the world and there is no current experience for comparison, then traditional market research will not suffice to assess its potential, conventional discounted cash flow finance cannot fund its development, and the decision-making process cannot rely on conventional rules. Direct customer use of prototypes or simulated prototypes in expeditionary marketing (marketing$_2$) is necessary to invoke and expose latent needs.

Competitive Architecture

Ideas must also be evaluated in the context of the existing competitive architecture to determine whether they may or may not have importance for the future of the organization:

Does this idea extend the current vector of the market, or does it represent a new vector?

Further, is it a new s-curve, or does it simply extend an existing one?

Is this idea going to happen anyway, regardless of whether our company chooses to do it, or does it depend on our unique capabilities and positioning in the market?

Are there other, competing ideas or technologies that might better fulfill the underlying customer problems that this idea addresses?

Why would we target our efforts in one channel versus another?

Do our predilections reflect underlying value to our customers, or simply internal biases that have come about based on organizational structure or the serendipity of history?

Some ideas will fit within the existing architecture as continuous and sustaining innovations, and these must be evaluated in terms of the relationship between cost to the vendor and benefit to the customer. Other ideas propose fundamental changes in the current architecture of processes and relationships in the market, so these will have to be viewed as discontinuous or disruptive. If fully developed, therefore, will these innovations lead the marketplace where it ought to go, and will they lead this company into markets where it ought to be?

Organizational Capability and Structure

Ideas that are determined to be worthwhile in terms of the architecture must then be assessed for their impact on organizational capability.

Does the needed capability presently exist, or must there be an investment in the development of new capability?

Is this new capability attainable?

Would it be worth the required investment?

Will it be a sustained source of value to the organization over the long term?

Can this product or service be marketed, sold, and delivered using existing organizational structures, or are managerial innovations required in the form of new departments, new divisions, new business units, or fully autonomous spin-off companies?

Can these costs be earned back?

Research and Business Development Process

What new research and business development activity must be undertaken to realize the idea?

How long is this likely to take, and how much is it likely to cost?

What are the incremental steps that can be taken in the research process that can be funded as options?

What external research will be required to fully develop the idea?

Can the success of that research be assured?

How great is the down side risk of failure if the research shows that the idea cannot be accomplished?

Product, Service, and Distribution Platforms

Can this new product or service be developed on existing platforms, or must new ones be developed?

In either case, what would the range of development costs be?

How will this impact on existing platform configurations?

Will it complement them, or render them obsolete?

Stakeholder Impact

How would this idea impact our various stakeholders, including our vendors, employees, investors, and the communities in which we operate?

Would implementation of this idea put us into competition with key suppliers?

Would this put us into competition with our investors or business partners?

If so, how would they respond?

Would it lead to significant changes in our workforce requirements?

Could our people learn the required new skills, or would it be necessary to displace them?

How would this impact on labor relations and existing labor agreements?

How will this be perceived in our community?

Will people welcome this as a worthwhile activity, or condemn it as
wasteful, destructive, or immoral?

Will we need to deal with significant environmental concerns or
problems?

Over the long term, what impact will this have on public relations?

Together, the answers to all these questions and others like them
compose an application and development scenario—a story that compares what is with how the world might differ if the possibilities inherent in this idea were to be realized. Sometimes the possibilities of
a new product are also visualized in detail using virtual reality or 3D
CAD to produce stills or animated video.

These scenarios and images may then be presented to possible research and development partners and lead customers or early adopters
to obtain their views. The question can then be asked: Are these customers willing to participate in the project early on so that their tacit
knowledge can be brought to bear during the subsequent stages of development, and so that their enthusiasm for the innovation will help
sustain it through subsequent developmental stages? If they will not participate, how should this be interpreted? Does it kill the project?

Independent laboratories can also be engaged to make their own
assessments.

As a synthesis of this inquiry, a reasonable assessment can be made
of the ultimate value that the innovation could offer to customers and
to all other stakeholder groups. The enthusiasm and creative tension
generated at the moment of invention may then be validated, rein-
forced, and amplified into an organizational imperative, or neutralized
into ambiguity, or even flatly contradicted and fully deflated.

In the latter case at this step or any other, definitive negative results
are cause to unhesitatingly terminate the project. In Chip Holt's view,
you must be prepared to terminate a large percentage of ongoing projects. "On average, the industry terminates 35 percent of everything
they identify in the option period. You need to reward the detection of
losing propositions instead of killing the chief engineer who comes to
corporate and says that it won't work. You need to have a huge basket

of alternatives. . . . Tell me on a scale of zero to one how unique this technology is. Is it something nobody else owns? Will it change the rules? Can we buy it? Give us on a scale of zero to one how probable you think this technology will be, and its yield."[8]

If a project is terminated, a wrap-up activity completes a full documentation of the process and its results, as this record may be useful for evaluating future ideas, or for resurrection should a future change in the marketplace return the project to relevance.

From the standpoint of learning and capability development, the exercise should have been valuable regardless of outcome, because asking and answering this demanding suite of questions can itself be a tremendous source of enduring learning value for the participants.

When an assessment team has been through this exercise a number of times, and they have had the chance to calibrate their findings in each case with the subsequent outcomes, they get closely attuned to the character of the markets they serve. This is a source of value as it is also a potential weakness. For as much as it is necessary to get close to customers, it is also necessary to keep some distance to avoid being swamped by changes resulting from new technologies and new competitors that customers do not foresee and do not plan for.

The ideas that have made it through this gauntlet become the innovation projects on which the future of the organization is to be built. As they have been evaluated with a focus on the question of competitive architecture, the evolution of the company then becomes a matter of managerial intention and design rather than the happenstance of events. Hence, the company's roles in the marketplace become the context in which it is meaningful to define strategic intent, and to see that intent carried out in the form of innovation.

Since a company's view of this architecture is both explicit and widely understood within the organization, it becomes a source of coordination and coherence among many different business units and communities of practice that actually constitute the organization, even as the pace of externally and internally driven change may be very fast.

In addition, the explicitly stated architecture becomes a framework through which each individual and each manager can develop new organizational capability in alignment with strategic intent. Each individual can then assess the meaning of change, and can direct their day-to-day work and long-term career paths accordingly.

Finally, the explicit architecture includes an expression of its underlying assumptions. Since they are exposed, anyone who discovers a discrepancy between an assumption and reality has a meaningful basis from which to raise strategic questions. Thus, the intelligence gathering function is not only directed outward, but also looks inward at the fit between strategic intent and marketplace reality.

Concept development ends and platform development begins when new questions, problems, ideas, discoveries, visions, and needs are indeed found to be the correct means to achieve strategic goals. When the interaction of these two knowledge sets suggests the concept of a new dominant design or product platform, this provides the seeds from which technology, tools, knowledge, new products, services, processes, and management practices may eventually sprout and mature.

When an apparently worthwhile idea does emerge, its very existence is an expression, whether tacit, explicit, or both, that current reality contrasts in some significant way with what could or should be. As explained in Chapter 3, this contrast between what already exists and the vision of a possible new future is often experienced as creative tension. This tension literally creates the compulsion to transform a seed into its full potential whose existence will change the world, or at least a part of it (see Figure 8.14).

The moment of insight from which an idea emerges, and the articulation of "difference" that the idea embodies, is therefore the very creation of a problem, and is the first step on the path to innovation. The stronger and more distinct the contrast, the stronger the motivation to proceed through the subsequent stages to bring the idea into reality.

Creative tension at first drives a hunger for knowledge, the need to learn about the difference between what is and what should be. This knowledge probably does not reside in any one person. Rather, the solution will come through the integration of diverse knowledge held by diverse people, a social process of mutually dependent problem solving

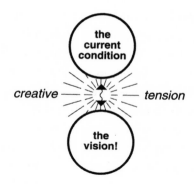

Figure 8.14 Creative Tension.

among communities of practice. Since the diversity of the coparticipants and their knowledge is vital to success, such diversity must be protected throughout an organization.

Similarly, the ambiguity that arises with creative tension must also be protected, although many people will feel a strong need to suppress it. Because it makes them thoroughly uncomfortable and the tension is too difficult to live with, managers too often make decisions in the form of a vote that relieves the tension. The choice they face, however, is between alternative courses of action that are insufficiently formulated, resulting in a choice no better than a guess.

In fact, there will always be a gap between what is and the possibilities for the future. Living with that gap, and the diversity of thoughts and opinions it engenders within an organization, helps to sustain the organization's emotional and intellectual vitality even while continuous work is done to transcend the gap.

The world-renowned Toyota production system, for example, was driven by a single vision, but developed over a period of more than 30 years. Progressive improvements were made by generations of workers, and even today a Toyota employee would tell you that the system is not complete, for there are always more needs and opportunities for improvement.[9]

On the other hand, if creative tension ever disappears from an organization altogether, it may indicate that permanent stagnation has set in.

As long as there is a robust and open dialogue about concepts and models, driven in part by research activities and in part perhaps by after-action reviews of ongoing activities throughout the organization, stagnation is unlikely to occur. Concepts continue to be studied and aggregated, ideas grow and mature, and at the point when creative tensions crystallizes around a particular idea, a need, or discovery, along with the possibility of its application in the market as a new dominant design or a new product platform, then Phase I is complete with respect to that particular idea, but the improvement$_2$ community continues as an ongoing function with many other possibilities that are not yet ready for action.

Having brought the idea to the inflection point of its development, the improvement$_2$ community moves on to look for the core concepts that will make up the next generation (see Figure 8.15).

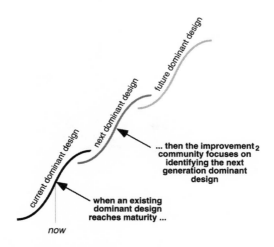

Figure 8.15 Improvement$_2$ Community Looks for the Next S-Curve. When an idea has become a mature dominant design in the marketplace, the improvement$_2$ community shifts its attention to the search for the next generation dominant design.

PHASE II. PLATFORM DEVELOPMENT

In 4th generation R&D practice, an iterative process is used to define exactly what tacit knowledge is currently needed for continuous and discontinuous innovation, and this is one of its most critical aspects. Each test and each step answers some questions, and raises others that must be answered in subsequent steps.

Designing the sequence of experiments through which questions are discovered and answered is done in the improvement$_1$ community in three steps. First, initial prototypes are tested by researchers and customers in research laboratories, followed by internal testing also by customers, and then full-scale external testing in actual customer environments with all the necessary infrastructure elements in place (see Figure 8.16).

Some observers recommend parallel processing or concurrent engineering in this phase and in Phase III. This may be feasible for certain kinds of innovations, particularly those that are continuous and sustaining.

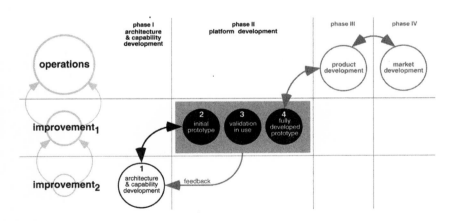

Figure 8.16 The Innovation Business Process, Phase II. In Phase II, the three steps of initial prototype, validation in use, and the fully developed prototype are done sequentially to ensure that all critical tacit knowledge is captured. Each step contains many iterations and may be done quickly, but it must be completed before beginning the next step.

For discontinuous or disruptive innovations, however, the learning curve is so steep that it is often better to follow a sequential path. While this may take longer, the full implications of a fundamental innovation may be hidden, and only a steadily building knowledge base will expose the real value. Each new discovery leads to new questions and opportunities that will not arise if taken out of sequence.

As with economic, learning, and market theory, an innovation in development is also a theory, so concept development must account for all observations. Its validity cannot be accepted if there are any unexplained or contradictory data. Although the iterative learning loops can be rapid as long as discrepancies do not emerge, this means a fundamentally sequential process in platform and product development.

For discontinuous innovation, the key in this phase is the discovery of the tacit knowledge of stakeholders through real experimentation. Until such knowledge is gained and understood, it is premature and possibly wasteful to push a project to the next stage of development.

To capture the tacit dimension, members of the research team observe firsthand and also record these tests on video. These are analyzed to find important tacit knowledge using techniques such as video ethnography and interaction analysis. Further, unconscious behavior by users and unnoticed but important interactions are observed. Using video allows the observers to leave the premises, so the impact of their research can be minimized.

In the concise history of airbags discussed in Chapter 4, on the other hand, the lack of testing led to misunderstanding about how the technology really performed, and this has cost more than 85 lives in airbag accidents. By rushing the technology into use before it was fully understood by the technologists and consumers, critical knowledge was gained only through actual use rather than in the safety of the laboratory.

To ensure that the right people are working on the future rather than the past, it is sometimes necessary for leaders to make dynamic organizational changes at this stage of the innovation process. This was accomplished at Hewlett-Packard with the creation of a Video Server Division, as led by Ned Barnholt and described in Chapter 5.

With his own team, Barnholt did the basic work in the development of a new competitive architecture, as they realized that the evolution of technology and of the market created an opportunity for HP in the video server market. He then created a platform team and seeded it with already developed video server capability from HP Labs. The resulting products and services took HP into a new market, were producing revenue within a year, and brought the company to a leadership position within 5 years.

On the basis of widespread managerial leadership of this character throughout HP, the company's pace of new product introductions has been accelerating throughout the 1990s, and now more than 75 percent of each year's sales have come from products that are three years old or newer. This "vintage chart," as they call it, shows the effectiveness of HP's commitment to innovation (see Figure 8.17).

Step 2: Initial Prototype Development

In the platform development of Phase II, multiple iterations of laboratory prototypes are rapidly built and tested to check feasibility, and to allow stakeholders, including customers, to experience real use. The

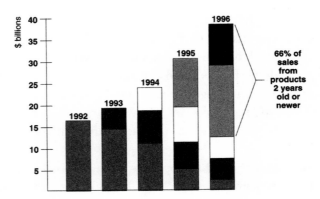

Figure 8.17 Hewlett-Packard's Vintage Chart.[10] Approximately 75 percent of Hewlett-Packard's sales come from products and services that are three years old, or newer.

consequences for competitive architecture and organizational capability are exposed and tested as more expertise is gained with the implications of this particular innovation.

Even if the circuitry is exposed on a bread board, or the labels are written by hand, or the pieces are not finely milled, feedback from real users will be invaluable for clarifying the potential value of an innovation and further specifying the key performance attributes.

This is design by interactive experimentation with users who are experts in the relevant domains, and whose tacit knowledge will be the key to ultimate success of the finished product in the marketplace. Since these are laboratory tests, however, considerable skepticism may be the first response to the results. The full impact of latent needs remains to be evoked in subsequent steps through use in real application environments.

Nevertheless, these initial tests will provide ample feedback, enabling an innovation team to verify (or to disprove) economic and emotive values, to assess the infrastructure that will be necessary to make effective use of the innovation, and to estimate the cost of full implementation.

In this step, estimates can also be made of the organizational capabilities that will be necessary to bring the innovation to market and effectively support it, including distribution, sales, manufacturing, service, and order fulfillment requirements.

Visualization tools are used to update application scenarios, and the consequences for market architecture, organizational capability, and user infrastructure are re-evaluated. Realistic assessments can then be made about the value that the innovation offers to stakeholders in current and future applications, and about how the innovation will affect the competitive architecture.

Through multiple successive cycles, the learning curve is applied to enable knowledge to be accumulated quickly, and to ascertain as quickly as possible whether there is something here that is worth continuing effort.

Since at each successive step resources are consumed, each step is also an opportunity to terminate a project, or conversely to reaffirm its potential value. In environments of great uncertainty, each step of the platform development stage can be funded as an option that may then be extended to the subsequent step only if both results and conditions warrant. Alternatively, a project may be tabled for the future until some anticipated changes in the market occur, or it may be terminated altogether.

For some projects, however, the results may be ambiguous. Some people will interpret the results as favorable and worthy of further effort, while others will be convinced that any further effort will be a waste of time. Deciding which path to follow is rarely easy.

Sometimes when a project gets officially terminated, one or two dedicated researchers continue working, perhaps even in secret, until they, too, give up or achieve a breakthrough that reincarnates the project.

Step 3. Validation of the Capability in Use

Although research labs and usability labs are useful for initial testing,[11] they are not sufficient for full development.

Therefore, having passed many iterations of tests at the laboratory prototyping stage, tests are now conducted on more refined prototypes. These again involve actual customers, and show diverse application scenarios for different target markets.

The products or services must be proven worthwhile and effective wherever they are to be used, whether that is in an office, on the road, in the home, or in the backwoods, because only there will all the tacit constraints of the actual use environment be present. Hence, Chip Holt offered the first Xerox DocuTech to the in-house print shop, where the development team could observe its performance in a real production environment.

In addition, an assessment is made of the requirements for production, both by the internal manufacturing group and by external vendors, who test their own capacity to produce key components. Knowledge is now being developed in three overlapping communities of practice: vendor, manufacturer, and customer. From these tests, detailed cost and benefit analyses can be developed.

Experience has shown that at least three iterations of validation in use are required to satisfactorily demonstrate the viability of a product or service.

Step 4. Fully Developed Product, Process, and Technology Platforms

After testing various configurations and capabilities, modular components and interfaces can be aggregated into platforms. This step must be comprehensive to expose as many assumptions and potential problems as possible.

Since all end user constituencies participate in this round of tests, this step will provide key input to both the product family and product development work of Phase III, and also to the market development activities of Phase IV. Members of the innovation team are therefore joined in the project by the operations personnel who will be responsible for transferring and managing innovation in full production and marketing.

At this step, fully developed prototypes must be validated through at least two iterations of large-scale tests by potential customers from multiple organizations. These tests involve customers who have not already participated in the development process to ensure that prior involvement in the project does not bias the test results. These customers should represent the full diversity of market segments and market locations. Only if these tests are successful can there be a high level of confidence in widespread market acceptance of the product, process, and technology platforms.

This phase of testing includes the full range of issues required in learning how to use the product or service, and all the communications that will be required to support the learning curve in deployment and use. Customer support and technical support capabilities must also be available and tested. Customer communications must also be tested, including selling the concept at trade shows, and training for sales, delivery, and maintenance.

All other related business processes that come into play on the part of vendor, seller, and customer must also be field tested. Hence, a key topic for inquiry concerns the management and capability innovations that will be required to ensure a successful product or service. The processes of production, delivery, and installation must approximate as closely as possible what would be required in a large-scale implementation; and in parallel, detailed models of marketing and selling show what new capabilities and infrastructure will be necessary for the innovation to be brought successfully to market. Therefore, members of the dealer or sales networks (if they exist) should also participate at this stage so that they, too, can assess the capabilities that they must develop to execute their part.

From this, it will be possible to measure the value created for all stakeholder groups, to assess the consequences for market architecture, dominant design, product, service, and distribution platforms, and to assess the consequences for organizational capability.

A learning curve model of the customer and other stakeholders is developed, and any project that is still alive after this stage must represent significant new value for customers and other stakeholders.

At the end of Phase II, the project passes the "wall of invention," beyond which there will be no fundamental research conducted, nor any significant conceptual development. What follows is the managed process of commercialization through the execution of ideas that have been proven through many iterations of refinement and testing. Should fundamentally new ideas emerge, they must be explored and developed in Phases I and II, but not in Phases III or IV.

PHASE III. PRODUCT FAMILY DEVELOPMENT—A STAGE-GATE PROCESS

Steps 5–7. Developing the Product Family in the Application of Capability and Platforms

In Phase II, each step has been very detailed, involving extensive tests and multiple iterations to fully prove a platform concept. In this third phase, the focus is on the rapid development of progressively more refined prototypes of product families and products. Since the platforms have already been fully validated, these test and prototyping iterations can be shorter and simpler than the interactions required in Phase II (see Figure 8.18).

Since the focus is now on developing the specific design attributes rather than deriving a platform architecture, Step 5 is the production and testing of an initial design. Step 6 represents the completed design, and Step 7 is production engineering, which includes tooling and preparation for distribution.

This phase more or less follows the logic of the "stage-gate" new product process,[12] although a key difference is that the stage-gate model does not account for the importance of dominant designs and product platforms that are taken as the basis of this phase of work. Nor does the stage-gate model recognize the importance of tacit knowledge in identifying unrecognized and unmet needs, its emergence in communities of practice, and the need for continuing after-sale knowledge interchange with customers using the knowledge channel.

Stage-gate methods have also been criticized as not reflecting the interpersonal relationships that support the way work actually gets accomplished in organizations. Joe Marone, Dean of Rensselaer Polytechnic

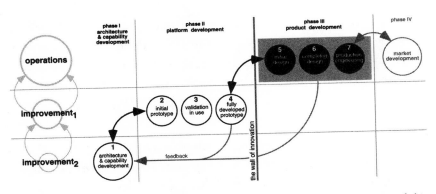

Figure 8.18 The Innovation Business Process, Phase III. The three steps of this phase are the initial design, the completed design, and production engineering, which includes tooling and preparation for distribution.

Institute has noted, "A lot of the work gets done not because of the formal authorities and process, but rather because of the relationships and knowing who to go to get something done . . . In our desperate hunt for stage-gate models we may sometimes lose sight that some of these relationships are much more important than the formal process in making these projects work."[13] These relationships are precisely where communities of practice are formed and where tacit knowledge is built, shared, and used as the basis on which to coordinate and accomplish work.

Since the underlying concepts were proven in Phase II, the work of Phase IV can begin while activity is still under way in Phase III. Concurrency between these phases supports a faster and more effective learning process for all participants, and a faster path to the market. The DocuTech technical and launch teams met together each week for a full 18 months before the product launch to ensure good mutual understanding and coordination. The key, again, is the development of a shared tacit understanding of the critical performance factors.

PHASE IV AND STEP 8. MARKET DEVELOPMENT FOR PRODUCT FAMILIES— A STAGE-GATE PROCESS

Market development must accomplish three sets of activities. Fully defining the revised competitive architecture is done concurrently with preparing the production and distribution systems for full activity, and commencing communication with the largest possible customer community via the knowledge channel (see Figure 8.19).

The Revised Architecture Framework: Implementation of New Competitive Architectures, Dominant Designs, and Product Families

The product families derived from platforms are implemented throughout the organization, which is likely to be a tremendously complex

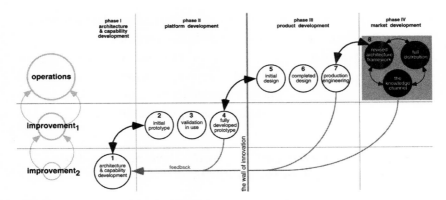

Figure 8.19 The Innovation Business Process, Phase IV. Phase IV is the concurrent development of a revised architecture framework, the establishment of full production and distribution, and initiation of the knowledge channel with respect to this particular product family.

activity. Perhaps the innovation is an entirely new dominant design, in which case the competitive architecture will be significantly impacted. Or perhaps it is a more modest innovation, a new product platform or product family within an existing dominant design.

Nevertheless, there will be a specific expectation of how this will impact the marketplace, and it is based on this expectation that the present allocation of resources reflects investments to bring this innovation to market. An innovation may require minimal or tremendous investment, but in any case all such funds are a trade-off against alternative investments that could have been made.

Many innovations require investment not just in tools and technology, as it may be necessary to fund the development of new organizational capabilities. Marketing materials and programs must be developed, while supply and manufacturing systems will be ramped up.

The innovation team transfers to the operations community the scientific and technological knowledge to operate and manage new manufacturing capabilities for new materials and technologies through joint participation in bringing new capabilities on line. As the operations staff prepare to take on new responsibilities, they will supplement this knowledge with additional education or training through universities, professional organizations, or in-house programs.

Internal and externally oriented information systems will be put on line to support internal development and external use, as well as the knowledge channel capabilities needed for meaningful dialogue between a company and new communities of its customers.

Transfer to Operations for Full Distribution, Sales, and Support of Product Families

When the first unit of a new family finally rolls off the line, the organization is fully prepared to support the new product or service families, and to support the customers who will soon be using them. Now success will come about if customers choose a product or service from this family.

Expectations are high, and sales reports are scrutinized daily, or even more frequently. Did we accomplish what we set out to do? Did we assess the market correctly? Did we understand the needs of customers, and did we communicate our value proposition to them effectively?

At this stage, an innovation is no longer protected as a source of future value. Rather, its value must be demonstrated in the here and now, and therefore it is evaluated according to conventional financial measures such as return on sales, return on investment, and profit and loss.

Now that a full cycle of design, production, and distribution has been accomplished, the meta-learning curve model has another data point. This learning curve is the one that shows how well the organization does at innovation. Is innovation a well-recognized characteristic of this organization, valued internally and by customers alike? Do competitors respect (or fear) the firm's capacity as an innovator?

While it may not be possible to draw a realistic learning curve that compares a company's learning capacity with its competitors, it is certainly possible to track a set of key variables, including patents awarded, product awards won, and percentage or dollars of sales from new products, as Hewlett-Packard has done with its vintage chart.

As each completed project has been an occasion for learning about a wide range of issues, the aggregation of this learning should represent a substantial body of knowledge. Is this aggregate impacting how the innovation process itself is managed? Or the performance of management in general? Is our rate of innovation consistent with or better than our competitors? Have we improved our position in the marketplace? Have we contributed to the development of the marketplace and have we facilitated productivity improvements for our customers?

Meanwhile, other projects are under way in $R\&D_1$ and $R\&D_2$, where new technologies are emerging with new possibilities. Do we have confidence that these can be turned into new products and services that will be valued in the marketplace? Are we keeping up with the external rate of change?

Supported by an effective process for architecture, capability and organization development, and a successful innovation process, management may no longer see change as a threat, but rather as an expanding source of opportunities to be discovered, developed, and commercialized.

The Knowledge Channel

Two-way communications with customers through the knowledge channel seek to spread the enthusiasm that was initially experienced in the testing phases to the broader community of customers who may now benefit from the new product families and products.

Full support for early adopters is provided here, along with support to all others as the innovation progresses toward the mainstream customer group.

The emphasis is on sharing knowledge and information that will enable customers to understand the philosophy behind the product, as well as it composition, use, and maintenance. In addition, dialogue through the knowledge channel becomes a source of new feedback to the ongoing development of the product family and platform, as well as the ongoing development of the architecture, capability, and the organization itself.

While the four phases and eight steps of the innovation business process are straightforward and usefully practical, making them effective requires a commitment to learning and the development of the proper context for learning to take place. This context is derived from the competitive architecture, and it is then reflected internally as organizational capability, organizational architecture, and appropriate business processes.

In the preceding chapters, we have discussed how these critical concepts emerge as aspects of the innovation business process, resulting in a description that is theoretically correct as an expression of critical new discoveries about the economy, learning, and management that are so fundamental to success (see Figure 8.20).

To properly describe the theory and the practice, we have unhesitatingly drawn on the work of numerous others whose insights on both levels have proven to be vital to composing a robust model of continuous and discontinuous innovation in a rapidly changing business environment. In addition to the complete Bibliography, we have provided a selected Bibliography of important reference works for each chapter.

Innovation—both continuous and discontinuous—is not a simple topic, nor is it a minor one. Achieving success at innovation requires

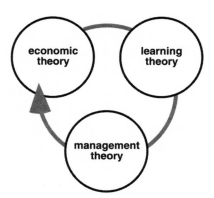

Figure 8.20 Three Critical Dimensions of Theory for Innovation. As noted in Chapter 2, the three critical theoretical dimensions of an effective innovation practice are the economy, the learning process, and management itself.

that one grapple with complexity, ambiguity, contradictions, unclear signals, and paradox, for neither innovation nor technology is black and white. As Roger Bohn shows, innovation evolves from fuzzy knowledge, and utilizes technology as the adjunct to knowledge rather than the other way around. Innovation is an intellectual process of defining what is the right thing to do in a murky, confusing environment. Sometimes you have to filter the noise from the signal, and sometimes the signal from the noise.

Innovation is the fusion of knowledge and technology into new platforms, products, and services. It is a competitively vital activity as well as a tremendously rewarding one that results at its finest in the creation of new value for customers and for all communities of stakeholders. It is only through innovation that new wealth is created, and it is only from new wealth that people in all cultures and on all continents are able to leave behind the constraints of chronic poverty and become participants in the vital and growing global economy.

Although there are certainly serious ecological problems with the economic model of the developed nations, and great concerns about the increasing environmental destruction that accompanies today's approach to economic development, economic development is also a powerful force for relieving human suffering.

As we move deeper into an economy that places increasing value on knowledge, we must master the discontinuous innovation process even as we use it to deal with the new problems of our own creation. To paraphrase Buckminster Fuller, when we solve our problems, what we get is really just new, more complex problems that we must then solve.[14] Such is the pattern of human history.

Creating and solving these problems occurs through another key pattern of history, the aggregation of knowledge from many different individuals, groups, and disciplines. These aggregations express important advances in our understanding and our ability to create products and services that meet real needs.

Notes

INTRODUCTION

[1] Jensen, Michael C., "The Modern Industrial Revolution, Exit, and the Failure of Internal Control Systems." *Journal of Finance* 48, no. 3: 831–80. As cited in Rosenbloom, Richard S.. and William J. Spencer, editors, *Engines of Innovation: U.S. Industrial Research at the End of an Era*. Boston, Harvard Business School Press, 1996.

[2] Stevens, Greg A., and James Burley. "3,000 Raw Ideas = 1 Commercial Success!" *Research•Technology Management*, May-June 1997.

[3] Cooper, Robert G., *Winning at New Products*. Reading, MA, Addison-Wesley Publishing Company, 1993. p. 19. Cooper cites: Booz, Allen & Hamilton, *New Product Management for the 1980s*. New York, Booz, Allen & Hamilton, Inc., 1982.

[4] von Hippel, Eric, *The Sources of Innovation*. New York, Oxford University Press, 1988.

[5] Matson, Eric, "Speed Kills (the Competition)." *Fast Company*, August-September 1996.

[6] National Science Board, *Science & Engineering Indicators–1996*. Washington DC, U.S. Government Printing Office, 1996. (NSB 96–21).

[7] Brown, John Seely, "Introduction: Rethinking Innovation in a Changing World." *Seeing Differently: Insights on Innovation*. John Seely Brown, editor. Boston, *Harvard Business Review*, 1997. p. xiii.

[8] Ackoff, Russell L., and Jamshid Gharajedaghi, "Reflections on Systems and their Models." *Systems Research,* Vol. 13 No 1, pp. 13–23 1996, and, Ackoff, Russell L., *Creating the Corporate Future.* New York, John Wiley & Sons, 1981.

[9] Data from the Frank Russell Company, Tacoma, WA.

[10] Drucker, Peter, *Post-Capitalist Society,* New York, HarperBusiness, 1993. p. 39.

[11] Data from Value Line Publishing, Inc. This topic is the subject of Chapter 5.

[12] Kodama, Fumio, *Analyzing Japanese High Technologies: The Techno-Paradigm Shift.* London, Pinter, 1991. p. 21.

[13] DeGenaro, William, Business Intelligence Workshop for the Industrial Research Institute, 1991.

[14] Holt, Chip, Corporate Vice President of the Joseph C. Wilson Center for Research and Technology, Xerox Corporation, in remarks to the annual conference of the Industrial Research Institute, May 23, 1996, Colorado Springs, CO.

CHAPTER 1

[1] Kodama, Fumio, *Analyzing Japanese High Technologies: The Techno-Paradigm Shift.* London, Pinter, 1991.

[2] Atkinson, Richard C., "How to Improve U.S. Productivity." *San Francisco Chronicle,* March 4, 1996.

[3] Drucker, Peter, *Innovation and Entrepreneurship.* New York, HarperBusiness, 1985.

[4] Thurow, Lester C., *The Future of Capitalism: How Today's Economic Forces Shape Tomorrow's World.* New York, William Morrow, 1996. p. 262. Thurow cites William Manchester, *A World Lit Only by Fire: The Medieval Mind and the Renaissance: Portrait of an Age.* Boston, Little, Brown, 1992, 1993. p. 5.

[5] Council on Competitiveness, Competitiveness Index 1995. Washington DC, Council on Competitiveness, 1995.

[6] Drucker, Peter, *Innovation and Entrepreneurship.* New York, Harper-Business, 1985. p. 33.

[7] Carley, William M., "To Keep GE's Profits Rising, Welch Pushes Quality-Control Plan." *Wall Street Journal,* January 13, 1997. p. 1.

[8] Data from the National Science Foundation as reported in, Buderi, Robert, "Corporate Research: It's Alive!" *Upside,* September 1997. p. 126.

[9] Porter, Michael, *Competitive Advantage: Creating and Sustaining Superior Performance.* New York, Free Press, 1985. p. 5.

[10] Hamel, Gary, and C.K. Prahalad, *Competing for the Future.* Boston, Harvard Business School Press, 1994.

[11] Collins, David, and Cynthia Montgomery, "Competing on Resources: Strategy in the 1990s." *Harvard Business Review,* July-August 1995.

[12] Marone, Joe, President, Bentley College, in remarks to the Discontinuous Innovation Special Interest Group of the Industrial Research Institute (IRI) at the IRI annual conference, May 25, 1996, Colorado Springs, CO.

[13] Yergin, Daniel, *The Prize: The Epic Quest for Oil, Money & Power.* New York, Touchstone, 1991, 1992.

[14] Utterback, James M., *Mastering the Dynamics of Innovation.* Boston, Harvard Business School Press, 1994.

[15] Marone, Joe, President, Bentley College, in remarks to the annual conference of the Industrial Research Institute, October 1997.

[16] Holt, Chip, Corporate Vice President of the Joseph C. Wilson Center for Research & Technology, Xerox Corporation, interviewed by Langdon Morris on August 19, 1997.

[17] Morris, Langdon, *Managing the Evolving Corporation.* New York, Van Nostrand Reinhold, 1995. p. 65. Used by permission.

[18] Murakami, Teruyasu, and Takashi Nishiwaki, *Strategy for Creation.* Cambridge, England, Woodhead Publishing Limited, 1991. p. 25.

[19] Pearlstein, Steven, "Have You Ever Dialed a Customer from Your Lab? You Will." *Fast Company* Magazine, February-March 1997. p. 54.

[20] Hounshell, David A., "The Evolution of Industrial Research in the United States." Rosenbloom, Richard S., and William J. Spencer, editors, *Engines of Innovation: U.S. Industrial Research at the End of an Era.* Boston, Harvard Business School Press, 1996. p. 40.

[21] Rhodes, Richard, *The Making of the Atomic Bomb.* New York, Touchstone, 1986.

[22] Rubin, Steven J., Presentation to the 3rd Generation R&D Special Interest Group at the Annual Conference of the Industrial Research Institute, May 25, 1996, Colorado Springs, CO.

[23] Groenveld, Peter, "Roadmapping Integrates Business and Technology." *Research•Technology Management,* Volume 40, Number 5, September-October 1997.

[24] Roussel, Philip A., Kamal N. Saad, and Tamara Erickson, *3rd Generation R&D: Managing the Link to Corporate Strategy.* Boston, Harvard Business School Press, 1991.

[25] de Geus, Arie, "Planning as Learning." *Harvard Business Review,* August-September, 1988.

[26] Hennessey, Joseph E., Program Manager for Management of Technological Innovation and Acting Deputy Asst. Director for Engineering, in conversation with Bill Miller, January, 1996.

[27] Luehrman, Timothy A., "What's It Worth? A General Manager's Guide to Valuation." *Harvard Business Review,* May-June 1997.

[28] Kodama, Fumio, "Technology Fusion and the New R&D." *Harvard Business Review,* July-August 1992.

[29] Morris, Langdon, *Managing the Evolving Corporation.* New York, John Wiley & Sons, 1995. p. 92.

CHAPTER 2

[1] Ackoff, Russell L., in conversation with Langdon Morris, October 23, 1996. See Russell L. Ackoff, *Creating the Corporate Future.* New York, John Wiley & Sons, 1981, and William L. Miller Ph.D. thesis.

[2] Arthur, Brian W., "Increasing Returns." *Harvard Business Review,* August-September 1996.

[3] Deming, W. Edwards, *The New Economics for Industry, Government, Education.* Cambridge, MA, Massachusetts Institute of Technology Center for Advanced Engineering Study, 1993. p. 104.

[4] Alexander, Christopher et al., *A Pattern Language.* New York, Oxford University Press, 1977.

[5] *Business Week,* "Two-Tier Marketing." *Business Week,* March 17, 1997.

[6] Taylor, Jim, and Watts Wacker, *The 500 Year Delta: What Happens After What Comes Next.* New York, HarperBusiness, 1997.

[7] Nadler, David et al., *Organizational Architecture: Designs for Changing Organizations.* San Francisco, Jossey-Bass, 1992.

[8] Morris, Langdon, *Managing the Evolving Corporation.* New York, Van Nostrand Reinhold, 1995.

[9] Patterson, Marvin L., with Sam Lightman, *Accelerating Innovation.* New York, Van Nostrand Reinhold, 1993. pp. 77, 87. Hartley, R.V.L., "Transmission of Information." *Bell Systems Technical Journal:* 535.

[10] Asthana, Praveen, "Jumping the Technology S-Curve." *IEEE Spectrum,* June 1995.

[11] Kodama, Fumio, "Technology Fusion and the New R&D." *Harvard Business Review,* July-August 1992.

[12] Kodama, Fumio, *Analyzing Japanese High Technologies: The Techno-Paradigm Shift.* London, Pinter Publishers, 1991.

[13] McLuhan, Marshall, *Understanding Media: The Extensions of Man.* Cambridge, MA, MIT Press, 1964, 1994.

[14] Zangwill, Willard I., *Lightning Strategies for Innovation.* New York, Lexington Books, 1993.

[15] Dogar, Rana, "Marketing to the Senses." *Working Woman,* April 1997.

[16] Utterback, James M., *Mastering the Dynamics of Innovation.* Boston, Harvard Business School Press, 1994.

[17] Utterback, *Mastering the Dynamics of Innovation.* p. 24.

[18] Utterback, *Mastering the Dynamics of Innovation.* p. 25. Italics in original.

[19] Edsall, Larry, "Mainstream Minivan." *Autoweek,* September 1, 1997.

[20] Rogers, Everett M. *Diffusion of Innovations.* New York, Free Press, 1962, 1971, 1983. pp. 243, 247.

[21] Utterback, *Mastering the Dynamics of Innovation.* p. 91.

[22] Miller, Karen Lowry, "Honda Sets Its Sight on a Different Checkered Flag." *Business Week,* August 17, 1992. p. 45.

[23] *Bloomberg Business News,* "Saturn to Start Selling GM's Electric Cars." *San Francisco Chronicle,* August 28, 1996.

[24] Meyer, Marc H., and Alvin P. Lehnerd, *The Power of Product Platforms: Building Value and Cost Leadership.* New York, Free Press, 1997. p. xii.

[25] Meyer and Lehnerd, *The Power of Product Platforms.* p. 10.

[26] Meyer and Lehnerd, *The Power of Product Platforms.* p. 15

[27] Ewasyshyn, Frank, Presentation at the University of Michigan Manufacturing Forum, October 28, 1991.

[28] Adapted from: Meyer, Marc H., and Alvin P. Lehnerd, *The Power of Product Platforms: Building Value and Cost Leadership.* New York, Free Press, 1997. p. 154.

[29] Hammer, Michael, and James Champy, *Reengineering the Corporation.* New York, HarperBusiness, 1993.

[30] Smith, Douglas K., and Robert C. Alexander. *Fumbling the Future.* New York, William Morrow, 1988.

[31] Williams, Tish, "Upside's Inferno." *Upside* magazine, November 1997. Foldout.

[32] Brown, John Seely, "Introduction." *Seeing Differently: Insights on Innovation.* John Seely Brown, editor. Boston, Harvard Business School Press, 1997. p. xi.

[33] Shook, Robert L., *Honda: An American Success Story.* New York, Prentice Hall Press, 1988.

[34] Tichy, Noel M., and Stratford Sherman, *Control Your Destiny or Someone Else Will.* New York, Currency Doubleday, 1993. p. 6.

[35] Siegmann, Ken, "Failure to Evolve Staggers Big Blue." *San Francisco Chronicle,* December 16, 1992. C 1.

[36] Brunner, Gordon F., Senior Vice President, Procter & Gamble, in conversation with Bill Miller.

[37] This story is based on the following sources:

Interviews with Chip Holt conducted by Langdon Morris on August 19 and October 7, 1997.

Chip Holt, remarks to the annual conference of the Industrial Research Institute, May 24, 1996, Colorado Springs, CO.

Esler, Bill, "Wonder Machine for Document Printing." *Graphic Arts Monthly,* February 1996.

[38] Klusner, Greg, Acting Director of Product Management, Kinko's, interviewed by Langdon Morris on December 2, 1997.

[39] Sihilling, Mike, Director of Production Systems, Kinko's, interviewed by Langdon Morris on December 3, 1997.

CHAPTER 3

[1] Ulrich, Dave, and Dale Lake, *Organizational Capability: Competing from the Inside Out.* New York, John Wiley & Sons, 1990.

[2] DeGenaro, William, Business Intelligence Workshop for the Industrial Research Institute, 1991.

[3] Morris, Langdon, *Managing the Evolving Corporation.* New York, Van Nostrand Reinhold, 1995. Reprinted by permission.

[4] Rothschild, Michael, *Bionomics: Economy as Ecosystem.* New York, Henry Holt, 1990. See Chapter 18.

[5] Dr. Pascal Baudry in conversation with Langdon Morris.

[6] Patterson, Marvin L., *Accelerating Innovation: Improving the Process of Product Development.* New York, Van Nostrand Reinhold, 1993. p. 11.

[7] Carroll, Chris, "Speed Kills (the competition)." *Fast Company,* August-September 1996.

[8] Eliot, T.S., *The Rock.* A pageant play first produced in London at Sadlers Wells Theater, May 28, 1934. *The Complete Poems and Plays of T.S. Eliot.* New York, Harcourt Brace.

[9] Morris, Langdon, *Managing the Evolving Corporation.* New York, Van Nostrand Reinhold, 1995. p. 74. Adapted from Dr. Russell L. Ackoff in presentation to the 10th annual conference of GOAL/QPC, November 8, 1993. Reprinted by permission.

[10] Jakab, Peter L., *Visions of a Flying Machine: The Wright Brothers and the Process of Invention.* Washington, DC, Smithsonian Institution Press, 1990. p. 138.

[11] Jakab, *Visions of a Flying Machine,* p. 195. The quote is from Orville Wright, "The Wright Brothers Aeroplane." *Century Magazine,* September 1908, p. 648.

[12] Ford, Henry with Samuel Crowther, *Today and Tomorrow.* Portland, OR, Productivity Press, 1988 (originally published in 1926,) p. 3.

[13] Bohn, Roger E., "Measuring and Managing Technical Knowledge." *Sloan Management Review,* Fall 1994. pp. 61–73.

[14] Gardner, Howard, *Multiple Intelligences: The Theory in Practice.* New York, Basic Books, 1993; and Burdman, Pamela, "Worth of SAT Exam Questioned." *San Francisco Chronicle,* November 11, 1997.

[15] Polanyi, Michael, *The Tacit Dimension.* Glouster, MA, Peter Smith, 1983.

[16] Polanyi, *The Tacit Dimension.*

[17] Dogar, Rana, "Marketing to the Senses." *Working Woman,* April 1997. p. 35.

[18] Pye, David, *The Nature and Art of Workmanship.* Cambridge, England, Cambridge University Press, 1968. pp. 1, 21. (Author's italics)

[19] Packard, David, *The HP Way: How Bill Hewlett and I Built Our Company.* New York, HarperBusiness, 1995. p. 156.

[20] Ziegler, Bart, "Old Market Research Tricks No Match for New Technology." *Wall Street Journal,* November 1, 1994.

[21] Internal Memo, Western Union, 1876.

[22] Although the exact quote presented here is unconfirmed, Fedex spokesperson Shirley Clark did confirm that the essence of this story is correct.

[23] Clark, Russell, Director of Marketing and Product Planning, Saturn Corporation. In presentation to the Product Development and Management Association (PDMA), Great Lakes Chapter, January 19, 1995.

[24] Brown, Warren, "Air Bags Favor the Driver's Side." *Washington Post National Weekly Edition,* November 10, 1997.

[25] Ottaway, David B., and Warren Brown, "The Air Bag Dilemma." *Washington Post National Weekly Edition,* June 16, 1997. The authors quote John D. Graham of the Harvard University School of Public Health.

[26] Christensen, Clayton M., *The Innovator's Dilemma: When New Technologies Cause Great Firms to Fail.* Boston, Harvard Business School Press, 1997. p. 183n.

[27] Nonaka, Ikujiro, and Hirotaka Takeuchi, *The Knowledge-Creating Company.* New York, Oxford University Press, 1995.

[28] Kuipers, Dean, "The Need for Speed." *Wired,* October 1997. p. 112.

[29] Jordan, Dr. Brigitte, "Etnographic Workplace Studies and Computer Supported Cooperative Work." Institute for Research on Learning, Report No. IRL94–0026, 1994.

[30] Institute for Research on Learning, *7 Principles of Learning.* Institute for Research on Learning, Menlo Park, CA, 1990.

[31] Wenger, Etienne, *Communities of Practice: Learning, Meaning, and Identity.* New York, Cambridge University Press, 1998.

[32] Shook, Robert L., *Honda: An American Success Story.* New York, Prentice Hall, 1988.

[33] Deming, W. Edwards, *The New Economics for Industry, Government, Education.* Cambridge, MA, Massachusetts Institute of Technology Center for Advanced Engineering Study, 1993. p. 104.

[34] Kuhn, Thomas S., *The Structure of Scientific Revolutions.* Chicago, University of Chicago Press, 1962, 1970.

[35] Linde, Andrei, "The Self-Reproducing Inflationary Universe." *Scientific American,* November 1994.

[36] The Arizona Republic, "Unprecedented Stress Making Americans Sick." *San Francisco Chronicle,* August 17, 1996.

[37] Drucker, Peter, *Innovation and Entrepreneurship.* New York, Harper-Business, 1985.

[38] Wiskerchen, Mike, former NASA scientist and Director of the California Space Grant Consortium, interviewed by Langdon Morris, January 5, 1994.

[39] Kodama, Fumio, *Emerging Patterns of Innovation: Sources of Japan's Technological Edge,* Boston, Harvard Business School Press, 1991, 1995. p. 9.

[40] Jordan, "Etnographic Workplace Studies.

[41] Hamel, Gary and C.K. Prahalad, *Competing for the Future.* Boston, Harvard Business School Press, 1994. p. 202.

[42] Nørretranders, Tor, *The User Illusion: Cutting Consciousness Down to Size.* New York, Viking, 1991 & 1998, Chapter 6. And: Zimmermann, Manfred, *Fundamentals of Sensory Physiology,* Robert F. Schmidt, editor, Berlin, Springer-Verlag, 3rd Edition, 1986, Chapter 3 and page 115.

[43] Gardner, Howard, *Multiple Intelligences: The Theory in Practice.* New York, Basic Books, 1993.

[44] Collins, Michael, *Carrying the Fire,* New York, Bantam Books, 1974. p. 306.

[45] Lovell, Jim, and Jeffrey Kluger, *Lost Moon: The Perilous Voyage of Apollo 13.* Boston, Houghton Mifflin, 1994.

CHAPTER 4

[1] Eckhouse, John, "Technofile." *Technology & Media* Newsletter, August 1994.

[2] Ziegler, Bart, "Old Market Research Tricks No Match for New Technology." *Wall Street Journal,* November 1, 1994.

[3] Ziegler, "Old Market Research Tricks.

[4] Huey, John, "Nothing Is Impossible." *Fortune,* September 23, 1991. p. 136.

[5] Nonaka, Ikujiro and Hirotaka Takeuchi, *The Knowledge-Creating Company.* New York, Oxford University Press, 1995. p. 72.

[6] Drucker, Peter F., *Post-Capitalist Society.* New York, HarperBusiness, 1993.

[7] Pearlstein, Steven, "Have You Ever Dialed a Customer from Your Lab? You Will." *Fast Company,* February/March 1997. p. 54.

[8] Thompson, Gordon, Director of Design, Nike. Interviewed by Langdon Morris, August 30, 1996. Thompson is responsible for the design of all footwear, apparel, equipment, and the image of the company. He designed the original NikeTowns in Portland and Chicago, and was codesigner of the New York NikeTown.

[9] Rogers, Everett M., *Diffusion of Innovations.* New York, Free Press, 1962, 1971, 1983.

[10] This story was written by Michael Maxtone-Graham, and originally appeared in *Hemispheres,* May, 1996. It is reprinted here by the kind permission of the author and *Hemispheres* Magazine.

[11] Although fewer than 200 Ford Tri-Motors were produced, the unique metal monoplane instantly became the standard for commercial flight and several of the sturdy aircraft were still in regular operation as late as the 1950s. At least one is still flying passengers today. From May through October, the Kalamazoo Aviation Museum schedules half-hour flights on Wednesday through Sunday. The cost is $35; 3101 East Milham Road, Kalamazoo, MI; Tel: 616–382-6555. Nonflying Ford Tri-Motors are on display at the Henry Ford Museum & Greenfield Village in Dearborn, MI (this is the aircraft in which Admiral Richard Byrd flew to the South Pole); The National Air & Space Museum in Washington, DC; The Naval Air Museum in Pensacola, FL; and The San Diego Air & Space Museum in San Diego, CA.

[12] Kearns, David T., and David A. Nadler, *Prophets in the Dark: How Xerox Reinvented Itself and Beat Back the Japanese.* New York, HarperBusiness, 1992. See Chapter 2.

[13] Ohno, Taiichi, *Toyota Production System: Beyond Large-Scale Production.* English Translation: Portland, OR, Productivity Press, 1988. p. 4.

[14] Perlman, Lewis J., "Opportunity Cost." *Wired,* November 1996. p. 133.

[15] This section is adapted from: Langdon Morris, *The Knowledge Channel: Corporate Strategies for the Internet.* Palo Alto, CA, Knowledge Venture Partners and San Ramon, CA, WDHB Consulting Group, 1997.

[16] Meeker, Mary, and Chris DePuy, *The Internet Report.* New York, HarperBusiness, 1996.

[17] Swartz, Jon, "PCs Plugging into Internet at a Furious Rate." *San Francisco Chronicle,* August 21, 1997. p. D1.

[18] Used with the permission of the Harvard University Program on Information Resources Policy.

[19] Adapted from remarks made by Robert Luff, formerly Chief Scientist, Scientific Atlanta, to the *Multimedia 1994* conference, San Francisco.

[20] Morris, Langdon, *The Knowledge Channel: Corporate Strategies for the Internet.* Palo Alto, CA, Knowledge Venture Partners and San Ramon, CA, WDHB Consulting Group, 1997. p. 29.

CHAPTER 5

[1] Becker, Gary, *Human Capital,* 3rd ed. Chicago, University of Chicago Press, 1993.

[2] Data from Value Line Publishing, Inc.

[3] Kodama, Fumio, *Analyzing Japanese High Technologies: The Techno-Paradigm Shift.* London, Pinter, 1991. p. 21.

[4] Edvinsson, Leif, and Michael S. Malone, *Intellectual Capital: Realizing Your Company's True Value by Finding its Hidden Brainpower.* New York, HarperBusiness, 1997; Sveiby, Karl Erik, *The New Organizational Wealth: Managing and Measuring Knowledge-Based Assets.* San Francisco, Berrett-Kohler, 1997; Stewart, Thomas A., *Intellectual Capital: The New Wealth of Organizations.* New York, Currency Doubleday, 1997; Brooking, Annie, *Intellectual Capital.* New York, Van Nostrand Reinhold, 1996.

[5] Sveiby, Karl Erik,*The New Organizational Wealth: Managing and Measuring Knowledge-Based Assets.* San Francisco, Berrett-Kohler, 1997; and Edvinsson and Malone. *Intellectual Capital.*

[6] Sveiby, *The New Organizational Wealth.*

[7] Edvinsson and Malone, *Intellectual Capital,* p. 42.

[8] Edvinsson and Malone, *Intellectual Capital,* p. 52.

[9] Marone, Joe, Dean of Rensselaer Polytechnic Institute, Rochester, NY, in presentation to the Discontinuous Innovation Special Interest Group at the annual meeting of the Industrial Research Institute, May 25, 1996, Colorado Springs, CO.

[10] Dixit, Avinash K., and Robert S. Pindyck, *Investment under Uncertainty.* Princeton, NJ, Princeton University Press, 1994. p. xi, 6.

[11] Hennessey, Joe, Director of R &D for Armstrong World Industries, in conversation with Bill Miller, January 1996.

[12] Faulker, Terrence W., "Applying 'Options Thinking' to R&D Valuation." *Research Technology Management,* May-June 1996, Vol. 39, No. 3.

[13] Kodama, Fumio, *Emerging Patterns of Innovation: Sources of Japan's Technological Edge.* Boston, Harvard Business School Press, 1991, 1995. p. 106.

[14] Howell, Robert A., Forward to *Japanese Management Accounting,* Yasuhiro Monden and Michiharu Sakuri, Editors. Cambridge, MA, Productivity Press, 1989. p. xix. Howell cites Hayes and Abernathy as the "thoughful academics."

[15] Mechlin, G., and Berg, D., "Evaluating Research, ROI Is Not Enough." *Harvard Business Review,* September-October 1980, pp. 93–99, as cited in Faulker, "Applying 'Options Thinking' to R&D Valuation."

[16] Drucker, Peter, *Innovation and Entrepreneurship.* New York, HarperBusiness, 1985. p. 166.

[17] Faulker, "Applying 'Options Thinking' to R&D Valuation."

[18] Adapted from: Faulker, "Applying 'Options Thinking' to R&D Valuation." *Research Technology Management,* May-June 1996, Vol. 39, No. 3.

[19] Source

[20] Moore, Dr. Gordon, "Lithography and the Future of Moore's Law." Presented at the SPIE Microlithography Symposium, February 20, 1995.

[21] Data from Sheth, Jagdish N., and Rajendra S. Sisodia, *The Consolidation of the Information Industry: A Paradigm Shift.* Chicago, International Engineering Consortium, 1996, and *New York Times,* April 23, 1994.

[22] "Raw Data." *Wired,* July 1995.

[23] Ross, Philip E., "Moore's Second Law." *Forbes,* March 25, 1996, and "The Tired/Wired 100." *Wired,* September 1996.

[24] Ross, "Moore's Second Law."

[25] Moore, "Lithography and the Future of Moore's Law."

[26] Ross, "Moore's Second Law."

[27] Moore, "Lithography and the Future of Moore's Law."

[28] Kirkpatrick, David, "Intel's Amazing Profit Machine." *Fortune,* February 17, 1997.

[29] Moore, Dr. Gordon, "Some Personal Perspectives on Research in the Semiconductor Industry." In: Richard S. Rosenbloom and William J. Spencer, editors, *Engines of Innovation.* Boston, Harvard Business School Press, 1996.

[30] Data courtesy of Dr. Gordon Moore.

[31] Berreman, G., "Anemic and emetic analyses in social anthropology." *American Anthropologist* 68 (2)1:346–354. p. 347.

[32] Koberg, Don, and Jim Bagnall, *The Universal Traveler: A Soft-Systems Guide to Creativity, Problem-Solving & the Process of Reaching Goals.* Los Altos, CA, Crisp Publications, 1991.

[33] Koestler, Arthur, *The Act of Creation.* New York, Macmillan, 1964.

[34] Shekerjian, Denise, *Uncommon Genius: How Great Ideas Are Born.* New York, Penguin Books, 1990. p. 6.

[35] Kaplan, Abraham, *The Conduct of Inquiry.* San Francisco, Chandler, 1964. p. 31. As cited in Rogers, Everett, *Diffusion of Innovations.* New York, Free Press, 1961, 1971, 1983.

[36] Grove, Andrew S., *Only the Paranoid Survive.* New York, Currency Doubleday, 1996. p. 50.

[37] Holt, Chip, Corporate Vice President of the Joseph C. Wilson Center for Research and Technology, Xerox Corporation, in remarks to the annual conference of the Industrial Research Institute, May 23, 1996, Colorado Springs, CO.

[38] Christensen, Clayton, *The Innovator's Dilemma: When New Technologies Cause Great Firms to Fail*. Boston, Harvard Business School Press, 1997. p. xii.

[39] Foster, Richard N., *Innovation: The Attacker's Advantage*. New York, Summit Books, 1986.

[40] Moore, Dr. Gordon E., "Some Personal Perspectives." p. 168.

CHAPTER 6

[1] Schein, Edgar H., "How Can Organizations Learn Faster? The Challenge of Entering the Green Room." *Sloan Management Review*, Winter 1993.

[2] Bank, David, "The Java Saga." *Wired*, December 1995, p. 169.

[3] Kuhn, Thomas S., *The Structure of Scientific Revolutions*. Chicago, University of Chicago Press, 1962, 1970.

[4] Suchman, Lucy, *Plans and Situated Actions: The Problem of Human-Machine Communication*. Cambridge, England, Cambridge University Press, 1987.

[5] Christensen, Clayton M., *The Innovator's Dilemma*. Boston, Harvard Business School Press, 1997. p. 173.

[6] Christensen, *The Innovator's Dilemma*. p. 54.

[7] Adapted from: Christensen, Clayton M., *The Innovator's Dilemma*. Boston, Harvard Business School Press, 1997. p. 16.

[8] Machiavelli, Niccolo, *The Prince*. Translated with an Introduction by George Bull, London, Penguin Books, 1961, 1975, 1981, 1995. p. 19.

[9] Murakami, Teruyasu, and Nishiwaki, Takashi. *Strategy for Creation*. Cambridge, England, Woodhead Publishing. 1991. p. 50.

[10] Wiskerchen, Dr. Michael J., Director, California Space Grant Consortium. Interviewed by Langdon Morris, January 5, 1994.

[11] Rogers, Everett M., *Diffusion of Innovations*. New York, Free Press, 1962, 1971, 1983. pp. 243, 247.

[12] Schein, Edgar H., "How Can Organizations Learn Faster? The Challenge of Entering the Green Room." *Sloan Management Review,* Winter 1993.

[13] Jaffe, Dr. Dennis T., and Dr. Cynthia D. Scott, *Mastering the Change Curve*. King of Prussia, PA, HRDG 1997.

[14] Ross, Dr. Elisabeth-Kubler, *On Death and Dying*. New York, Collier Books, 1997.

[15] Ken Cox, Assistant to the Director, Engineering Directorate, NASA, Lyndon B. Johnson Space Center, Houston, interviewed by Langdon Morris, July 5, 1996.

[16] Askew, Ray, Space Station Senior Scientist, in presentation to the Strategic Aviation Technology Working Group, Auburn, Alabama, April 7, 1997.

[17] Working Paper of the Employment Policies Institute, Washington DC.

[18] Marshall, Jonathan, "Work Team Under Attack." *San Francisco Chronicle,* July 5, 1996.

[19] Kim, Gary, Probe Research, Denver, CO, in presentation to the Western Cable Conference, November 1994.

[20] Sveiby, Karl Erik, The *New Organizational Wealth: Managing and Measuring Knowledge-Based Assets*. San Francisco, Berrett-Kohler, 1997. pp. 10–11.

[21] Nonaka, Ikujiro and Hirotaka Tekeuchi, *The Knowledge-Creating Company: How Japanese Companies Create the Dynamics of Innovation*. New York, Oxford University Press, 1995. p. 15.

[22] Drucker, Peter, *Innovation and Entrepreneurship*. New York, HarperBusiness, 1985. p. 162.

[23] Holt, Chip, Corporate Vice President of the Joseph C. Wilson Center for Research and Technology, Xerox Corporation, interviewed by Langdon Morris, August 19 and October 4, 1997.

[24] Rohzin, Donna, Worldwide Product Development Manager, HP Home Products Division, in presentation, January 21, 1996.

[25] Packard, David, *The HP Way: How Bill Hewlett and I Built Our Company.* New York, HarperBusiness, 1995. pp. 195–199.

[26] Hewlett-Packard Company

[27] "The Fortune 500." *Fortune* Magazine, April 29, 1996.

[28] This story is based on an interview with Ned Barnholt conducted by Langdon Morris on August 9, 1996. The interview is supplemented by the following material:

- An interview with Susan Curtis, TMO Manager of Strategic Programs, August 6, 1996.
- Zell, Deone, *Changing by Design: Organizational Innovation at Hewlett-Packard.* Ithaca, NY, Cornell University Press, 1997.
- Groves, Martha, "A Road to Renewal." *Los Angeles Times,* August 6, 1995.
- Ned Barnholt's presentation to the annual meeting of the Industrial Research Institute, May 23, 1996.
- Excerpts from a presentation given by Ned Barnholt, May 25, 1995.

[29] Zell, Deone, *Changing by Design: Organizational Innovation at Hewlett-Packard.* Ithaca, NY, Cornell University Press, 1997. p. 107

[30] Zell, *Changing by Design.* p. 124

[31] Drucker, *Innovation and Entrepreneurship.* p. 151.

CHAPTER 7

[1] Engelbart, Douglas C., "Toward High-Performance Organizations: A Strategic Role for Groupware." *Proceedings, Groupware '92 Conference,* San Jose, CA, August 3–5, 1992. Morgan Kaufmann.

Note that Engelbart calls his approach the "ABC Model," and he has not endorsed our application of the concept at levels of organizational recursion beyond the individual department.

[2] Engelbart, Douglas, C., Bootstrap Management Seminar: *Boosting Collective IQ: A Design for Dramatic Improvements in Productivity, Effectiveness, and Competitiveness.* The Bootstrap Institute, January 31, 1996.

[3] Packard, David, *The HP Way: How Bill Hewlett and I Built Our Company.* New York, HarperBusiness, 1995. p. 124.

[4] Bloomquist, Lee G., "Learn from Warren Buffett's 'Way'" *Research•Technology Management,* March-April 1996. p. 8.

[5] Merrifield, D. Bruce, "Economics in Technology Licensing." *les Nouvelles,* June 1992.

[6] Chatterji, Deb, "Accessing External Sources of Technology." *Research•Technology Management.* Volume 39 Number 2, March-April 1996.

[7] Brandenburger, Adam M., and Barry J. Nalebuff, *Co-opetition.* New York, Doubleday, 1996.

[8] Leeke, Steven D., Director and General Manger for Internet Content & Service Businesses, New Enterprise Group, Motorola. Interviewed by Langdon Morris on September 9, 1997.

[9] Nicholson, Geoff, Vice President, International Technology Operations, 3M and Karl Zaininger, Senior Partner, Thomas Group, Inc. in presentation to the Global Management of R&D Workshop, January 30–February 1, 1992.

[10] Stevens, Greg A., and James Burley, "3,000 Raw Ideas = 1 Commercial Success!" *Research • Technology Management,* May-June 1997.

[11] Roussel, Philip A., Kamal N. Saad, and Tamara J. Erickson, *Third Generation R&D: Managing the Link to Corporate Strategy.* Boston, Harvard Business School Press, 1991.

[12] Groenveld, Pieter, "Roadmapping Integrates Business and Technology." *Research•Technology Management,* Volume 40 Number 5, September–October 1997.

[13] Miller, Karen Lowry, "Honda Sets Its Sights on a Different Checkered Flag." *Business Week,* August 17, 1992. p. 45.

[14] Foster, Richard, *Innovation: The Attacker's Advantage.* New York, Summit Books, 1986. p. 162.

[15] Diaz, Michael, and Joseph Sligo, "How Software Process Improvement Helped Motorola." *IEEE Software,* September/October 1997.

16 Curtis, Bill, William E. Hefey, and Sally Miller, "People Capability Maturity Model." Software Engineering Institute, Carnegie Mellon University, September 1995. Document #: CMU/SEI-95-mm-02.

17 Prahalad, C.K., and Gary Hamel, "The Core Competence of the Corporation." *Harvard Business Review,* May-June 1990.

18 Gallon, Mark R., Harold M. Stillman, and David Coates, "Putting Core Competency Thinking into Practice. *Research • Technology Management,* May-June 1995.

19 Roberts, Edward B., "Generating Effective Corporate Innovation." *Technology Review,* October-November 1977.

20 Prahalad and Hamel, "The Core Competence of the Corporation."

21 "Unprecedented Stress Making Americans Sick." *San Francisco Chronicle,* August 17, 1996.

22 Ross, Judy, Presentation to the École Nationale des Ponts et Chaussées Graduate School of International Business, July 17, 1996.

23 Murakami, Teruyasu, and Takashi Nishiwaki, *Strategy for Creation.* Cambridge, England., Woodhead Publishing, 1991. p. 21

24 Burgess, John, "The Realities of Simulations." *Washington Post,* April 12, 1993.

25 de Geus, Arie, "Planning as Learning." *Harvard Business Review,* March-April 1988.

26 Wick, Daniel L., "Strategic Impotence." Review of *Dereliction of Duty* by H.R. McMaster as published in the *San Francisco Chronicle,* August 17, 1997.

27 Pascale, Richard, "Fight•Learn•Lead." *Fast Company,* August-September 1996.

28 Pascale, "Fight•Learn•Lead."

29 Carbonara, Peter, "Hire for Attitude Train for Skill." *Fast Company,* August-September, 1996.

30 Carbonara, "Hire for Attitude Train for Skill."

31 Swartz, Jon, "Technology Takes the Wheel." *San Francisco Chronicle,* September 7, 1996.

[32] Ricks, Thomas E., "Lessons Learned: Army Devises System to Decide What Does, and Does Not, Work." *Wall Street Journal,* May 23, 1997.

[33] Schein, Ed, "How Can Organizations Learn Faster? The Challenge of Entering the Green Room." *Sloan Management Review,* Winter 1993.

[34] Schein, "How Can Organizations Learn Faster?"

[35] Argyris, Chris, *On Organizational Learning.* Oxford, England, Blackwell 1992, 1994. p. 102.

[36] Mintz, John, "Betting the Company on a 21st Century Jetliner." *Washington Post National Weekly Edition,* April 3–9, 1995. The cost estimate was made by Joseph F. Campbell of Lehman Brothers Inc. The quote is from Joseph Ozimek, marketing chief of Boeing's commercial aircraft.

CHAPTER 8

[1] Adapted from: Meyer, Marc H., and Alvin P. Lehnerd, *The Power of Product Platforms: Building Value and Cost Leadership.* New York, Free Press, 1997. p. 154.

[2] Cooper, Robert G., *Winning at New Products: Accelerating the Process from Idea to Launch.* Reading, MA, Addison-Wesley, 2nd ed., 1993. p. 83.

[3] Kodama, Fumio, "Technology Fusion and the New R&D." *Harvard Business Review,* July-August 1992. p. 75.

[4] Miller, Joseph A., "Discovery Research Re-Emerges at Du Pont." *Research•Technology Management,* January-February 1997.

[5] Drucker, Peter, *Innovation and Entrepreneurship.* New York, HarperBusiness, 1985.

[6] Drucker, *Innovation and Entrepreneurship,* p. 151.

[7] Morris, Langdon, *Managing the Evolving Corporation.* New York, Van Nostrand Reinhold, 1995.

[8] Holt, Chip, presentation at the annual meeting of the Industrial Research Institute, May 23, 1996, Colorado Springs, CO.

[9] Ohno, Taiichi, *Toyota Production System.* Portland, OR, Productivity Press, 1988.

[10] Hewlett Packard Company

[11] Landauer, Thomas K., *The Trouble with Computers: Usefulness, Usability, and Productivity.* Cambridge, MA, MIT Press, 1995.

[12] Cooper, *Winning at New Products.*

[13] Marone, Joe, Dean, Rensselaer Polytechnic Institute, in remarks to the Discontinuous Innovation Special Interest Group at the annuual meeting of the Industrial Research Institute, May 25, 1996, Colorado Springs, CO.

[14] Fuller, R. Buckminster, *Critical Path.* New York, St. Martin's Press, 1981.

Index